THE AMERICAN WINE SOCIETY PRESENTS

THE COMPLETE HANDBOOK
OF WINEMAKING

Published by G.W. Kent, Inc.
3667 Morgan Rd.
Ann Arbor, MI 48108 USA

© Copyright 1993 The American Wine Society

1st Printing 1993

ISBN# 0-9619072-2-3

Printed in the United States of America

FOREWORD

As the American Wine Society concludes its 25th anniversary celebration, this book is a fitting tribute to the authors who have contributed their time, talents and energies to create outstanding technical articles for the Society's Journals, manuals and special publications during the Society's 25 years. The authors have shared their viticultural, oenological and wine appreciation expertise with Society members, wine educators and others without compensation. This publication is a small, but fitting recognition of their contributions.

The American Wine Society had its humble beginnings in 1966, when a few home winemakers met in Ithaca, New York, to form the Ithaca Oenological Union. In October 7, 1967, a meeting was held at Dr. Konstantin Frank's (the Society's Founder) Vinifera Wine Cellars near Hammondsport, New York, where 200 growers, winemakers and wine lovers met to broaden the scope of the Ithaca Oenological Union into a new organization with a new name, the American Wine Society. On December 3, 1967, the Society was formally chartered with its first President, Mr. A.W. (Lauby) Laubengayer. Under his leadership the Society began to recognize members who not only made home wines, but included individuals who enjoyed wine and were interested in promoting the production of superior domestic wines.

Today, the American Wine Society has over 3,600 members from all corners of the globe and has expanded its wine interest to all wines of the world. It has maintained its educational focus and has steadfastly rejected commercializing its operations.

There are 21 regional Vice Presidents and over 70 active chapters serving the Society members by providing wine tastings, luncheons, winery tours, wine competitions and a host of educational and social events. Members are also supported by a National Board of Directors who provide publications, winery tours, annual conferences, a wine judge certification program, amateur and commercial wine competitions, and many other services normally expected of a national organization.

Today, the American Wine Society remains a nonprofit organization devoted to educating individuals on all aspects of wine. Membership is open to all interested persons: wine experts, grape growers, amateur wine makers, wine appreciators, wine educators, and wine enthusiasts who want to learn more about wine.

If you are interested in wine, and value the information presented in this book, why not join the American Wine Society and enjoy the fellowship of a local chapter and the support of a national organization. A membership application is provided at the back of this book for your convenience. If you want more information about the Society, call or write the National office using the phone number and address provided on the membership application.

Please let us know if the information included in this book have been helpful. If you would like to become a contributor to American Wine Society publications, please call or send your manuscript for review.

Alcide L. Porell
PRESIDENT
American Wine Society

The American Wine Society Presents

THE COMPLETE HANDBOOK OF WINEMAKING

Table of Contents

About The Authors

E. S. Phillips
Professor Emeritus at Cornell University. One of the first members of the American Wine Society.

Jim Gifford
General manager and winemaker at Fox Run Winery. He has previously been winemaker at Glenora and Domaine Mumm. His sparkling wines have won many awards.

Les Sperling
Professor of Chemical Engineering at Lehigh University. Avid home fruit winemaker, grows peaches, plums, pears, raspberries, blueberries, strawberries and grapes.

Werner Roesener
Founded several wine circles in Ontario. Canada Grand Champion Winemaker in 1988. Graduate American Wine Society wine judge.

James Knap
Received PhD. in Chemical Engineering from the University of Illinois. Now retired from Union Carbide. Now a wine educator and regional director of Les Amis du Vin for Virginia and West Virginia.

J. Donald Cooper
Award-winning Ontario home winemaker. Believes that what started out as a hobby has become an obsession.

Emile Peynaud
Chief of Research Services at the Enological and Agricultural Station of Bordeaux. Professor Peynaud is one of the foremost wine researchers in the world.

Harold E. Applegate
Retired medical research scientist. Has grown grapes and made wine since 1948.

Robert A. Plane
Earned PhD. from the University of Chicago. Has served as Professor of Chemistry at Cornell University, President of Clarkson University and Wells College and Director of the New York State Agriculture Experiment Station. President of Plane's Cayuga Vineyard Winery.

Leonard R. Mattick
Earned PhD. from the University of Connecticut. Now Professor Emeritus of Chemistry at Cornell University. Internationally recognized expert on acid control in wines. Honorary Lifetime member of the American Society for Enologists and Viticulturists.

Douglas P. Moorhead
Co-owner of Presque Isle Wine Cellars, a winery and home-winemaking supply company. He is also president of Moorhead Vineyards, Inc., a 160 acre grape farm, and is on the board of directors of National Grape Co-op (Welch's Grape Juice). Secretary of the Pennsylvania Wine Association. He and his wife Marlene were awarded lifetime membership in the American Wine Society.

Philip F. Jackisch
Earned PhD. in Organic Chemistry from the University of Michigan. Author of "Modern Winemaking" and over 100 magazine articles on wine. Commercial winery consultant.

Vernon L. Singleton
Earned PhD. in Protein Biochemistry. Professor Emeritus at University of California–Davis. Internationally renowned enologist.

Jacques Recht
Winemaker at Ingleside Plantation Winery in Virginia. Studied enology at Ingenieur Fermentation Institute of Brussels. Winemaking experience in several countries around the world.

Phillip E. DeVore

A home winemaker for 25 years he is a chemical engineer who believes experimentation and good record keeping are keys to steady progress.

Chester H. Page

Earned a PhD. in Physics at Yale University. Author of many scientific papers and textbooks. Has developed electronic equipment for automatic titration of free SO_2 in wine, for accurate acid titration (without using a pH meter), and a simple, precise ebulliometer for alcohol content of wine.

G. Hamilton Mowbray

Earned a PhD. in the field of human sensory perception from Cambridge University. A pioneer in research related to guided missile systems for the U.S. Navy. Has run Montbray Wine Cellars, a winery in Maryland since 1966. Consultant on wine for Time-Life Books, he has received the French Government's highest award for agricultural endeavors, "The Order of Merit in Agriculture", for excellence in wine production and education, an honor bestowed on only two other American winemakers.

Alton L. Long

A chemist and wine educator. American Wine Society Graduate Certified Judge and a leader in the American Wine Society.

An Outline of Still Wine Making from Grapes

An Outline of Still Wine Making from Grapes

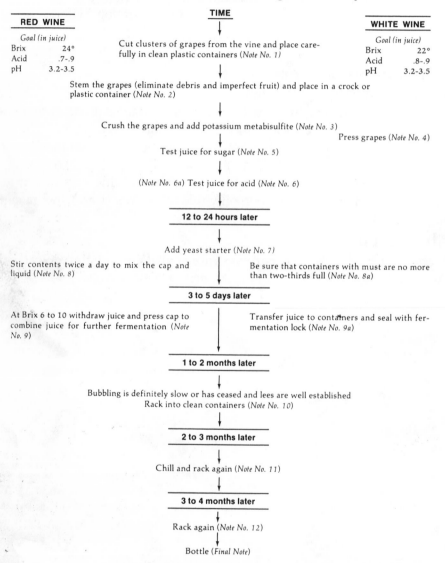

TIME

RED WINE

Goal (in juice)
Brix   24°
Acid   .7-.9
pH   3.2-3.5

WHITE WINE

Goal (in juice)
Brix   22°
Acid   .8-.9
pH   3.2-3.5

Cut clusters of grapes from the vine and place carefully in clean plastic containers (*Note No. 1*)

Stem the grapes (eliminate debris and imperfect fruit) and place in a crock or plastic container (*Note No. 2*)

Crush the grapes and add potassium metabisulfite (*Note No. 3*)

Press grapes (*Note No. 4*)

Test juice for sugar (*Note No. 5*)

(*Note No. 6a*) Test juice for acid (*Note No. 6*)

12 to 24 hours later

Add yeast starter (*Note No. 7*)

Stir contents twice a day to mix the cap and liquid (*Note No. 8*)

Be sure that containers with must are no more than two-thirds full (*Note No. 8a*)

3 to 5 days later

At Brix 6 to 10 withdraw juice and press cap to combine juice for further fermentation (*Note No. 9*)

Transfer juice to containers and seal with fermentation lock (*Note No. 9a*)

1 to 2 months later

Bubbling is definitely slow or has ceased and lees are well established
Rack into clean containers (*Note No. 10*)

2 to 3 months later

Chill and rack again (*Note No. 11*)

3 to 4 months later

Rack again (*Note No. 12*)

Bottle (*Final Note*)

CHAPTER ONE

STILL WINE FROM GRAPES

E.S. Phillips, Ph .D.

PART 1

HARVEST

THE TIME OF HARVEST varies with the climate, grape variety and the area. Recent investigations also pose questions concerning the optimum degree of maturity for winemaking. These will be influenced by the type of wine made as well as personal tastes. Among these would be the degree of sweetness desired — bone dry, modestly sweet or definitely sweet. Experienced winemakers hope that nature may be kind and give grapes at harvest-time with 22% sugar and an acidity of about .8 to .9. Such conditions give what is loosely termed a "balanced" juice that will yield a dry wine (0–1/2% sugar) with enough acid to leave a delicate clean taste and enough alcohol to preserve the final product. Imbalances of sugar, acid or alcohol will mask the delicate aromas and flavors inherent in nature's product.

It may well be that in some cases harvesting at a sugar content of about Brix 18 may produce a more fruity wine. In such cases additional sugar must be added to the pressed juice to achieve a Brix of 22. In addition, some grapes may deteriorate rapidly and a lower (than 22% sugar) Brix is often desirable. An example would be Delaware grapes.

In general, northeastern or midwestern grapes should be harvested as late as possible (before a killing frost) to allow the fruit to attain as high a sugar content as possible with a corresponding decrease in acidity. Western and southern producers will normally have enough sugar in their grapes but may encounter a greater problem retaining enough acid to develop a crisp, well-rounded wine. This may be particularly true if the grapes are harvested too late in the warmer regions or seasons. Thus, this area leaves room for experimentation.

If you purchase juice from commercial processors you must depend on the supplier to harvest at the optimum time for each variety. However, the supplier has the problem of outguessing "Mother Nature" in advance of the actual harvest and fitting his flow of juice to some predetermined date for his customers. If harvested too soon the sugar may be down and the acid up, too late a harvest may, with some varieties, have more sugar than normal with low acidity.

Cleanliness at Harvest

There is little question but what the historic foot-stomping, wood-crushing, and hand-squeezing of the past makes this section hard to write. One can always point to such practices and make the statement that wine was made despite such crude methods. A rebuttal might question the percentage of high quality results. My father made far more vinegar and poor quality wine with practices of the past than he had unqualified successes. Frankly, it was his lack of success that discouraged me from following in his footsteps. It was until retirement gave me more free time (plus the insistence of friends who were experienced winemakers) that I embarked on what has resulted in an exciting and stimulating avocation. With success a winemaker produces a delectable table wine that enhances any meal. Even wines that are less than satisfactory may be excellent cooking ingredients. Since we can't lose, let's look further.

It is likely that fully developed bunches of ripe grapes will be free from the preceding negative statements. If, however, birds, hail, molds or other factors cause some of these grapes to be less than perfect, it would appear logical to avoid potential troubles by eliminating these undesirable elements. If such grapes are left for any length of time, molds, enzymes, bacteria, and some wild yeasts may jointly make the final wine less than perfect. If, as some authors suggest, you hold the grapes for a day or two to increase the sugar content before crushing, suggestions about cleanliness would appear necessary to preclude the possibility of contaminating healthy grapes. Furthermore, grapes, unlike some fruits, do not continue to ripen after harvest. Any improvement in the harvested grape would be caused by a loss of water that, therefore, changes the percentage of sugar and acid in the berry.

Plastic containers to hold the harvested grapes are suggested because they are easy to clean.

PART 2

Stem the Grapes

Grapes for white wine will be crushed and pressed immediately. Grapes for red wine will be crushed and partially fermented in a crock or plastic container.

It should be emphasized that although plastic containers hold liquids, some are porous to gases and may retain or accumulate odors that can influence the final flavor of the wine if the juice is retained in the container.

PART 3

The Role of Metabisulfite

There is little argument that if many grapes have to be processed, a commercial crusher is desirable. With but a few grapes, many improvised methods have been tried. However, anyone who has pursued the elusive grape at a crushing bee will relate that grapes tenaciously resist a change of shape. If wooden posts or similar porous mashers are used, coat the implement with hot paraffin until the pores are filled. Wash immediately after each use.

One word of caution. As soon as grapes are crushed, all the prerequisites are present for two changes. One is the ability of the materials to absorb oxygen to the detriment of both the color and flavor of the finished wine. Secondly, because the grape skin is covered with wild yeasts, molds and bacteria, the conditions are set for an uncontrolled fermentation.

Both can be prevented by judicious use of SO_2 that is most readily available from potassium metabisulfite or sodium metabisulfite that yields about half its weight as SO_2. Two grams of sulfite for each uncrushed bushel of grapes is adequate. A more meticulous method results when 18.1 grams of sulfite is dissolved in 100 ml of water. One ml of the solution per liter of juice or kilogram of grapes gives 100 parts per million.

100 ppm of sulfite in the fresh juice is a desired level. The SO_2 released will inhibit the wild yeasts, molds and bacteria. After standing 12 to 24 hours a cultured yeast is added and produces the first fermentation. Do not overdose the fresh juice. Excessive doses of SO_2 can produce adverse effects that will plague the winemaker even to the final product.

Although we have just said that 100 ppm SO_2 is desirable there are certain conditions where lesser concentrations are desirable. As will be seen later some wines will improve with a malolactic fermentation in which harsh malic acid is converted to softer lactic acid. In such a case 50 ppm would be a more desirable level. This method of acid reduction is more prevalent with red wines than with white. More about this later. As a further help:

1 gram of metabisulfite (1/4 teaspoon) = 150 ppm per gallon

1 Campden tablet = 30 to 50 ppm per gallon.

PART 4

Press Grapes

As with crushing, many improvised as well as commercial presses are available. Commercial basket presses are popular and can be improved by using plastic window screen as a liner. To get more juice from your grapes remember to press, stir the cake and press again.

One word of caution — do not allow metal, other than stainless steel, to come into contact with the juice. Iron and copper are particularly troublesome. If either of these metals is used in the press, paint with an acid resisting enamel.

Many persons now buy juice from nearby sources and thus skip the preceding steps. The following may be helpful:

1. If the supplier has not treated the fresh juice with sulfite, place 1 or 2 grams in the bottom of a 5 gallon carboy to reduce potential oxidation and prevent the start of fermentation if the juice warms in transit.

2. In rare instances, pressure within the carboy may rise while transporting it home, and if tightly sealed the glass may break. A safer method is to make the closure with material such as Saran wrap held with a rubber band, etc.

PART 5

Test for Sugar

Only a few pieces of laboratory equipment are necessary to produce wine. Most essential is a hydrometer and a cylindrical hydrometer jar (or 100 ml graduated cylinder) with which to determine the sugar content of the fresh juice. One can not rely on taste to even come close. Hydrometers most commonly used read in % sugar, degrees Balling, or degrees Brix. For our purposes consider them all equivalent.

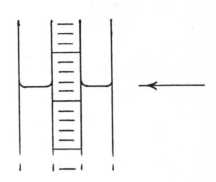

Filter through cheese cloth enough liquid to fill a hydrometer jar to within a few inches of the top. Adjust the juice to the temperature at which your hydrometer is calibrated (usually about 68° F–20° C). Insert the clean hydrometer, give a slight spin, and read the number at the juice level.

Your goal is to ferment juice that has a Brix of 22. This will yield an alcohol content of about 12%. If the sugar content is less than desirable, add cane sugar to make up the shortage.

A 22% sugar solution can be made by placing two pounds (4 cups) of granulated sugar in a gallon jar and adding water to the one gallon mark. This is particularly useful when one has to ameliorate a high acid juice to reasonable levels. This will be discussed in more detail in part 6.

If the sugar is added to a gallon (as one would do in winemaking) add 1.5 to 1.6 ounces of sugar for each point of Brix short of the ideal. Because we are dealing with a living biological product our forecasts of alcohol and residual sugar can only be approximate. I well remember one year fermenting 9 different grapes at Brix 24 with the hope that a bit of residual sugar might be left. Measurements at the end of fermentation showed a sugar range from 0 to 2%. Part of the variation may have been caused by the variation in the types of grapes used.

Since white wine is made from the juice only, the sugar can be added immediately unless further amelioration with water is necessary to correct high acid juice. Hence it is desirable to test for acid before acting on the sugar needs.

For white wine dissolve the sugar in some of the juice and stir carefully. For red wines make a record of the sugar needed but do not add until the juice has been pressed from the pulp.

Some writers suggest phasing in the addition of sugar to the juice during early fermentation. If one is attempting to derive more than 12% alcohol, this may have its advantages. For those attempting to produce a fine, delicate, dry wine the practice of producing more than 12% alcohol is questionable except possibly with certain vinifera varieties such as Pinot noir. Note: 13 pounds of sugar adds volume equivalent to 1 gallon of water. Therefore, if 2 pounds of sugar is needed to correct 5 gallons of juice, the resulting volume will increase by 2/13 of a gallon (about 20 ounces of juice).

PART 6

Test For Acid (White Juice)

The proper acid level for a finished wine varies with personal taste, wine type, grape used, climactic conditions where the grapes are grown, fermentation, and a host of others. Too little acid in the final wine produces a flat and insipid product that leaves an unclean or soapy, flat taste in the mouth. Too high acid produces an excessively tart wine. Residual sugar tends to mask acidity. Thus, even with these few generalizations, it becomes obvious that knowledge of the juice's acidity is essential to produce a good wine. This author firmly believes that a capital investment of about $15 for an acid test kit can make a dramatic improvement in any amateur's wine.

Without detailing all the reasons for such results we can say that the acidity of California grapes usually ranges from a low of .4 (calculated as tartaric acid) to an occasional 1.0. On the other hand, northeastern grapes often range from .7 to nearly 2.0. Within these ranges varietal differences exist. If nature is kind, jubilation among winemakers is at its peak when a sugar of 20–22% with an acid that ranges from about .7 to .8 is measured. With these brief remarks let us look at the steps necessary to measure total acids in white juice.

In its simplest terms titration for total acids is simply the addition of a known alkali or base to a specific quantity of acid until the resulting liquid is neither acid nor alkaline. Kits to perform this measurement are sold by most winemaking supply shops and include:

One 25 ml or 50 ml burette or plastic syringe

One 5 ml pipette

Sodium hydroxide 0.1 Normal

Phenolphthalein solution

In addition I like to use several glass, heat resisting Ehrlenmeyer flasks of 125 ml capacity and several 1 oz plastic or glass measuring jars in which to collect 6 or 8 ml of juice or wine. Because it is best to boil the juice and water to eliminate any dissolved gases (such as CO_2) one should have a small source of heat. An old electric heater used for a glass coffee maker is excellent. The steps for titration of white wine are as follows:

1. Fill the burette with sodium hydroxide.

2. Pour into the flask about 75 ml of distilled water and 5 ml of the juice.

3. Bring the water-juice mixture to a boil.

4. Add 4 or 5 drops of phenolphthalein indicator to the mixture.

5. Record the level of the sodium hydroxide in the burette and slowly add the sodium hydroxide to the flask. As you begin, it is possible to release several ml of the sodium hydroxide, but near the end a few drops at a time will suffice.

6. Swirl the mixture in the flask. When the faint pink end point holds for 30 seconds, record the sodium hydroxide position from the burette.

7. Subtract the first from the last burette reading. This is the exact volume of solution of sodium hydroxide to neutralize the acidity in the juice.

8. Multiply the results by 0.15 for the total acid. The entire process takes but a few minutes and will return great dividends. Treatment of juice that is far from 0.8–0.9 will be covered later. Most acid test kits available at winemaking shops have complete instructions and equipment included.

PART 6A

Test For Acid (Red Juice)

Pigmentation in the red juice makes titration a bit more difficult than with colorless juice. There are 3 methods to cope with the problem: 1) decolorization of the red juice; 2) the use of both red and blue litmus paper to help determine the end point; 3) the following method that is recommended by the author.

Follow the method for white juice through the first 3 steps. Do not add the phenolphthalein as in step 4. At step 6 you will note that suddenly the dark-reddish solution turns to a blue-green color. This means that you are now close to the end point and can safely add the phenolphthalein. Continue to add the sodium hydroxide, a few drops at a time, swirl, and when the entire solution turns pink and holds you have achieved neutrality. Compute as with white juice.

I would be remiss to omit one other method of measuring acidity used by professionals and some advanced amateurs. Let me point out again that the methods described here, for both white and red wines, constitute a relatively cheap way to determine total acidity. It is a measure of potential acidity and loosely stated does not take into account the relative strengths of acids present. The other method of measuring acids determines the effective acidity and is compared on a scale that ranges from 0 to 14 with 7 being a neutral point. It is called pH measurement. Numbers less than 7 show increases in acidity and numbers greater than 7 show increasing alkalinity.

In addition to total acidity, pH measurements can be extremely helpful in determining future action. Chapters 8 and 9 will cover pH in great detail.

PART 7

Amelioration and Yeast

By now it is obvious that although the winemaker has certain goals that he hopes will be reached at harvest, nature does not always oblige. The outline in the beginning of this chapter shows that for white wine we hope for a sugar of about 22% with an acid that titrates to from .7 to .9. If pH is measured it hopefully may be from 3.1 to 3.6. Red wines can run a bit higher in sugar and hopefully slightly lower in acid. When these conditions are not achieved, the winemaker is called on for adjustments — called amelioration.

If the sugar is low one can correct by adding 1.5 to 1.6 ounces of sugar per gallon for each point of Brix below the ideal. If the sugar is high (and it shouldn't be if harvest is carefully timed) one can dilute the must by adding about 5 ounces of water per gallon per point of Brix above the ideal. Unfortunately, this dilutes elements other than sugar but is better than making no adjustments at all.

The problem of adjusting for an acid imbalance is more complicated particularly in the northeastern states. Here the acids often exceed optimum conditions for winemaking. The warmer climates, such as parts of

California, have the reverse situation; they more likely hope for enough acid to approach the ideal conditions. In addition to these variables, the fermentation and stabilization process normally lowers the acid, thus making the decisions on treatment far from simple.

Before we go further it might be well to place all of the elements discussed so far into a graphic relationship with time. The graph is highly generalized because seasonal and varietal differences may differ drastically from the norms. The two predominant acids in grape juice are tartaric (that remains relatively constant whether grapes are harvested early or late) and malic (that decreases as the grapes ripen).

We see from this graph three important changes that occur during fermentation:

1. Yeasts convert the sugars into alcohol in about a 2 to 1 ratio.

2. Bacteria (malolactic) convert the harsh malic acid into the milder lactic acid.

3. The deposition of potassium bitartrate (that may be encouraged by low temperatures). Although shown after the malolactic fermentation it may occur earlier and/or later and in varying degrees.

These three stages are called Primary Fermentation (#1), Secondary (or malolactic) Fermentation (#2), and Stabilization (#3).

Going back to the chart; adjusting for sugar is no problem. High acid, on the other hand, is more difficult. With simple titration and primarily two acids involved several options are available. Let's look at a few and come to some generalizations that can be refined with more experience.

The simplest procedure is to ignore the acid, ferment, and after the wine is made if high acid still persists blend with another low acid wine. However, as often as not the final wine is considerably lower in acid than

Some Changes that Occur During Fermentation and Aging

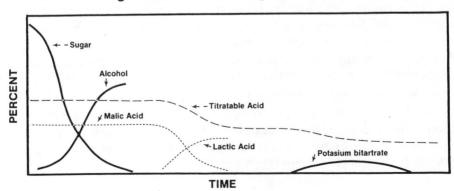

showed in the juice. More than likely a malolactic fermentation took place (explaining the prolonged fine bubbles that persisted for several months) and the conversion of acids gives a lower total acid when titrated. Several conditions can prevent this fortunate circumstance. One could be a heavier than recommended use of sulfite. Secondly, a total acid above 1.2 or 1.3 may simply defy a secondary fermentation. This may be more true with white wines than with reds.

Another easy way to adjust acid balance is to dilute the juice with water. Grapes with strong flavors and aromas can stand this treatment better than those whose juice is more delicate and subtle. Use sugar water (2 lbs sugar + water to make 1 gallon) so that further sugar adjustments are unnecessary. I have found that northeastern Delaware, Diamond, and Steuben grapes often benefit with about 15% amelioration with sugar water. Catawba can be carried to from 30–50% sugar water.

Chemical adjustments constitute a third method of acid reduction but are more complicated than one might suspect. One can assume that fermentation and cold stabilization will normally reduce the acid in the original juice by about .2. Therefore, if the juice is between .8 and .9 before fermentation do nothing to change the acid. (It is preferable to make acid adjustments before fermentation but they must be done with caution). It is far better to fall short of a desired level than to overshoot and have a flat wine. Also, minor changes can be accomplished after fermentation if desirable.

Two chemicals are commonly used for acid reduction. Each has its virtues and its faults. Calcium carbonate (precipitated chalk) has been used for years, but does not reduce acid uniformly. If a malolactic fermentation follows the chemical treatment, lactic acid will predominate leaving an insipid wine. If no malolactic occurs and the treatment has been applied with a heavy hand the wine may end up with a chalky, apple flavor not typical of the grape variety.

If calcium carbonate is used it is preferable to treat from 1/5 to 1/2 of the juice (before fermentation) with the carbonate computed for the whole batch. For 5 gallons I normally treat 1–2 gallons. The quantity of carbonate to use is calculated as follows: 2.5 grams (0.09 oz.) lowers acidity by 0.1% (I seldom exceed 5 grams per gallon). Place the carbonate in a container and slowly add the juice; stir or swirl until the foam abates. Store in a cool place for a day or two and add to the rest of the juice.

The second chemical that can used to reduce acidity is potassium bicarbonate. For each point of reduction use 3.4 grams (0.13 oz.) and follow the same procedure as above. The bicarbonate method also precipitates some of the potassium bitartrate.

Yeast

To use active dried wine yeast one should use approximately 5 grams per 5 gallons. Pour the dried yeast into a cup of warm (110° F) water and wait 10–15 minutes; then stir well and pitch into the juice. Rehydrating the yeast as such will allow the yeast to reproduce and ferment at a faster rate and will prevent off-flavors that can occur if the dried yeast is pitched directly into the sweet juice. The yeast cells can burst their cell walls and mutate rapidly if pitched directly into liquid containing sugars if they have not yet rehydrated and become healthy living cells.

PART 8

Fermentation (Red)

At this point the making of red wine differs markedly from white. The crushed grapes are fermented on their skins for about 3 to 5 days in crocks or pails until the Brix drops about 10 points. In this way the color is extracted from the skins. A desirable by-product is an additional extraction of tannins.

Because the fermentation of crushed grapes occurs in open crocks or plastic pails, one has to worry about fruit flies and acetic bacteria. Although the juice has to be stirred twice a day, it is highly desirable to tightly cover the container with a tight fitting cloth. A tight string around the top to hold the cloth in place may be sufficient. Be advised that the brew will froth and seemingly increase in size, so never fill the pail to the top. Several pails only partly filled are a better plan than a clean up after an eruption.

Red grapes may be fermented at about 70° F.

PART 8A

Fermentation (White)

The initial fermentation (in which the yeasts convert the sugars to alcohol) is by all odds the most spectacular part of wine making. It is best viewed in glass containers. Its duration is normally short (5–12 days) and may be a source of trouble if the carboys and jugs are too full and allow the froth produced to erupt violently. Below are suggestions on how to handle 5 gallons of juice for this initial period.

It might be well to backtrack a bit and include here alternate methods of handling grapes and juice. Some commercial wineries leave the stem on the hand-picked white grapes. Crushed and pressed, this adds a bit of tannin to the juice. Other grapes are fermented briefly on the skin and then pressed. Results are similar.

For those who buy juice it should be pointed out that without agitation in the storage tank, the juice may stratify and deliver a variable product. Also, I have seen white juice with so many solids that it looked like light colored mud. In other cases the juice has been relatively clear. Thus, the practice of allowing the juice to settle for 24 hours and racking before adding the yeast. Commercial wineries commonly centrifuge the juice leaving variable amounts of solids.

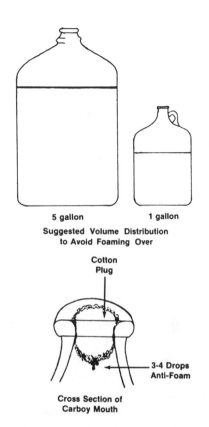

5 gallon   1 gallon

Suggested Volume Distribution
to Avoid Foaming Over

Cotton Plug

3-4 Drops Anti-Foam

Cross Section of
Carboy Mouth

After the initial fermentation has quieted to a simmer it may be advisable to swirl the juice in each bottle. Often this will reactivate the fermentation. Such a practice prevents a violent renewal when the contents of the small containers are returned to the large ones.

If additional sugar water has been added to the juice to reduce the acidity, a second bottle or smaller carboy must be used.

In general, white juice may be fermented at from 60° F to 70° F. However, many enologists are of the opinion that with delicate grapes too much flavor and aroma is lost at these high temperatures. Some are using 50° F. Some are experimenting with even lower temperatures. Many have settled at 55° F.

PART 9

Fermentation (Red)

The red juice under the cap should be siphoned into carboys. Press the cap through cheesecloth (or a press) to extract more juice and combine the total. It is at this step that the sugar is added to the liquid as previously determined. If necessary to ameliorate the juice to lower its acidity this is also done now. This may pose a problem if the juice before amelioration equals the capacity of available carboys. The total of the sugar and the sugar water mixture will exceed your capacity. More important, you have the problem of adding the supplements equally. It has been a fairly common practice to add the contents of the juice, sugar, and sugar water to a large plastic pail and then pour back into carboys. However, in so doing, quantities of air get into the mixture. Red wine can tolerate the added air better than white wine. If this type of mixing is followed, it would be far better to siphon all liquids. The added sugar will again produce a violent fermentation and the practice as outlined in part 8a should be followed for a few days prior to installing a fermentation lock.

PART 9A

Secondary Fermentation

You may or may not want to encourage a secondary (malolactic) fermentation. For the pros and cons of malolactic fermentation see Chapter 14. For the methods for testing for malolactic fermentation see Chapter 15.

PART 10

Racking

Ask a dozen winemakers when the first racking should take place and you will get a dozen different answers. They will range from immediately after the alcohol fermentation to shortly before bottling. Reasons for this variation may be in a preference for or against a malolactic fermentation. With low total acid one might rack and sulfite early. With high total acid one might prefer to leave the wine on the lees (sediment) to encourage a malolactic fermentation and naturally reduce the acidity to a desired level. In this case the enologist does run some risk that contaminated lees may produce off-flavors. Sulfiting at the first racking is likely to inhibit a malolactic fermentation that desirably should follow soon after the primary fermentation. If delayed it may be the source of off-odors.

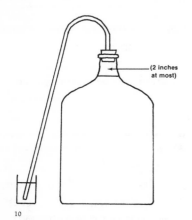

(2 inches at most)

10

As a generalization, we recommend the first racking in from 4 to 8 weeks. If you want to experiment, rack one carboy (of the same juice) early and another late; then after a few years of experimentation, make your own rules. Remember that conditions will vary from year to year.

Some rack at the end of 5 or 10 days. This leaves behind heavy products with enough solids in suspension to give a good malolactic fermentation.

Racking is the process of siphoning the liquid from one container to another in such a way that air makes but minimal contact with the wine. It may also be considered as partial purification of the wine. In the process the liquid is removed from the settled accumulation of dead yeast, fragments of the pulp and skin of grapes, tartrates and other impurities. Equipment includes a flexible tube of plastic or surgical rubber that is more than twice as long as the carboy is high and a stiff plastic or glass tube a bit higher than the carboy and formed as the nearby drawing. Try to prevent the lees from getting sucked up into the hose and thus transferred into the new container. Leave only about 1 1/2 inches at the top of the new container.

PART 11

Second Racking

By now the wine will be fairly clear and the lees will be but a fraction of the first deposit. In many cases they are formed by tartaric and other crystals.

Prior to this racking in late winter, great benefits accrue from a cold treatment of about 27° F for a period of several weeks. Place the carboys in garage and achieve the desired temperature by adjusting doors or windows. Some use a spare refrigerator for this purpose.

This racking is much simpler than the first. The amount of sulfite varies with the enologists questioned and likely with the variety of grapes used. In general from 15 ppm to 30 ppm is enough.

Sugar content of finished wine (or at stages through the second fermentation) may be readily measured by sugar testing kits available from drug stores or winemaking shops.

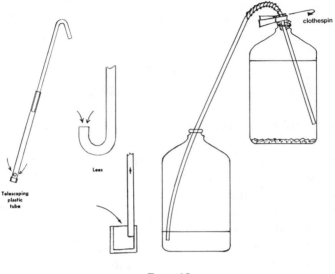

PART 12

Final Notes

The third racking is debatable and in many cases may be omitted. However, where a fairly heavy deposit occurs late in the process, bottling will be easier without the need to fight such sediment at bottling. Red wine is more likely to need this racking than is white.

Now that we have been so positive about handling the wine and particularly about racking, let us raise a few questions (and possibly some eyebrows). It would appear from reading this chapter that we classify oxygen as the worst of the bad. Is that really true? Wine in a barrel may lose as much as 5% of its volume in a year. Sure it is topped, but unless an automatic unit is attached to the bung isn't it likely that a bit of air intrudes? If this is so, might it not be possible that a minute amount of air at racking will help the wine to develop in glass carboys as well?

Some even advocate that at the first racking the wine should splash down the side of the carboy. For further rackings this is taboo. Your author splashes at the first racking, usually immediately after the alcohol fermentation is complete. I also used CO_2 in the empty carboy to prevent undue oxygen absorption but have given this up because the splashed wine usually releases quantities of sulfite.

This does not mean that one can be careless. Far from it. But a bit of oxygen will do no harm and may help the aging process.

We haven't discussed fining. This is the process of using one of various materials to clear wine that stubbornly refuses to become clear. The most commonly used material is bentonite. Unfortunately, it leaves light fluffy lees and one may lose part of the wine unless the racking is accompanied by filtration. If used, the usual dosage for 5 gallons ranges from 5 to 10 grams. Other materials for fining include gelatin, Sparkolloid, isinglass, blood, eggs, caseins, and others. Frankly, in many cases, time alone is the best agent without introducing the possibility of contaminants to a potentially fine product.

Filtration is another subject of many facets. In general, filtration is only infrequently essential. However, there are circumstances where it can improve the wine. Occasionally, wine fails to clear properly and often filtration will quickly rectify the problem. Used for this purpose filtration is usually done in the spring or summer following fermentation. Most filters made for amateurs are so made that even 5 gallons can be transferred with but minimal air contact and no loss of flavor. The exception is when one wishes to retain a bit of sweetness by interrupting the fermentation. Because such use is early in the process, many solids still remain and a series of filters, from coarse to sterile (or near sterile), must be used. In this case multiple filtration could cause excessive oxidation; thus the practice is questionable for amateurs.

However, this author has had single filtration adequately clear Dutchess, Chardonnay, and Seyval using a microfine cartridge. The objection to filters is their cost. If you make a lot of wine and have problems, the amortized cost-per-gallon may be insignificant compared to the cost of the raw product. For a small amount of wine I question the economics involved.

Any filtration should be preceded by ample washing and sterilization of the equipment. Three steps should be followed:

1. Run water through the filter until the "pass-thru" water has no residual taste.

2. Run a mild citric acid-sulfite solution through and let stand for 10 or 15 minutes.

3. Run water through to dissipate the acid and sulfite. Now filter the wine.

Fining and/or filtration helps remove most of the suspended material (observed when a focusing flash-light beam is directed through the wine) that may cause off flavors at a later date.

Bottling

When to bottle is sometimes a problem. It is possible to have a wine that tastes good but which fails to come up to acid and sugar goals. This is possible because such goals may be average for a variety of conditions. If one waits in the hope that goals will be achieved, the final result may fall short of your hopes. For instance, it is possible to have a wine slightly high in acid, with a trace of sugar (1/4 to 1/2%), that smells and tastes good. However, while still in the carboy an occasional bubble will be emitted. The question is whether the yeast is still converting sugar to alcohol or whether a malolactic fermentation is underway or whether some bacterial action is in progress.

So long as the wine has a good clean aroma and the taste is equally good without a strong acid bite, it is likely that bottling immediately (with about 30–40 ppm of sulfite) is desirable. Delay may cause the aromatics to dissipate thus losing one important organoleptic factor.

Clean all bottles and siphoning equipment and sterilize with sulfite before use. Treat the carboy of wine with 30 ppm of sulfite 12 to 24 hours before bottling.

There are three types of closures that are commonly used by winemakers. Crown caps, screw caps and corks. Crown caps and screw caps are easy to apply and should be treated with sulfite before use. Corks can be soaked in scalding water for 10 to 20 minutes and rinsed in fresh water before inserting with a corker. There are a large number of corkers available in home winemaking shops. The type that compress the cork before inserting it work the best, but cost the most. Wine bottles that are corked should be laid down on their sides to prevent the corks from drying out and leaking.

With one exception all of the foregoing suggestions have centered on the production of still, dry table wines. If a sweet wine is desired, make a sugar syrup and mix it in the carboy with some potassium sorbate (a preservative) at bottling time. The potassium sorbate is available at home winemaking shops and will prevent the yeast from activating and consuming the added sugar. If that were to happen you would end up with a dry wine and blown corks, because the yeast would produce CO_2 in the corked bottle.

Don't expect the new wine to be ambrosia from the Gods until it has a chance to age a bit. Set a few bottles aside for longer aging and have a yearly comparative tasting of your own product.

CHAPTER 2

SPARKLING WINE: A HOME WINEMAKER'S GUIDE TO METHODE CHAMPENOISE

Jim Gifford

NOTICE: Certain parts of sparkling wine production require extreme care. Failure to follow the safety precautions stated in this chapter may result in serious bodily injury. Neither the author, the American Wine Society, nor G.W. Kent, Inc. will be responsible for any injuries that might result from a failure to follow safety precautions.

WHEREVER WINE IS MADE, sparkling wine is made by various methods. It is known by different terms: Champagne in France; Cava in Spain; Asti Spumante in Italy; Sekt in Germany. The Methode Champenoise described here was developed in the Champagne district of France and is used throughout the world. It is the only method employed in Champagne.

Sparkling wine as we know it today has been produced for over 300 years. The oldest Champagne firm in continuous existence, Ruinart P'ere et Fils (Rheims), was founded in 1729. The rudimentary steps of the process, later to be called Methode Champenoise, were probably developed by the monk Dom Perignon in the later part of the seventeenth century, 60 years before the founding of Ruinart.

The Methode Champenoise process evolved over time through a combination of accidental discoveries, trial and error experiences and complex scientific revelations which led to important technical developments. Today, the Methode Champenoise is a unique combination of labor intensive operations and scientifically automated convenience.

Sparkling wine is thought to be the most complicated of wines to make, and with good reason. It is actually made twice-first as a still wine which is closely followed by a second prise de mousse fermentation (literally, "the taking on of the sparkle"). Each of these two winemaking processes has its own requirements and specifications with concomitant difficulties and risks. It is the wine which requires the most decisions of its creator, and which takes the most time to master.

Sparkling wine production is, therefore, best performed by experienced winemakers (whether professional or amateur). The making of sparkling wine requires equipment, materials and space beyond that of still winemaking. Safety precautions should be taken once the second fermentation has occurred, since the bottles will be under pressure, and therefore could explode accidentally. High temperatures will increase the pressure and, therefore increase the potential of explosion. Obviously dropping bottles at this stage, and later, risks explosion of the bottle. It is therefore imperative to always wear eye protection along with long sleeve shirts and long pants or slacks when working with or handling bottled sparkling wine.

This chapter is a detailed description of the Methode Champenoise, with explanations of the reasoning involved in its development, as well as a beginner's guide to each process involved. They are in no way prescriptions for guaranteed success, nor are they the only specific methods that will bring success. Success in making sparkling wine requires a patient attitude as well as willingness to make slight adjustments to the described processes when required, such as when the raw materials are less than perfect or the equipment for ideal winemaking is unavailable. Even commercial wineries have to make these kinds of adjustments at times.

What is important for all winemakers to have is openness to innovation and a good mind for experimentation. The trial and error axiom used to develop the present Methode Champenoise process still applies. Don't be afraid to alter a step slightly. Just remember what you did and how you did it. Make notes. That way the Methode Champenoise process described here will become a guide, not a dictum.

The Grapes

There are, in theory, no restrictions upon which varieties of grapes can be used for making sparkling wine. Technically speaking, the major concerns of the winemaker involve only the maturity level, fruit quality, acidity, and pH of the grapes when picked.

Realistically, however, the accepted style range for sparkling wines is rather narrow. For practical purposes this limits the number of grape varieties suitable for making sparkling wines.

TABLE 1

GRAPE VARIETIES FOR SPARKLING WINE		
MOST DESIRABLE		
Vinifera	Hybrid	Native
Chardonnay	*Vidal blanc*	*Dutchess*
Pinot noir	*Seyval blanc*	
Pinot blanc	*Vignoles*	
Muscat (for spumante)		
Riesling (for sekt)		
LESS DESIRABLE		
Vinifera	Hybrid	Native
Chenin blanc	*Cayuga*	*Catawba*
Thompson Seedless	*Baco noir*	*Isabella*
	Aurora	*Concord*
LEAST DESIRABLE		
Vinifera	Hybrid	Native
French Colombard	*DeChaunac*	*Delaware*
Cabernet Sauvignon	*Chelois*	*Elvira*
Carignane	*Chancellor*	
Petite Syrah		
Zinfandel		

Why is this style range so narrow? One reason is because the effervescence in sparkling wine greatly enhances the aroma and bouquet of the wine. This factor eliminates strongly scented grape varieties which are too intense in character after the second fermentation.

Another factor which influences varietal selection is that of the carbonic acid found in sparkling wines. Carbonic acid creates a rather bitter feeling on the palate.

Many red varieties are high in phenolic compounds which, among other things cause a wine to be astringent or bitter. Therefore, tannic red varieties (tannin is a phenol based compound) such as Cabernet Sauvignon or Petite Syrah are not desirable for making sparkling wine since they become offensively astringent in the presence of carbonic acid.

Table 1 is a listing of varieties of grapes (organized by species) commonly available to the home winemaker, with ranking of desirability for making sparkling wine.

Picking The Grapes

Once the variety/varieties have been chosen for making the sparkling wine, criteria for when and how to pick them need to be established.

The single most important factor to use when determining when to pick the grapes is that of percent sugar. Sugar determines the potential alcohol of the base wine after fermentation. Because an alcohol level of between 10 and 11% is desired for the base wine, a sugar level of no less than 17.5% and no more than 19.0% is most desirable.

The sugar level of the grapes is also an indication of fruit maturity and indicates rather consistently (with some vintage variation) whether the grapes are at optimum ripeness.

Low levels of natural sugar in the fruit can be altered by chaptalizing the juice, which consists of adding a measured amount of sugar in order to raise the potential alcohol to a desired amount. The formula for this practice is discussed in detail coming up in a couple of pages. This means that low sugar levels should not deter the winemaker from picking the grapes, if the other criteria of maturity are at or near the levels desired.

Other important considerations for picking the grapes include total acidity levels and pH. In the Champagne region of France, a cool region with a short, fast growing season, fruit harvested at 17.5–19.0% sugar will normally contain 10–12 grams per liter total acidity (expressed as tartaric acid), and have a pH as low as 2.8–2.9. Almost all Champagne houses

TABLE 2

PRESSING REGIMEN FOR SPARKLING WINE				
CAKE MIXING	**PRESSURE**	**FRACTION**	**VOLUME/TON**	**%**
1st	free run	first	66 gallons	39%
2nd	light press	first	40 gallons	23%
3rd	light press	first	26 gallons	15%
		TOTAL	**132 gallons**	**77%**
4th	medium press	second	13 gallons	8%
		TOTAL	**13 gallons**	**8%**
5th	heavy press	third	13 gallons	8%
6th	heavy press	third	13 gallons	8%
		TOTAL	**26 gallons**	**16%**
		GRAND TOTAL	**171 gallons**	

The total yield per ton will vary from vintage to vintage and between varieties in each vintage. Any increase or decrease will effect the heavy press fraction only. In other words, a theoretical yield of 171 gallons of juice per ton should be used when calculating when to switch fractions during each press load.

Note: The time required for realizing the volumes per fraction increases as the press cycle progresses.

complete malolactic fermentation, however, which along with normal cold stabilization, lowers the total acidity to around 8.5 grams per liter and raises the pH to around 3.05–3.15.

The goal of the winemaker is to have a cuvee ready for bottling that will have an alcohol level of 10–11%, a pH of 3.1–3.3 and a total acidity of 7.5–8.5 grams per liter. If a pH meter is not available, use total acidity as a guide for harvesting and later wine processing.

Finally, one of the most important criterion for when to harvest grapes to be made into sparkling wine is fruit quality. There should be very little mold, mildew or rot in the grapes when pressed. If rain and high humidity levels occur toward the end of the ripening period, the resultant infections of mold or rot may progress rapidly and force the harvesting of the grapes earlier than anticipated. The maximum level of mold or bunch rot allowable is 10% of the total crop.

Sparkling wine grapes should be picked by hand into small boxes. This is required by law in Champagne and is being utilized by more and more of the serious wine houses in the U.S. Hand

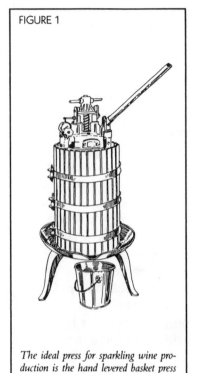

FIGURE 1

The ideal press for sparkling wine production is the hand levered basket press commonly used by home winemakers.

picking is necessary to reduce the extraction of many types of phenolic compounds (phenolic compounds found in grapes are responsible for red wine color, act as substrates for browning reactions, and as discussed earlier, organoleptically are astringent and bitter).

The handling of the grapes is thought to be the most important step in determining the quality and aging potential of the wine. If grapes are not available, juice may be purchased from various home winemaking shops. If possible, ask for the lighter press fractions (the first 2/3 to 3/4 of the yield) to be separated from the heavier press juice. Add metabisulfite as needed using the pressing regime described here as a guide, but use limited amounts if you are planning a malolactic fermentation.

Pressing should occur within a few hours of picking, if possible. Ideally it should be performed in a basket press (see Figure 1) or small bladder/membrane press, and should be performed with slowly increasing pressure at each stage with the cake being broken up several times per the regimen in Table 2.

The grapes should not be destemmed, but rather pressed "whole cluster". The stems act as a press aid by helping to increase the flow-rate of the juice, thus increasing the percentage of juice classified as "light press". This is important for minimizing the extraction of phenolic compounds such as oxidases, pectins and mineral salts.

The highest quality juice is the "free-run", followed by the "light press" and the "medium press" fractions. If the grapes are sound and at the optimum maturity, the free run and light press fractions combined will equal approximately 3/4 of the entire yield possible. For a commercial winery (using the following protocol) this

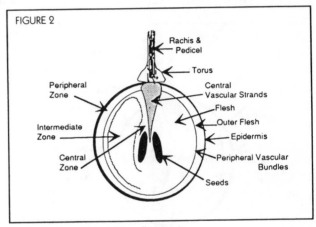

FIGURE 2

Reprinted with permission of Cornell University

is about 132 gallons out of approximately 171 gallons per ton average yield. When the grapes are not sound or harsher methods of pressing (i.e. screw press) are employed, less of the juice can be classified as light press. The home winemaker can calculate his yield per press load by weighing his grapes per load and estimating one gallon juice/12.5 lbs of grapes.

The purpose of breaking up the cake frequently during the first press cycle is to increase the quality of the light press fraction. Breaking up the cake at frequent intervals during the early stages of pressing ensures that all mature berries will be broken before continuing to the medium press fraction. This ensures that only the highest quality juice will be separated during the first fraction.

Figures 2 and 3 are illustrations of the inside of a mature grape berry. Only the juice from the "intermediate zone" is desired for making sparkling wine. The reason for this is illustrated in Figure 3. The "central zone" contains the seeds which are full of oils and tannins. The "peripheral zone" contains pectins, lipids, mineral salts, oxidases, astringent anthocyanin pigments, as well as browning precursors.

The Juice

The largest and most important fraction of the juice is the first one out of the press. It is lowest in phenolic compounds and therefore lowest in color, bitterness and browning potential. The pH is lower and the total acidity higher than the other fractions. It has the most finesse and elegance and best potential for aging.

In normal years it is not necessary to fine this portion of the juice. Merely add 20–25 ppm sulfite (see Table 3), chill to 40–45° F and settle overnight.

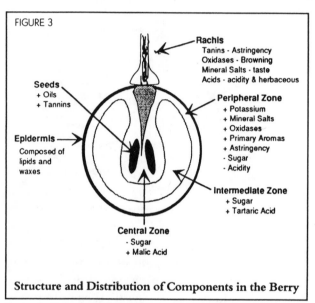

FIGURE 3

Rachis
Tanins - Astringency
Oxidases - Browning
Mineral Salts - taste
Acids - acidity & herbaceous

Seeds
+ Oils
+ Tannins

Peripheral Zone
+ Potassium
+ Mineral Salts
+ Oxidases
+ Primary Aromas
+ Astringency
- Sugar
- Acidity

Epidermis
Composed of
lipids and
waxes

Intermediate Zone
+ Sugar
+ Tartaric Acid

Central Zone
- Sugar
+ Malic Acid

Structure and Distribution of Components in the Berry

Reprinted with permission of Cornell University

The second or medium press fration is separated from the first fraction and fined. It should be fined with bentonite /casein or PVPP. Bentonite/ casein (50/50 solution) should be added at a rate of .25–.50 oz./ gallon. PVPP should be added at a rate of .25 oz./gallon. Once fined, settled and racked off the lees, the juice may be added back to the first fraction for fermentation, or may be fermented separately. If a cuvee is light or thin bodied, this fraction may be an appropriate addition to fill out the body, but it will also make it one that will age more quickly. Waiting until after fermentation to decide what to do is the ideal situation for the winemaker. Sulfite addition is the same as for the first fraction (20–25 ppm).

The most difficult fraction to obtain (especially with a hand powered basket press) is the third and last fraction. It has the highest phenolic content as well as the least amount of acid, highest pH and is the least desirable to utilize for quality sparkling wine. This fraction should be fined, settled and fermented separately from the first two fractions. If it is to be fermented(not discarded), it should be heavily fined with bentonite/casein (1oz./gallon), as well as a decolorizing carbon at the same rate as bentonite/casein. It should be sulfited at a higher rate than the first two fractions (over 50 ppm).

TABLE 3

GRAMS OF KMBS TO ADD TO ACHIEVE DESIRED PPM IN A KNOWN VOLUME OF WINE					
AMOUNT OF WINE TO BE ADJUSTED					
PPM SO$_2$ DESIRED	10L	50L	100L	500L	1000L
5 ppm	.11	.55	1.10	5.50	11.00
10 ppm	.22	1.10	2.20	11.00	22.00
15 ppm	.33	1.65	3.30	16.50	33.00
20 ppm	.44	2.20	4.40	22.00	44.00
25 ppm	.55	2.75	5.50	27.50	55.00
30 ppm	.66	3.30	6.60	33.00	66.00
35 ppm	.77	3.85	7.70	38.50	77.00
40 ppm	.88	4.40	8.80	44.00	88.00
45 ppm	.99	4.95	9.90	49.50	99.00
50 ppm	1.10	5.50	11.00	55.00	110.00

Potassium metabisulfite (KMBS) is the water soluble potassium salt of sulfur dioxide, and is the commonly used form of sulfite in the wine industry. Theoretically, available sulfur dioxide makes up 57.6% (when fresh) of the total weight of the potassium metabisulfite molecule. Standard tables use this factor when developing guides for addition. Personal experience and observation has determined that closer to 45% of the weight of KMBS actually becomes available upon hydration. Table 3 uses the factor .45 in its formulation, rather than the theoretical figure of .576. Therefore, the values of grams of KMBS suggested will be a bit higher than those of most other tables to reach the same level of addition.

Chaptalization

In vintages when the grapes have not attained a sugar level high enough to produce a base wine of 10–11% alcohol, sugar may be added to bring the juice to the desired potential alcohol level.

To determine how much sugar to add (cane sugar is easiest and most commonly used) you must first know what the percent sugar of the juice is prior to yeast inoculation. The sugar reading of the juice is multiplied by the factor .58, because about 58% of the sugar will be fermented to alcohol. For instance, a refractometer or hydrometer reading of 16.2 will have a calculated potential alcohol as follows:

$$16.2 \times .58 = 9.4\%$$

The formula for chaptalization is based upon the fact that 17 grams of cane sugar will raise one liter of juice one percent in potential alcohol. Therefore, if an alcohol level of 11.0% is desired it is necessary to raise the potential alcohol as follows:

$$
\begin{array}{rl}
11.0 & \text{(desired alcohol level)} \\
-\ \ 9.4 & \text{(actual potential alcohol)} \\
\hline
1.6 & \text{(amount to raise)} \\
\times\ 17.0 & \text{(grams sugar to raise 1 liter by 1\%)} \\
\hline
27.2 & \text{(grams/liter needed to raise alcohol by 1.6\%)}
\end{array}
$$

If you have 100 liters of juice then:

$$
\begin{array}{rl}
100 & \\
\times\ 27.2 & \\
\hline
2720 & \text{grams sugar are needed (metric/English conversion} \\
 & \text{formula at end of this chapter)}
\end{array}
$$

Fermentation Of Juice

Following settling overnight at 40–45° F, the juice will be racked to another container and inoculated with an appropriate yeast. A relatively new theory developed in France concerning the selection of yeast is as follows: use a low foaming yeast for the primary yeast fermentation, but use a high foaming, pressure and alcohol tolerant yeast for the second yeast fermentation. These choices are now available to the home wine-maker. There are many "Champagne" yeasts to choose from, just be certain to follow manufacturer's recommendations regarding rates of addition and hydration methods.

Today most Champagne firms ferment in glass-lined or stainless steel tanks. A few, such as Bollinger, Gosset and, most notably, Krug are exceptions to the rule. These firms still ferment and age a large portion of their wines in wood.

Fermenting in small oak cooperage, when it is an option, is a stylistic consideration of the winemaker and can be performed on all or part of the blend. It produces a distinctive character in the wine and will impart a stronger bouquet that may be considered unique or at least distinct for modern-day sparkling wine.

Undoubtedly, 5 or 10 gallon glass containers are the most commonly used fermentation vessels for the home winemaker. 50 gallon food-grade plastic drums or 55 gallon wooden barrels are also used by home wine-makers. Whatever type of container is used, it should be kept about 3/4 full during fermentation (Figure 4). A container too full will most likely overflow at the height of fermentation. If it is much less than half full it will have an increased poten-tial for acquiring hydro-gen sulfide, or acquire a "leesy" character.

Malolactic fermenta-tion is often used in Champagne. This fermen-tation is desirable in Champagne because it lowers the total acidity, raises the pH of the wine and adds a characteristic flavor that is readily dis-

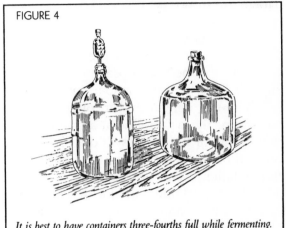

FIGURE 4

It is best to have containers three-fourths full while fermenting.

cerned as typical French earthiness, and complexity. It has only recently been experimented with in the U.S. for sparkling wines.

As in most microbiological work, experience and proper equipment are required for successful malolactic fermentation. It is risky to deal with because only small amounts of sulfite can be utilized if the bacteria are to grow.

Commercial malolactic cultures are available with instructions, and often consulting services are offered customers. Many advances are being made in this area presently to simplify this process, including development of active-dried cultures which are much less complicated to use. The curious home winemaker should be aware of this trend and ask about available strains just coming onto the market. Malolactic fermenta-tion should always be completed prior to the second yeast fermentation.

It is important that the components of the blend be racked off fermenta-tion lees into a full airtight container and sulfite added to 20–25 ppm free sulfite. At this time the wine should be chilled at 28–30° F for 20 to 30 days.

The wine should then be racked off the tartrate crystals and .25–.50 oz. of bentonite/gallon should be added to remove excess protein for heat stabilization. Please note that these instructions are for larger home winemaking operations. Unless the home winemaker produces wine for special competitions and/or ships wine relatively long distances, it is not necessary to heat or cold stabilize the wine, although it is still recom-mended as good winemaking procedure. Wines consumed locally will probably not experience the temperature extremes that will cause problems in the wine.

Tirage (bottling)

Sugar has to be utilized at three different steps in the Methode Champenoise process: for the yeast work-up; for the second fermentation; and for the final dosage (sweetening). Typically, granulated cane sugar is the type used for sparkling wine production.

There is a danger and inconvenience inherent in adding granulated sugar directly to the wine at any time during processing. The danger is that not all of the sugar will dissolve and/or invert so that it can be fermented by the yeast during the first two steps (yeast work-up and bottle fermentation). The inconvenience is obvious when dry sugar is added to a bottle of sparkling wine for the purpose of sweetening it. This usually causes excess foaming and product loss.

To solve both problems it is best to make your own syrup, using a small portion of the base wine (cuvee). The low pH of the wine will break (by inversion) the bonds of the long polysaccharide chains of the sucrose molecules. The process takes 3–5 days to complete with all but the higher saccharides inverting into fermentable sugars. Typically 99.6% or more of the saccharides in sucrose are fermentable after inversion.

The concentration of the syrup should be 50%, or 500 grams/liter wine to make calculation of addition as easy as possible. Making a 50% syrup is not as simple as adding 500 grams of sugar to a liter of wine. This is because the weight of the sugar causes the volume of the wine to expand. The rate of expansion is 7.908 gallons/100 lbs. of granulated sugar.

A rough calculation for making 50% syrup is as follows: Add 25 lbs. of sugar to 4 gallons of wine to get about 6 gallons of syrup at 500 grams/liter, or reduce amounts proportionately.

Riddling aids of various types have been developed to enhance the speed and efficiency of sliding the yeast into the neck of the bottle. The dynamics of the various materials used for this purpose consist of an inert material being added to the wine at time of bottling, usually just minutes before the beginning of bottling. This material will settle out in the bottle underneath and with the yeast lees. It has a weak negative charge (the same as the glass), and is therefore repelled slightly by the glass. The lees has a weak positive charge and therefore is slightly attracted to the glass. When used, riddling aid will speed up and increase the efficiency of subsequent riddling by neutralizing the overall charge attraction of the lees to the glass.

Most riddling aids use bentonite, either alone or mixed with other proprietary ingredients such as alginates. The following is the formula for a food grade bentonite to be used as a riddling aid in a 100 bottle tirage preparation.

Hydrate 8 grams food grade bentonite in 1 liter warm water.

Let set for 24 hours.

Add to adjusted base wine per later instructions.

Sparkling wine bottles are a special type made to withstand high pressure, and are, therefore, much heavier than still wine bottles. Sparkling wine bottles often have a punt or pushup at the bottom, which is traditional and does perform the function of deflecting pressure away from the bottom of the bottle.

The neck of the sparkling wine bottle is made to receive either a crown cap secured around the outside lip, or a standard champagne cork. This cork would necessarily have to be secured by a wire hood, if used. Most home winemaking shops have a selection of this type of bottle for your use. Under no circumstances should standard still wine bottles be used.

Yeast Propagation/Inoculation

The most delicate operation to perform during the making of sparkling wine is the propagation and inoculation of the yeast. In sparkling wine production, as opposed to still wine production, a "training" of the yeast prior to inoculation is required. That is, even though a yeast has been selected for high alcohol tolerance (as well as pressure tolerance) it is important that the culture used become acclimated to the wine and sugar medium into which it will soon be introduced. It is also helpful to "retrain" the yeast to the higher alcohol level so that they are not shocked by this rather inhospitable component of the medium.

There are many different yeasts available to the commercial winemaker for making sparkling wine. These strains are selected for their ability to withstand high pressure, for alcohol tolerance, for ease of riddling, for flavor enhancement and other reasons. Most home winemaking shops will have several to choose from.

All sparkling wine yeasts should have a manufacturer's recommended work-up for that yeast. Some are several days in length, others are as short as 2–3 day work-ups. Rather than try to prescribe one yeast protocol over another, a few general rules or guidelines will be given here.

1. Be sure free SO_2 of wine is below 15 ppm.

2. Hydrate yeast per manufacturer's recommendation.

3. Sweeten small portion (less than 5% of total volume) of base wine to 3–4% sugar.

4. Add hydrated yeast to sweetened base wine and aerate. Yeast should become active within a few hours.

5. May want to allow fermentation to proceed until fermentation rate is slowing down and only a small amount of sugar is left. At this time the inoculum may be diluted with water to bring the alcohol level to 9–10%, sweetened per step 3 and allowed to ferment again.

6. Or, if it is felt that the culture is healthy, alcohol tolerant and is not producing off odors, it can inoculated at this time (without the dilution and refermentation).

7. The volume of the yeast culture should be about 5% of the total volume to be bottled that day. This may seem like a very small amount, but if the yeast is healthy and viable it is the ideal amount. A very active culture added a 3–5% of total volume should have about 1.5 million cells/ml. of wine. This amount of yeast encourages faster riddling and gives a balanced fruit and yeast character to the wine. Higher cell counts/ml. of wine will give heavier yeast character up to a point, but risk H_2S production.

8. It is recommended that the yeast culture be added to the adjusted base wine one day prior to bottling. This mixture should be aerated frequently during the period between inoculation and bottling.

The adjustment of the base wine consists of sugar addition of 24 grams/liter of wine added in the form of syrup. (This amount will produce a pressure of approximately 90 psi and should never be exceeded. Lower pressures may be obtained using the following formula: 4 grams sugar/liter of wine=1 atmosphere or about 14.7 psi) In addition, the riddling aid should be added just prior to the bottling process. The wine should be stirred occasionally during bottling to keep the riddling aid in suspension. The recommended rate of addition is 3 to 5 grams per 100 liters of wine.

Bottling

Equipment needed: Sparkling wine bottles, crown caps, filler, bottle capper.

1. Fill bottle to approximately 2 inches from bottom lip of bottle, remembering to stir the yet-to-be-bottled wine occasionally.

2. Crimp crown cap snugly around lip of glass. Test by twisting with hand. It should not move or twist around lip of bottle.

3. Lay all bottles on side and store in dark area at 55–60° F. Storage can be sturdy cardboard boxes, specially constructed wooden crates, or stacked on side on lath runners.

Fermentation And Aging

The bottles will remain on their side for 12–48 months. They should remain at a constant temperature in a slightly humid area, such as a cellar or basement.

The actual fermentation will be completed in 3–6 weeks. Most yeast autolysis (degradation of the individual cells which flavors the wine and makes it "yeasty") occurs between the 6th and 12th month after bottling. A small amount of autolysis (about 5% of the total) continues after bottling. When the winemaker feels that the wine is at its peak it will be prepared for yeast removal and disgorging.

Riddling

The gradual manipulation of the yeast from the sides of the bottle to the cap is called riddling. The sediment, both gross and fine, is gradually maneuvered down the side of the glass bottle by twisting and tilting it until the sediment is deposited against the crown cap.

If riddling aid has been added in the appropriate amount this process will be speeded up considerably. The riddling aid is especially efficient in clearing the wine of the finest, most difficult to remove sediment.

Note: Face protection should be worn during all subsequent processing.

Before the bottles are to be riddled, each one should be shaken. This is accomplished by inverting each bottle in such a way as to use the air bubble in the bottle to "wash" the deposited sediment until all of it is suspended. Usually 8 to 10 inversions are enough. The term shaking does not mean vigorous movement.

The shaken bottles should be laid horizontally for 6–7 days or until the sediment has redeposited on the side of the bottle. This accomplishes two things: the breaking of any loose bonds between the glass and sediment, and allowing the heavier riddling aid to settle out first so it can act as a carrier for the finest sediment.

After the resting period, the bottles are carefully placed in an A-frame type riddling rack in as horizontal fashion as possible. (See bottom bottle, Figure 5). The sediment will deposit on the bottom side of the bottle.

The bottle will now be marked with a white line (usually made of water soluble paint) on the punt bottom of the glass. The line will go from the middle of the punt, perpendicular to the floor, bisecting the sediment as in Step 1, Figure 6. The bottles will rest again for 1–2 days prior to commencement of riddling.

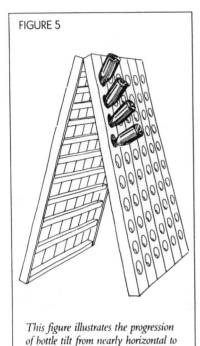

FIGURE 5

This figure illustrates the progression of bottle tilt from nearly horizontal to nearly vertical that occurs gradually during the riddling program. Progression is bottom bottle to top bottle.

Figure 6 is a standard riddling program for easy to remove sediment. It has 22 steps; at least 7 hours should elapse between each one. Therefore, a program of turning once in the morning and once in the evening would require 11 days to complete. If, for one reason or another, this schedule can not be adhered to, do what is possible.

The diagram consists of circles divided into 8 equal sections, 3 on the right, 3 on the left and 1 at the top and bottom. The circle with one line at the bottom (the upper left one) corresponds to the starting point of the program. The diagram progresses at incremental turns each step with a 5 degree tilt occurring frequently, but not every time.

If followed properly the sediment will be tight against the crown cap at the end of the program and the bottle will be almost vertical, and upside down. (See top bottle, Figure 5).

For difficult-to-riddle sediment, the diagram in Figure 6 would be divided into 16 equal sections with smaller incremental turns. A 2–3 degree tilt would be utilized with this program. This type of program would have twice as many steps as the standard one illustrated here.

An alternative for winemakers who have not added riddling aid and/or do not have a riddling rack is suggested by C. Devitt Ward, an experienced home winemaker. He has found that inverting the bottles in a cardboard box then picking up each bottle a few inches and dropping it back into the box once or twice a day often will achieve the same results as those described here.

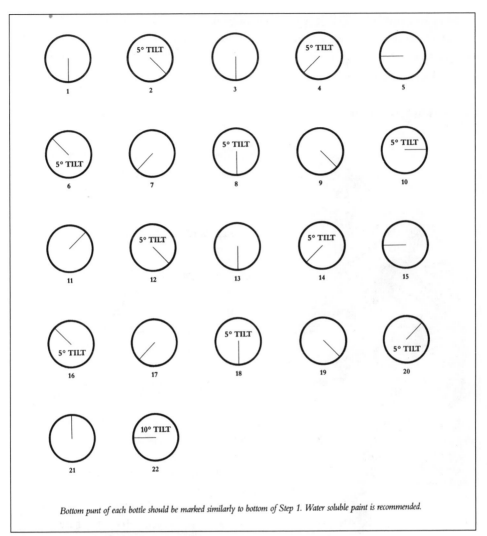

Bottom punt of each bottle should be marked similarly to bottom of Step 1. Water soluble paint is recommended.

Figure 6. Standard Riddling Program

Disgorging

Removing the sediment from the wine is called disgorging. There are two types of disgorging: flying disgorgement and iced disgorgement. In both processes the wine is chilled to about 40–45° F first. It is best to use an authentic decrowner like the one in the illustration. This is similar to a "church key" type bottle cap remover, except that it removes the crown cap from the bottom up (as the bottle points horizontally) which is the opposite of the more common church key. This makes the decrowner safer and cleaner to use.

In both methods of disgorging the actual yeast removal should take place inside a barrel or keg modified with a hole cut in its side where the sediment will be directed by the disgorger. The only other safe place to remove the sediment would be outside, away from people or breakable items.

Flying Disgorgement

Figure 7

1. Hold punt of bottle firmly against abdomen or upper thigh and point crown downward. (See Figure 7)

2. Place decrowner around crown cap and seat so as to just begin to remove cap. (See Figure 8)

3. When pressure begins to build and is about to blow sediment out, steadily swing neck of bottle up toward opening in barrel so that air bubble nears neck of bottle. As air bubble reaches neck let crown cap fly, followed by sediment and small amount of wine. (See Figure 9)

Iced Disgorgement

A simplified version of a "bac a glace", the French machine used for freezing an ice plug in the neck of the bottle is fairly easy to adapt at home. A wash basin or styrofoam cooler (or similar type container) may be used. A salt brine solution consisting of concentrated salt water will be placed in the container. This will be chilled via dry ice (amount to be determined by trial and error). A wooden lattice work with openings just large enough to fit the neck of the bottle through should be fitted into the container resting just above the salt brine. The properly riddled and chilled sparkling wine will be placed in the opening in the lattice so that about 3 to 4 inches of the neck is submerged. The chilled brine will freeze a plug in 5-10 minutes for each bottle. Once the ice plug is formed the wine can be stood upright and disgorged into the opening in the barrel.

Alternative suggestion for this procedure is: Dip the bottle neck in a mixture of crushed ice and rock salt, which will produce an ice plug in the pre-chilled bottle. Note: The brine solution will be below freezing and, therefore extreme caution must be used with this process. Insulated rubber gloves, protective outer clothing and face protection are a must.

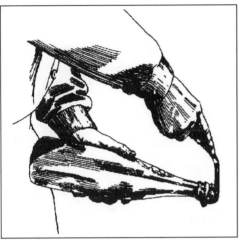

Figure 8

Dosage

Sweetening with syrup is performed by quickly adding, with a pipette or syringe, the desired amount according to the taste of the winemaker, and closing as quickly as possible in order to eliminate frothing. A typical dosage in France contains sugar, SO_2 and Cognac. Use of this method is the choice of the individual winemaker. Sulfite may be added to protect the wine from premature aging due to oxidation. The suggested level is 20–25 ppm. The bottle will either be corked and have a wire hood attached, or another crown cap will be placed on the bottle. The bottle should then be inverted several times to mix the syrup well.

The wine should lie on its side or upside down for at least 3 months. This gives the cork time

Figure 9

to soften for easy removal. In addition, the syrup will have time to "marry" with the wine.

Metric Conversion Values

1 gallon = 3.7853 liters

1 liter = 0.2642 gallon

1 hectoliter = 26.4172 gallons

1 pound = 0.4536 kilograms

1 pound = 454 gram

1 kilogram = 2.205 pounds

1 ounce = 28.35 grams

1 gram = .0353 ounces

100 grams = 3.53 ounces

CHAPTER 3

HOW TO MAKE FRUIT WINES
Les Sperling Ph.D.

Getting Started in Fruit Winemaking

T HERE ARE MANY kinds of wine. While most commercial wines are based on grapes, many home winemakers have developed the art of fruit winemaking. Thus, the home winemaker can delight his or her friends with an unusual drink, a fruit wine. Properly made, fruit wines can be as good as grape wines. However, because much more material has been written about making grape wines than fruit wines, interested amateurs often have difficulty finding reliable information about making fruit wines. This chapter combines basic information about fruit wine-making with the expertise of a number of American Wine Society members, especially national amateur competition prize winners in the fruit wine category.

The importance of fruit wines on the American scene should not be underestimated. Out of some 400 wines submitted to the American Wine Society every year for the amateur wine competition, about 15% are fruit wines. This makes it one of the largest categories in the competition. It must be emphasized that in cold climates, where grapes may grow poorly, fruit wines often dominate the scene. Note, for example, hard cider and apple wines, which were popular in Colonial times in New England, and still are.

Suggestions For Beginners

Perhaps the number one suggestion in starting to make any wine, grape or fruit, is to select sound, ripe fruit. Use the quality of fruit that you would serve guests after dinner. If any portion is rotten, cut it out.

Not so widely noted among fruit winemakers is the variety of fruit being used. Few grape winemakers use just any variety of grapes: they use Chardonnay, Riesling, Baco noir, etc. However, apple, peach, raspberry, etc. wines rarely show the variety of fruit used. Some fruit varieties are preferred over others, and sometimes, especially for apples, blends are better than varietals.

Fruit Winemaking

For the beginner, perhaps the easiest fruit wine to make is apple. Apple cider is available in season in fruit markets throughout much of North America. An important criterion is that no preservatives have been added. Preservatives will prevent the yeast from fermenting the juice into wine. The source of the cider is also important. Cheap ciders may have been made from fallen apples, now bruised, dirty or oxidized brown. Many apple ciders, however, are made from good quality apples.

Of course, the simplest drink to make is hard cider. Just pour the cider into a large crock and let 'er rip! The product ought to be ready to drink in about a month. However, its quality will vary greatly, and because of its low alcohol content, about 6%, it will not last long.

Some Basics, Apple Wine

Since the volume shrinks slightly upon fermenting, and some wine is lost in racking, about 6 gallons of juice should produce 5 gallons of finished wine. The average apple cider will have a specific gravity of 1.050–1.055 as measured by a hydrometer. To make a 12% alcohol wine the specific gravity should be about 1.090. One pound of sugar per pint of water, boiled and then cooled makes a suitable concentrated solution for this purpose. Approximately one pound of sugar will be needed per gallon of cider to make a quality wine. If the wine is later to be sweetened and hence diluted, slightly more sugar should be added, so the alcohol content will be high enough after dilution.

For many apple ciders, the acidity is a bit low, as determined by titration. It should be in the range of 0.7–0.8% acidity, expressed as tartaric acid. As a rough guide, one ounce of tartaric or similar acid will raise the acidity of 5 gallons of juice approximately 0.1. Since the main acid in apples is malic acid it is the preferred acid to add by most apple winemakers. Alternatively, and sometimes recommended for the home winemaker is tartaric acid, because it does not undergo malolactic fermentation. For commercial apple wines the BATF permits only malic acid to be added.

Regardless of the fruit type, early in the fermentation the must should be stirred twice a day to introduce a limited amount of oxygen, required by the growing population of yeast. If solid fruit is present, it should be punched down each time, wetting all portions.

It must be pointed out that during the fermentation process, the wines are cloudy, and may look terrible. After the primary fermentation is finished, the yeast will settle out over a period of weeks, and the wine should be racked off the sediment.

Fermentation of fruit wines often takes longer than the corresponding grape wines. In part, this can be speeded up by the addition of nutrients, just like fertilizing plants. However, most apple fermentations continue for weeks, rather than the few days needed for grapes.

Additional Points

While winemakers differ somewhat on the level of sulfur dioxide to add, for the beginner one Campden tablet per gallon of juice is recommended. This should be dissolved first using one ounce of water per tablet. Pectic enzyme should also be added to the juice so the wine will be clearer when finished. After 24 hours, the yeast is added to the juice. Again, there are umpteen different wine yeasts. Many will produce slightly different flavors in the wine. These can be bought as dry-active packets just for the home winemaker, and start 5–10 gallons of juice.

Most commercial ciders are blends of apples, which may vary from place to place, and as the season progresses. Tom Petuskey of New Jersey and Earl Deveney of Pennsylvania both recommend blends of apples, if a choice can be made. Deveney recommends 50% of high acid varieties, such as Winesap, 25% aromatic apples, such as Jonathan for their "nose", and 25% Red Delicious, for their sweetness.

In his article which appeared in the American Wine Society Journal (Volume 20, issue 3) Tome Petuskey points out that there are 4 classifications of apples:

1. Sweet Subacid Group: Baldwin, Rome Beauty

2. Mildly Acid to Slightly Tart: Winesap, Jonathan, Stayman

3. Aromatic Group: Delicious, Golden Delicious, McIntosh

4. Astringent Group: Florence Hibernal, most crab apples

A blend of at least 3 different classifications is recommended, providing a balance of sweetness, tartness, and tannin, along with a fresh, fruity aroma. If the beginner can not select his or her own apples, Petuskey recommends careful selection of the source of the cider. Late selection of cider makes for a higher content of apples with higher acidity in many cases. Petuskey points out that whole apples kept in cold storage seem to produce a better balanced and better tasting cider.

While blends of apples are often recommended for apple wines, the Joseph Cerniglia Winery, Inc. in Vermont is known for its "varietal apple wines of distinction". The taste of each variety does come through. Thus, the interested amateur has a choice of preparation methods.

One particular "trick" in making a custom wine might be to substitute honey for white sugar in making the wine. About 10 pounds of honey seems just right under many circumstances for six gallons of initial cider. The honey, which by itself makes mead, needs a bit of treatment first. This involves addition of an equal quantity of cider to the honey, and boiling for ten minutes. This causes the proteins to precipitate, and rise as a foam, which should then be spooned off. Then, the mix is cooled and stirred into the cider.

After completion of the fermentation, the wine may be "dry", i.e., there is little or no sugar left, known as residual sugar. The hydrometer reading may be at 1.000 or slightly below. While some people like their wines dry, and this goes especially for grape wines, many people like their fruit wines slightly sweet. Each winemaker should sweeten to taste. At about 3% sugar, for most people the wine will definitely take on a distinctive sweet taste. However, sweetened wines should have potassium sorbate added, to prevent re-fermentation.

Another method of sweetening wines involves the use of the "sweet reserve" method. Here, some of the juice is saved (reserved), frozen or under heavy sulfur dioxide levels to prevent fermentation. Later, the wine is sweetened with this juice. The use of the sweet reserve method produces a significantly more "fruity" wine. While this concept is widely practiced for grape wines among amateurs and professionals alike, relatively few fruit winemakers have tried it.

If the wine exhibits a haze, it can be filtered or fined by any of several commercial fining agents, such as bentonite, Sparkolloid, or Kaolin. A home-made clarifying agent uses an egg white beaten up with a pint of the wine and a pinch of salt, good for 5 gallons. The egg white depends on its protein content, which reacts with tannin to cause a precipitation. For "white" wines, most fruit wines, tannin content is low, and may have to be added. Most of the clarifying agents require a month or so to settle, after which the wine should be racked off.

Much has been said about aging of wines. Since apple wine is really a "white" wine, it is ready to drink after a month or two in the bottle. Since it may take 8 or 10 months before bottling, the entire process may be a year. Apple wine, properly stored cool and at constant temperature, may last a year or more after bottling. The following is a simple recipe for apple wine:

6 gallons of cider

12 lbs. of honey (or sugar to specific gravity 1.090)

2 oz. of tartaric or malic acid (to 0.7–0.8% acidity)

6 Campden tablets

24 drops of pectic enzyme

1 packet of wine yeast

Ferment at 60–70° F

Other Fruits

While the above discussion emphasized apple wines, most of the comments can easily be translated into other fruit wines. One point of argument, however, relates to the amelioration of the juice with water, particularly the addition of a solution of sugar and fruit acids to the juice, diluting it. Some winemakers prefer to work with straight juice, generally true for apple wine, but others prefer to ameliorate strawberry, raspberry, or elderberry wines.

There are two points to the argument: First, the juice of some fruits is too strong in taste to make into the desired wines, and second, the cost of some fruits, raspberries for example, may be very high. A possible solution involves a blend of the fruit juice with cider. For example, cider and raspberry juice can be fermented separately and blended later. Or, through freezing the raspberries, the two can actually be fermented together. At a 50/50 blend, the mild apple wine taste will be swamped by that of the raspberry, yet it will not appear "thin" as a result of dilution.

Various fruits contain different acids. While grapes are known for having tartaric acid, citric and malic acids predominate in many other fruits.

TABLE 1

Acid Type of Some Common Fruits

Citric	Malic
Oranges	Apples
Raspberries	Pears
Currants	Cherries
Elderberries	Plums
Strawberries	Peaches

Citric, malic and tartaric acids can be determined quantitatively by titration. It must be noted that the acids differ in strength somewhat. To raise the acidity of a must or wine by 0.1%, approximately 0.12 ounce of citric or malic acid must be added per gallon, or 0.14 ounce of tartaric acid per gallon. As a rough guide, natural grape juice has about one ounce of tartaric acid per gallon.

Most importantly, the acids differ as to what happens in the fermentation. Citric acid tends to be consumed during normal fermentations, and hence after a fermentation the acid level may be significantly below that anticipated. Malic acid is subject to malolactic fermentation, which must be avoided in the fermentation of such fruits. Thus, when needed, tartaric acid may make a safer substitution acid, bringing acidity back to the normal range.

Another important way that fruit wines differ from grape wines is their behavior during cold stabilization. Grape wines contain excess amounts of potassium bitartrate, which is soluble in the wine at room temperature, but slowly crystallizes out at refrigerator temperatures, making the wine cloudy. This unsightly phenomenon can be avoided by cooling the wines to 32° F or slightly below for periods of up to two weeks, then racking the wine off the precipitate. For fruit wines there is also sometimes a precipitate, but the chemistry may be far different.

A Study of a Fermentation: Black Raspberries

Fruit wines tend to be much more "recipe" oriented than grape wines, because the natural ingredients usually will not by themselves yield a quality wine. The following paragraphs describe two aspects of fruit winemaking: a typical recipe, and notes during the actual fermentation.

Black raspberries will be used as the example, because they make a particularly interesting berry wine, very dark in color. A recipe for 5 gallons of wine goes as follows:

13 quarts of black raspberries

5 Campden tablets

10 nutrient tablets

15 pounds of white sugar

1 pectic enzyme tablet

3 lemons, juice of

Water to 5 3/4 gallons

1 packet of wine yeast

Dissolve Campden tablets and nutrient tablets separately in 1/2 glass of water each. Dissolve sugar (one pound of sugar to a pint of water), heat to boiling and cool. Mix all ingredients except yeast. After 24 hours, sprinkle yeast on must.

The following is a typical fermentation record:

Days Elapsed	Temp F	Sp. Gravity	Comments
1	84	1.112	Rapid fermentation
2 1/2	83	1.083	
3	84	1.072	Removed seeds
4 1/2	81	1.057	
5 1/2	79	1.048	
7 1/2	78	1.034	
9 1/2	78	1.028	
11 1/2	79	1.019	Fermentation slow
13 1/2	78	1.010	

General comments: Fermentation was in mid-summer, with surrounding temperatures of 72–75° F. Thus, the temperature of the fermentation was a bit high; 70° F might have been better. It should be noted that rapidly fermenting musts give off a lot of heat. The acidity of the must was a bit low, 0.6% acidity. Two ounces of tartaric acid added would have been better. Final specific gravity was 1.000. Wine tasted reasonably good.

Gordon Gribble of Vermont notes that black raspberry wines and also blueberry wines, especially when made dry, rapidly clarify and do not require fining. Because they do not have tartaric acid, they do not present a tartrate problem later in the bottle. Thus, cold stabilization, although still desirable, will not precipitate potassium bitartrate.

General Suggestions

In principle, fruit wine fermentation utilizes the same concepts as grape wine fermentation in that certain ranges of sugar, acidity, and nutrients must be attained, sterilization is required (through addition of sodium metabisulfite or boiling), and that wine yeasts are used. However, fruits as grown are quite different from grapes in chemistry, because the acid type and content, and sugar levels are different, etc. And, to complicate things further, the fruits are all different from each other.

If the reader has made grape wines, much has been learned which will be useful for making fruit wines. If the reader is a novice, the perhaps good advice is to follow a general, reliable recipe at first. Of course, the reader should find out about the specifics of the fruit to be fermented.

However, many times the winemaker may be confronted with a basket of fruit a friend or neighbor has brought over, and there may not be time to become an expert. To summarize what is needed in such cases, the following may be helpful:

The specific gravity of the must should be brought to about 20-24 Brix, corresponding to a specific gravity of 1.080–1.100, which will yield from 11% to 14% alcohol, assuming that all of the sugar is fermented. The acidity should be in the range of 0.7–0.9% acidity. If the fruit is ameliorated with significant amounts of water some nutrient is helpful. Sulfites are needed, followed by inoculation with wine yeast. Temperatures should be in the range of 50–70° F for the fermentation, with the temperature preferably decreasing as the fermentation proceeds. Protection against air is essential. Racking should be done as soon as the fermentation in the primary fermenter is complete, and at least once more later after the sediment falls out.

It must be noted that these points are essentially the same, whether the fruit is grape or non-grape. Thus, there are general procedures which should be followed, and there are specific suggestions for each type of fruit, to bring the wine to the best possible quality. Some of these specific suggestions will be discussed below, particularly quoting American Wine Society prize winners.

Juicy Suggestions

Rett Oren of Pennsylvania points out that there are two challenges to fruit winemaking:

1. Attain a degree of complexity. A possible approach is through blending of wines, both from different varieties of the same fruit, and from different fruits.

2. Bring out the aroma. He recommends cold fermentation, 55–60° F as a way of preventing the aroma from escaping during the fermentation.

One problem is that the fermentation may stick (stop) before completion. Oren does acid titration before and after fermentation, wanting about a 0.85% acidity reading at the end. Usually with fruit wines, he has to add acid, using a blend of tartaric and citric.

Oren won his prize with frozen strawberries, which he said he bought bulk from a supermarket. Werner Roesener of Ontario, also used frozen fruit, raspberries from the store which he blended with red grape concentrate in a 75/25 ratio. He believes that the addition of some grape materials gives fruit wines more of a vinous character. The better frozen fruits, especially bought in bulk, provide a mechanism of getting quality fruits nearly free from oxidation.

William Dabney of New York ameliorates fruit wines 30% and highly recommends pectic enzymes for clarity. He makes dessert wines, which require sorbates to prevent re-fermentation. For his strawberry wine, Dabney emphasizes the need for fully ripe fruit, and adds yeast nutrient and tannin powder as recommended, and citric acid is added to 0.6–0.7% acidity, which also lowers the pH. Dabney points out that the color fades at high pH, and longevity is reduced. The wines are fined with bentonite and filtered before bottling.

Oxidation is a big problem with fruit wines, as much or more than with white grape wines. Larger quantities of wine are safer than small quantities, because the larger volume to surface ratio reduces oxidation rates. David Torso of Pennsylvania recommends keeping wines covered with carbon dioxide, with liberal doses of sulfur dioxide in the wine. He uses carbon dioxide even in the pressing basket. Certainly, a most important use of carbon dioxide is in the bottling of the wine, because of the surface exposure during the filling process.

Shirley Martin, also of Pennsylvania, recommends using acid blends when in doubt. For apple wines, she recommends 2/3 tartaric and 1/3 citric, and for strawberry wines a mix of tartaric and malic. Charles Brooks of Pennsylvania adds hot water to ameliorate his wines, which is probably responsible for the very deep colors he is able to bring out. Of course, very hot water also sterilizes the fruit.

The aging characteristics of fruit wines differ very greatly. In a panel discussion on fruit winemaking, Al Cristy pointed out that his apricot dessert wine, more than 10 years old at the time, was still getting better! However, most fruit wines, being really "white" wines, are better consumed within a few years or less. Thus, each winemaker should test their wines regularly to see how they are aging.

It must be pointed out that the wine of each fruit differs from each other as much as each differs from grapes, because they are each different species. Thus, the range of differences expected between different varieties of grapes is expected to be smaller than the differences between, say, apple and peach, or raspberry and elderberry. Therefore, each kind of fruit has to be examined on its own merits.

William Wilen of Ohio wrote, "... a major misconception exists about making fruit wine. Some winemakers I know consider fruit winemaking more appropriate for beginners — something to practice with before "graduating" to real winemaking (that is grape winemaking). They perceive fruit winemaking as unsophisticated and, as such, not worthy of extensive analysis or discussion. I think they are wrong because I have judged fruit wines in competition and found many of them to be better than some of the grape wines I judged."

Indeed, some of the problems of fruit winemaking is the public perception of the art. However, the complexity of the task, more complex than grape winemaking, makes it a greater challenge. And a top fruit wine does equal a top grape wine, able to score a 20 (perfect score) in competition.

A Few Recipes

While many fruit wines win prizes in the American Wine Society fruit category as such, some win in other categories, such as dessert wines. A recipe for 5 gallons of elderberry dessert wine is as follows:

15 pounds of crushed elderberries

12 pounds of sugar, boiled in water

1 quart crushed, pitted plums, from Japanese variety

3 pectic enzyme tablets

5 nutrient tablets

water to 5 1/2 gallons

1 packet of wine yeast

Boiling sugar water was poured over the crushed elderberries and plums to sterilize them. The must has a specific gravity of 1.128 at 85° F and an acidity of 0.7% acidity. After fermentation, the wine had a specific gravity of 1.001. The wine was racked three times. The first time, the volume was reduced to fill a 5 gallon carboy. On the second two rackings, the ullage was filled with boiled, cooled sugar water. After the second racking, the wine was fined with one egg white and a pinch of salt. Potassium sorbate was added to prevent re-fermentation from the added sugar. On the third racking, one Campden tablet was added as the only sulfur. During this time , the wine was cold stabilized by temperatures of 24–40° F for two weeks. At bottling, the wine had a specific gravity of 1.028. After aging for 2 years, the wine was still improving.

A wine made from elderberries and plums will have lots of tannin, and hence is really a red wine. Elderberries were the stuff used in "Arsenic and Old Lace". The old ladies knew that the flavor of the wine was strong enough to hide most anything!

Harold Panuska of Minnesota points out that berries should be measured by the pound, more accurate than measuring by the quart. He uses Heritage raspberries, which ripen in the fall and have higher acidity than most. His recipe and procedure are as follows:

42 pounds frozen raspberries

30 pounds sugar, boiled with part of the water

1/4 tsp. metabisulfite for every 5 gallons of must

10 gallons of water

Acid adjusted to 0.6% acidity with tartaric acid

15 tsp. of nutrient

5 tsp. of pectic enzyme

2 tsp. of ascorbic acid (prevents oxidation)

Wine yeast

After fermentation:

Rack and filter (under carbon dioxide gas)

Adjust for sweetness to 1.010 specific gravity

Add potassium sorbate, 100–250 ppm

Clear with Polyclar to reduce tannin

Adjust metabisulfite level to 25 ppm, before bottling.

Notes: After the primary fermentation is nearly complete, he removes the pulp and seeds and racks the juice into carboys. Fermentation is at 65–70° F.

Ed Stopper of Pennsylvania makes a peach wine out of Belle of Georgia peaches, which are very sweet. Because the peaches are white fleshed the wine is very pale. Stopper says he uses the peaches without water. He peels and seeds them, then immediately adds 100 ppm of sulfur dioxide to minimize oxidation. The fruit is heated to boiling, cooled, and dry sugar added to 21 Brix (11 % alcohol). It must be emphasized that the peach seeds (stones) must be removed. The seeds from peaches, plums and apricots are toxic.

Stopper uses champagne yeast, and pectic enzyme at 1/2 teaspoon per gallon. After the fermentation is started, and the pulp begins to break up, the must is depulped, and the fermentation run to dryness like a white grape wine. The wine is racked 3 or 4 times with shorter intervals at the beginning. About 35–40 ppm of sulfur dioxide is added at each racking. This can be in the form of Campden tablets. The wine is fined and filtered. Later, extra acid is added, if needed, and the wine sugared to 5–6% just before bottling, with potassium sorbate added, making a type of dessert wine.

Stopper points out that the peaches must be skinned, as the skins will make the wine bitter.

Ed Levis of Pennsylvania has one bit of good advice for any fruit winemaker: "Make it taste like the fruit itself." He made cherry and raspberry wines, and then blended them. He uses about 50% water, then adds sugar to about 22 Brix, ferments it dry (about 10 1/2% alcohol), then adjusts it to 0.8% acidity (adding the same acid as was in the fruit) and 5–6% sugar, making a low alcohol, sweet wine.

Earl Deveney makes peach wine with Sunhigh peaches because it yields a good aroma. He also makes apple wine and likes to ferment it at cellar temperatures to start, then reduces the temperature every 3 days to 45–48° F, which he maintains in a converted freezer.

Betty and Tom McCarthy contributed a raspberry wine recipe, interesting because it involves a blend of red and black raspberries. The frozen fruit was fermented in winter, which held the temperatures down. After initial clarification, the wine was sterile filtered. The final wine was sweetened to a specific gravity of 1.004.

Shirley Martin volunteered her favorite recipe for dandelion wine. Strictly speaking, dandelion is not a "fruit" wine, but a flower wine. However, in competitions they are often grouped together. Flower wines differ from fruit wines in that the flowers usually contribute aroma or taste only. Indeed, a well-made dandelion wine should smell like a new mown hay field. For one gallon of dandelion wine:

3 quarts of dandelion heads (no stems)

1 gallon boiling water

2 to 2 1/4 pounds of corn sugar

1 Campden tablet (crushed and dissolved)

1/2 tsp. grape tannin, dissolved in boiling water

2 tsp. nutrient

4 tsp. acid blend

1 packet of wine yeast

Dandelions should be picked in sunshine or afternoon when they are fully opened. Use only the heads. Measure and put into the primary fermenter. Dissolve the sugar in the boiling water and pour over the flowers. Add the Campden tablet. Cover with a cloth. Stir each day for two days and then strain. Do not leave the dandelions soaking for more than 48 hours or foul odors will develop. Return the liquid to the primary fermenter. Stir in the tannin, acid blend, nutrient and wine yeast. Cover. Stir twice daily for 4–6 days or until the specific gravity drops to 1.030. Then siphon into the secondary fermenter, attach an airlock and let set until the specific gravity reading is 1.000, then siphon off the sediment and stabilize by adding one Campden tablet. Once fermentation is complete it will begin to clear. Siphon in 2 weeks and again in 4 weeks. When clear and stable, bottle. Drinkable in 6–9 months.

Other recipes recommend addition of lemons, oranges and raisins in various amounts, substituting for the acid blend shown above. Some recipes also add the orange peel, but with no pith. These fruits contribute complexity to the taste and aroma.

By way of summary, some of the suggestions specific to fruit wine-making include:

1. Use of good wine yeasts is recommended.

2. If a significant amount of water is added, use a yeast nutrient.

3. Pectic enzyme should be added, which will break down the pectin, leaving a clearer wine.

4. Ferment the wines as cold as possible, preferably in the range of 45–60° F to preserve the aroma.

5. Make sure the acid level is correct, both before and after the fermentation.

6. If the wine is sweetened, add potassium sorbate to prevent re-fermentation.

Whether the fruit is home-grown, purchased, or the gifts of neighbors, quality wines can be made easily. This makes a wonderful hobby, useful especially for fall and winter months. And for the busy person (except for the brief fermentation period), will wait for that snowy evening or quiet time at home for attention. And when the wines are ready, enjoy!

CHAPTER 4

PORT STYLE HOME WINEMAKING

Werner Roesener

T HE FULL BODIED sweet red wines from the city of Oporto in Portugal have always been admired and enjoyed by wine wine lovers all over the world, so much so that wine producers in different parts of the globe were inspired to emulate these luscious wines. So we find products like California Port, Australian Port, South African, Canadian and many more on the wine shelves in various countries. However, commercial wine producers often are handicapped by restrictive local laws, telling them what base materials and methods are acceptable or forbidden. As a result, few of these emulations are satisfactory alternatives to the real thing. The amateur winemaker does not face these restrictions, but often lacks directions and know-how for achieving this style of wine. A few of us, however, were sufficiently determined to overcome such obstacles. This chapter will show how to produce excellent Port style wines at home.

Production Techniques

As with any other wines, the first step in producing Port-style amateur wines is the selection of suitable base materials. As a rule, any red vinifera or French hybrid grape can be used. Native American grapes are less desirable because of their overwhelming fruitiness, but blending in small amounts of native grape wine at the finishing step can be beneficial. Many non-grape fruits are also well suited, in particular blackcurrants, boysenberries and elderberries. Single ingredient Port-style wines typically lack depth of character; the name of the game is to have a variety of different wines at hand to achieve a pleasing end result by blending.

Three different methods will be described for producing stock wines which will in turn be used in the blending and finishing process. Since the final product will require an alcohol level of 17–20%, the target level of each blending stock should be in the range of 15–22% alcohol.

Method A

This is close to the traditional method used by Port wine producers in Portugal. Fermentation of the pulp/juice mixture is started at SG (Specific Gravity) 1080 to 1100. The SG is monitored frequently, and when about half the sugar has been converted at an SG of 1040–1050 the must or juice is separated from the pulp and 120 ml of 190 proof grain spirit is added to each liter of juice, or 15 ounces to each US gallon. This will raise the alcohol level to the 17–18% range and will stop the fermentation, leaving the unfermented sugars for natural sweetness. A check for rising bubbles should be made after 24 hours. If continued fermentation is observed, another 1% grain spirit should be added. 50 ppm sulfite should also be added at this stage. Racking off the sediment and aging completes production of the stock wine.

Method B

This method avoids the cost of adding grain spirits, but in the process forgoes the benefit of natural sweetness by unfermented fruit sugar. We start with fermenting a pulp/juice mixture at SG 1080–1100. It is necessary to inoculate with a yeast of 16% minimum alcohol tolerance for this method. Long skin fermentation is to be avoided unless lengthy aging is acceptable. When the SG drops below 1010, small amounts of SG 1300 sugar syrup or grape concentrate are added, about 4 oz. for a 5 gallon carboy. This process is repeated as often as necessary until fermentation stops. This usually results in a wine with 16–17% alcohol. Again this wine is to be racked, sulfited and aged.

Method C

This method is particularly suited for salvaging a finished red table wine which has failed to reach expectations by way of being flat and uninteresting, but without major flaws. The starting point is a finished table wine, red preferred, aged or not, alcohol typically around 12%. The wine is poured into a soft or semi-soft plastic container, taking care to leave about 10% air space at the top for expansion. The container is then placed in a freezer. After 48 or more hours it is removed from the freezer, suspended inverted over a receiving vessel. The frozen wine begins to thaw and drip into the receiver. When about 50–60% of the volume is dripped out, the process is stopped. The still frozen part is discarded since it is mostly water. The dripped out portion is now a concentrated wine of 20–24% alcohol. It is used as blending stock.

Aging, Blending, Finishing

Having built up a stock of a number of blending wines, now comes the chore of putting it all together. The decision whether to age the component wines or the finished blend requires some thought. I find that arriving at a final blend with very young stock adds an element of uncertainty, so I prefer to work with blending stock of two years age or over. A port wine of purple color and a youthful grapey aroma is not likely to be appreciated. Also the aging period gives me an opportunity to do such things as oaking. Oak is an essential element in the complexity of ports. I purposely over-oak some of my component wines, like 30 grams (1 oz.) of oak chips into one gallon, left there for two weeks or so. Toasting the chips avoids a raw sawmill type flavor. The so-treated wine is labeled "oaked" and is at the blending stage complimented with other component wines that were not oaked. The ratio of oaked to non-oaked wine is found by experimentation. Another helpful blending ingredient is Brandy or Armagnac, about 2–5% imparts one of the essential flavor components to the wine. Keep in mind that 5% of 80 proof Brandy will raise the overall alcohol level by about 2%, say from 16% up to 18%. All blending experimentation should be done on a small scale, meticulously writing down the relative quantities of each component. The final alcohol level must also be taken into account; for instance, blending equal parts of a 15% wine with one of 23% will yield a wine of $(15 + 23)/2 = 19\%$.

Materials for touching up the final sweetness, besides sugar, include fruit syrups of blackcurrant, blackberry, etc. available in grocery and delicatessen stores. Refermentation is of no concern at these alcohol levels, so don't bother using sorbates. All experimental blends should be re-tasted after a few days of storage because some of the sugars invert and other ingredients marry together. When tasting blends it is always helpful to have a glass of genuine Port at hand for reference. Frequently, a blend comes out with too much acidity, so minor adjustments can be made by adding small amounts of potassium bicarbonate. When it is far out, the wine is sent back to the drawing board to rethink the blending strategy to include more of some low acid blending stock. It is not uncommon that I produce 10 samples of blends in 4–6 ounce lots at one session, number them, put them away for a week, and then have a blind tasting session usually involving a panel of family members or friends. The winemaker should resist the temptation of relying solely on his/her own senses when evaluating blends. I find that the knowledge of what efforts and ingredients went into a product affects my ability to judge my own wines objectively.

Measuring Alcoholic Strength

The traditional methods for determining alcoholic strength involve relatively elaborate lab procedures. The method that I have devised is fast, with its only drawback being that it requires a brix calibrated refractometer, a gadget that most grape growers have on hand to quickly read the sugar level in grape juice. Further it requires a narrow range hydrometer (SG 980-1020). A standard range hydrometer can also be used, but will yield less accurate results.

The procedure is to measure the SG, deduct 1000 from it, note the result. Then obtain a brix reading by placing a couple of drops of the wine on the refractometer prism, this will yield a number of 0–32; multiply it by 4.17, deduct the SG derived number from it, multiply the result by 0.365, equals alcohol in vol%. Example: SG1016, Brix 14 equals 15.47% alcohol by volume.

If this sounds too complicated, then get a simple programmable calculator and program the formula into it; presto the result is available with the push of a few keys. One warning is in order: Some winemakers add glycerol to their port in order to increase body and viscocity. The optical characteristic of glycerol is similar to that of alcohol. The above method is fooled to think the glycerol is alcohol and so produces an erroneous reading. In this case the alcohol measurement should precede the addition of glycerol. The small amount of glycerol normally produced during fermentation is already compensated for in the formula.

CHAPTER 5

MAKING SHERRY-TYPE WINE

James Knap, J. Donald Cooper, and Werner Roesener

THERE ARE SEVERAL distinct types of sherry, made by somewhat different procedures for different uses. All sherries are wines from many vintages blended into a single consistent product. Some of the blends involve wines of more than one grape. Sherries are oxidized wines, and they are all fortified, some more than others. We generally use sherry as an aperitif, a sipping wine or a dessert wine, but in Spain the lightest, least-fortified are used as food wines.

This chapter deals with procedures for making 3 wines that are similar to 3 of the most common types of sherry. These processes do not involve soleras which the Jerezanos use to blend vintages; nevertheless, they make wines that approximate the taste and sensory qualities of the Spanish wines.

Fino: A very pale, dry wine from the Palomino grape usually about 15–16% alcohol.

Amontillado: A full-bodied, amber, medium-dry wine from the Palomino grape but often sweetened with wine from the Pedro Ximenez, often 18–20% alcohol.

Oloroso or cream: A rich, smooth, deeply-colored, sweet wine from Palomino sweetened with Pedro Ximenez, near 20% alcohol.

Making A Fino-type Sherry — Don Cooper

My endeavor in this type of winemaking is towards the dry or fino-type which we quite often enjoy before dinner. For those who enjoy this type of wine, you will know you are on the right track as the fermentation and aging proceed. The aroma will be your first hint of success.

To make sherry one must have the proper grape or juice. That is Palomino just as used in Spain. In the Toronto area this is readily available as juice in 20 liter pails, shipped from California. It is quite inexpensive, $31.00 Canadian for a pail. I usually purchase the juice in January or February, after I organize my table wine production. By that time, the juice has already started a slow preliminary fermentation, although the distributor has kept it well-refrigerated.

The juice usually has a gravity of 1065–1075 and an acidity of 0.65% (as tartaric). To this I add pectic enzyme, gypsum powder, tannin and yeast nutrient. I start the fermentation in an open vessel with a plastic sheet cover, using Lalvin EC-1118 yeast already prepared as a starter.

When the gravity drops to 1040, I feed the fermenting juice with sugar syrup (two parts sugar to one part water). Enough is added to increase the gravity to 1050 or so each time. I don't believe this is too important as long as there is good, active fermentation. After I have used up the sugar syrup (two pounds of sugar in 8 days), the gravity is around 1030. The wine is then racked into a carboy, and flor yeast is added. An 8 inch air space is left at the top of the carboy, and the neck is plugged with cotton wool. At this time oak chips or strips can be added. Any leftover wine can be put in gallon or half-gallon jugs with the same procedure as for the carboy. The yeasts I have used cause flor formation, but it doesn't last. It disappears like magic in a few weeks. I leave this carboy for about a year before racking. During the year, I slowly fortify with about 25 ounces of brandy or grain alcohol. Both are 80 proof.

My first attempt at this style of wine was in 1983, and with great patience I did not filter or bottle it until 1987. The batch I started in 1987 has now been fined and filtered, and I am running out of patience (and my pre-dinner sherry). The 1987 lot seemed a bit darker in color, so I fined it with casein (skim milk powder) followed a couple of days later with bentonite. This fining was done at freezing temperatures during cold stabilization, and it did lighten the wine's color. I had been reading about decoloring wine with charcoal, so I tried it on a couple of bottles of the 1987. I used an aquarium-filter type of charcoal. It worked, but unfortunately removed some of the bouquet as well.

I recommend cold stabilization of fino-type sherry because it lowers the acidity and eliminates the tartrate crystals that would otherwise show up when the wine is refrigerated to prepare it for serving.

Making an Amontillado-type Sherry — Jim Knap

The style my wife and I prefer is Amontillado, a light-amber, semi-sweet, high-alcohol, nutty-tasting sherry; we use it as an aperitif, in cooking and for sipping. When I began, Dry Sack was my model, but I gradually moved nearer to the "Wisdom and Warter Amontillado". We like about 20% alcohol, 2% sugar and 0.5% acid.

I have always used grape concentrates in making sherry. The slightly caramelized flavor that concentrates have adds to the nutty, full-bodied nature when the wine is done. I prefer concentrates of Palomino and Pedro Ximenez grapes, a batch of each. Palomino concentrates have been unavailable in recent years so I have used Spanish-white concentrates. Products labeled Palo Cortado, Carrascal or Amontillado also satisfy the Palomino role, but they are usually very dark and require treatment to lighten the color of the wine.

Late spring is my usual starting time. I want to have wine to put in my garage attic by June when it begins to warm up. The reconstituted concentrates are adjusted to 1.092 specific gravity and 0.5% acid (as tartaric). I add tannin, gypsum, yeast nutrient, and pectic enzymes. I always use flor yeast, but have never developed a flor. When the gravity of the fermenting juice drops to 1.04, I add a pound and a half of sugar and yeast nutrient. At 1.00, I rack into a secondary fermenter, and add portions of sugar and yeast nutrient until the alcohol rises to 16% in the white and 18% in the Ximenez. Then I rack off into 1 gallon jugs (2/3 full), and add 1 tablespoon of gypsum and 4 teaspoons of oak sawdust. The mouths are covered with a piece of paper towel held on by a rubber band, and the jugs placed in the attic of my garage. The temperature there cycles between 70 and 120° F in the summer, which causes the jugs to "breathe", encouraging oxidation.

When I am finished with the fresh grape vintage in late October or November, the jugs are beginning to develop varying degrees of sherry character, so I rack them into carboys, clarify with Sparkolloid and bentonite and analyze. Adjustments in oak, alcohol (with grape brandy), and sugar are made to approximate my goal. Then the carboys (half-full) go to the attic.

As the wines get close to my sensory requirements, they are recovered, blended, sweetened to 2–2.5% sugar and the alcohol again adjusted to 19–20%. Often I find it necessary to add some of my previously-made sherries to achieve that last flavor adjustment. In this way I guess I achieve some of what the Jerezanos get in their soleras. I leave the final blend in the carboys until it is convenient to bottle it, typically a few months. Sometimes the final blend requires another fining. Total elapsed time is 1 1/2 to 2 years.

On occasion when a concentrate is very dark, or when I have tried a baking technique much cruder than that described in the next section, I have had to lighten the color of the wine. I have done this with activated charcoal (pure stuff from a chemical supply house). The carbon takes a long time to settle so it can be racked, and still some dark haze is there. So I follow the carbon with Polyclar AT, which also settles slowly, and then with Sparkolloid and bentonite. All that fining strips the wine of some of its sensory values as well as lightening the color, but a few months back in my "attic solera" and the nose and flavor return.

Because I feel that blending is the critical operation to achieve uniformity of product, I have decided to establish a fractional blending system not unlike a solera. Only half of my now-aging wine will be bottled and half of the now-fermenting batch will ultimately be added to the remainder to blend and age until next year when some will be bottled and more new wine added.

Making Oloroso or Cream-style Sherry — Werner Roesener

I make heavier and sweeter wines than the preceding two authors. Mine resemble Oloroso and Cream Sherry. These sweeter wines are sipped after dinner in place of liqueurs.

My base ingredients include Palomino juice from California, Pedro Jimenez concentrate from Australia and other wine bases sold specifically for sherry making that may contain such things as figs and bananas. I also came across recipes calling for a concoction from dried apricots, dried figs, banana chips, and raisins, augmented with grape juice concentrate. When concentrated wine bases are the starting point, I disregard the instructions that come with them.

I dilute the concentrates to a gravity of 1.110 to start fermentation with sherry yeast. To increase body and alcohol, I feed the wine with grape concentrate whenever the gravity dips below 1.005. When I start with grape juice, I proceed in a similar way with whatever gravity the juice had. Since the additions of concentrate add extra acid, I try to keep starting acidity around five grams per liter.

When fermentation finally ceases, alcohol may be 16–18% and the body may still be on the thin side. To remedy this, I subject part of the batch to a freeze-concentration process: one gallon of wine is placed in a freezer for 48 hours, then inverted over a receiving vessel to let 50–75% drip out while it thaws. See Figure 2. The rest, being mostly water is discarded. This yields a concentrated wine with 20–25% alcohol. This I blend back into the original batch in a ratio determined by tasting experiments. Final sweetening is done with fructose and/or grape concentrate. I have also found it useful to sweeten with a syrupy extract made by boiling chopped raisins.

A Madeira-like flavor is achieved by baking the wine for 6 months at 100° F. This I do in a specially-constructed oven heated electrically and with an electronic temperature controller. My oven is a two story design built from plywood and insulated with Styrofoam. See Figure 3. Each of the two compartments has its own heating element and independent control and can hold one 5 gallon carboy, a primary fermenter pail, or 8 one gallon jugs. The oven also doubles up for promptly starting fermentation of grape or grape juice in the cool season by heating to 80° F.

My overall strategy is to produce a number of sherry batches, different by way of base ingredients and process, and to try to achieve pleasing end results by experimenting with blends of these different batches. The freeze-concentration process also lends itself to converting the odd batch of over-the-hill or oxidized white wine into useful sherry-blending stock. However, care must be exercised to avoid inflicting a bad taste into an otherwise decent wine. This is best done by preceding all blending with experiments on a very small scale.

Advice For Beginners

The secret of successful sherry making is knowing what taste and sensory values you desire. Pick a commercial sherry you like, and use some of these procedures to try to reproduce it. Much of your success will depend on your skill at blending, and that will increase as you experiment. You are bound to have a lot of fun as you learn.

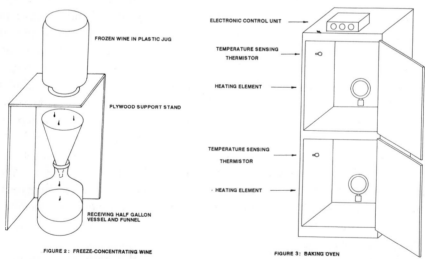

FIGURE 2 : FREEZE-CONCENTRATING WINE

FIGURE 3: BAKING OVEN

Figure 2. Freeze-Concentrating Wine

Figure 3. Baking Oven

CHAPTER 6

THE USE OF SULFUR IN THE PRESERVATION OF WINES

Translated and adapted with permission by G.H. Mowbray from
"Connaissance et Travail du Vin" by Emile Peynaud

T HE RATIONAL use of anhydrous sulfur, more commonly known as sulfur dioxide (SO_2), is the very foundation to the preservation of wines. Sulfur dioxide is a gas that is formed when sulfur is burned. It is a very ancient preservative, but its wide-spread use and the thorough understanding of its mode of action is of relatively recent date. The types of table wines we know today have only been made possible through its careful use.

Preservation techniques create the style of wine. Wine does not keep by itself. Left alone, it alters rapidly and at best becomes vinegar. Without the use of some preservative, it could not withstand the manipulations and transportations necessary for its commerce. In all ages it has been necessary to resort to artificial means of preservation. The ancient Greeks gave us retsina, in which pine pitch was used as an antiseptic. Following the discovery of distillation, the addition of high-proof ethanol gave us fortified wines. The alcohol protects them from micro-organisms but not from oxidation, and it is the oxidation that gives these wines their character. Wines preserved by the use of SO_2 gas from burned sulfur sticks are of more recent origin. The practice developed in the warmer climates where preservation was more difficult. It is the use of sulfur dioxide that has made possible long storage in barrels followed by bottle aging, and more recently still, the conservation of fruitiness and freshness.

The Beneficial Properties of SO2 in the Preservation of Wine

As an antiseptic — Provides an inhibiting action on yeasts and bacteria. That fraction of anhydrous sulfur that exists in the state of dissolved SO_2 gas is alone endowed with antiseptic properties.

As an anti-oxidant — This power is due to its reducing properties. It hoards oxygen which it then converts to sulfuric acid. It is the totality of the titratable free SO_2 that acts as a reducing agent and thus prevents yellowing and maderization.

As a flavor preserver — In reacting with acetaldehyde, and in blocking this substance under the form of a stable sulfite compound, sulfur dioxide ameliorates the taste and conserves the freshness of the aroma. It opposes the transient changes in wine, such as bottle-sickness, that accompany manipulation in the presence of atmospheric oxygen.

The measurement of SO_2 in wines must be precise. In practice, it is easy to make mistakes of either one of two kinds which has led to a saying that it can be at once the best and the worst of things. If the dose added to a wine is too strong, and this may be only by a dozen parts per million, the wine takes on the sharp, acrid odor of burning sulfur along with a disagreeable aftertaste — the so-called "sulfur taste", spoken of by professional winetasters. On the other hand, if the quantity added is too small, again by a matter of about a dozen parts per million, dry wines are not protected from oxidation, nor sweet wines from renewed fermentation.

People new to wine are often disturbed or even mildly outraged when they learn that SO_2 is a frequent additive to table wines. They shouldn't be. It is a practice of long standing that, when properly employed, carries with it no health hazards. The development of modern technology has led to smaller and smaller doses being required, resulting in wines of higher and higher quality. Besides, the governments of all wine-producing nations have strict regulations concerning the amount of sulfur dioxide wines may contain and still be marketed.

The States of Sulfur Dioxide in Wines

Sulfur dioxide exists in wine in two states — one is free and the other is in organic combination with certain constituents of wine. Total anhydrous sulfur, or total SO_2, is the sum of SO_2 free and SO_2 combined.

To a first approximation, only free SO_2 has any effect as an antiseptic or an anti-oxidant. Combined SO_2 has neither the properties nor the reactions of free SO_2, nor can it be properly spoken of as SO_2

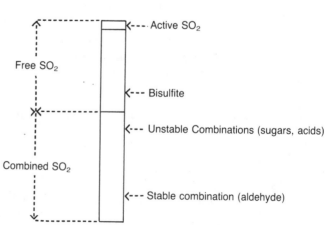

in this state. It has neither odor nor taste and only a mild anti-bacterial power.

Free SO_2 — This is the fraction titratable by iodine in acidified wine. The major part of free SO_2 exists in wine as a salt under the form of acid salts or bisulfites. In this form it has a minimum antiseptic power, at least on yeasts, and it has no odor.

For a wine to contain 1.5 mg of active SO_2 per liter, which is barely sufficient to preserve a sweet white wine, it must possess the following quantities of free SO_2 as function of its pH:

pH 2.8 — 15 mg
3.0 — 25 mg
3.2 — 40 mg
3.4 — 64 mg
3.6 — 100 mg
3.8 — 150 mg

It is that part which is present in the form of dissolved SO_2 gas that is active. Only it is antiseptic and possesses the disagreeable odor of sulfur. For a given dose of free anhydrous sulfur, the proportion of SO_2 dissolved and, in consequence, its antiseptic efficacy and the odor of the wine depends on the real acidity of the wine — on its pH.

Combined SO_2 — Sulfur dioxide combines in wines with a great number of substances belonging to the chemical group of aldehydes or the ketones. With these substances it produces two types of compounds with different stability.

With the acetaldehyde produced by yeasts it forms a very stable, irreversible compound (said to have a weak constant of dissociation) which is called sulfurous acid aldehyde or ethanosulfonic acid. Acetaldehyde is an intermediary substance in the fermentation of sugar. Adding SO_2 to the juice blocks acetaldehyde under the form of a sulfite compound. In the same way the refermentation of a sweet wine, followed by the addition of SO_2, increases considerably the proportion of sulfur dioxide combined with acetaldehyde. It is by this fashion that combined SO_2 accumulates in certain wines.

Sulfur dioxide also forms unstable, reversible compounds with other constituents of wine, compounds with a high constant of dissociation. It is a question of the equilibrium of the reaction. The equilibrium depends in part on the proportion of substances which fix SO_2, and in part on the level of total SO_2. The equilibrium is also temperature dependent. To satisfy this equilibrium, the proportion of combined SO_2 increases when SO_2 is added to wine and decreases as free SO_2 diminishes. It increases when the wine is chilled and decreases when it is warmed. For example, a white wine which titrates 85 ppm of free SO_2 at 15° C, will titrate 68 ppm at 0° C and 100 ppm at 30° C.

Combined SO_2 in a weakly stable form provides a sort of reserve which acts to replenish free SO_2 in proportion to its loss through oxidation. The constituents of wine that fix sulfur dioxide (about 20 are known) have several origins.

1. Substances present in healthy grapes and in juice such as glucose, arabinose, galacturonic acid, polysaccharides and polyphenols.

2. Substances in grapes attacked by Botrytis cinerea or by a bacterial microflora, such as diacetogluconic acid, ketofructose, etc.

3. Substances formed by yeasts under normal conditions or accumulated in the fermentation of juices from rotted grapes, such as pyruvic acid and alpha ketoglutaric acid.

A distinction thus is made between normal, limited combinations which are those generally resulting from the use of healthy grapes, and those abnormal combinations which intervene in wines from rotten or deteriorated grapes and which are due to a deficiency of nutritive elements for the yeasts.

The state of anhydrous sulfur in a white wine: reducing sugars 74 g, acetaldehyde 104 mg, pyruvic acid 93 mg, alpha ketoglutaric acid 74 mg, uronic acids 400 mg, pH 3.20.

	Quantities In mg
Total SO_2	392
Free SO_2	68
Active SO_2	2.5
Combined SO_2	324
with Acetaldehyde	151
with Sugars	13
with Pyruvic Acid	41
with Alpha-ketoglutaric Acid	17
with Uronic Acids	3
Known Fraction of Combined SO_2	225 (68%)
Unknown Fraction of Combined SO_2	99 (32%)

The major inconvenience of sulfur dioxide as a preservative is tied to its chemical reactivity which renders it inactive for the most part. To maintain a sufficient level of active SO_2 in wine, it is necessary to accumulate several dozens of mg of free anhydrous sulfur and several hundreds of mg of total anhydrous sulfur.

The Combination of Supplementary Doses of Sulfur Dioxide

What happens when sulfur dioxide is added to a white wine that already contains some at the time of racking, say? Each addition results in the combination of a part of the added dose with certain constituents of the wine. A few hours after the addition, the total dose added can not be found. Suppose we have a wine that titrates 40 mg of free SO_2 and we add 60 mg. After 3 or 4 days, we can not find 100 mg of free sulfur (40 + 60), but only an amount sensibly less — 80 mg as an example. A certain quantity, here 20 mg, has been combined.

In practice, it is vital to know the fraction of SO_2 that can combine when it is desired to adjust with precision to the chosen level for free SO_2 content of a sweet wine, for instance. The proportion of combination is variable according to the wine (according to the nature and the quantity of substances which fix it). It varies also with the level of free SO_2 already contained in the wine. In the normal case, half of the added anhydrous sulfur combines when the level of free SO_2 is below 30 mg, about a third when the free SO_2 is 60 mg, about a quarter when it is 100 mg and about 1/10 when it is above 120 mg. These values are only guidelines. In certain abnormal cases, the combined amount can be double the figures indicated.

In practice the following rule can be adopted, allowing the calculation of the addition to make a normal wine, within customary limits: " When adding SO_2 to a wine, 2/3 of the dose added will remain in the free state and 1/3 will combine." Thus, if it is desired to bring a wine titrating 40 mg of free SO_2 to a level of 100 mg free SO_2 it will be necessary to add to it 100 - 40 = 60 plus half of 60, or in reality 90 mg. Without being absolutely rigorous, this method of calculation results in practice in bringing the free SO_2 content of a wine to a desirable level.

Doses of Sulfur Dioxide to Use

To ensure the preservation of red wines, it is generally sufficient to maintain a level of free SO_2 somewhere slightly above 0 mg, whereas white wines should not fall below 16–20 mg and white, sweet wines not below 40–50 mg per liter.

Functionally, the amount of free SO_2 does not remain constant. It decreases steadily during the course of aging due to its progressive oxidation. This diminution is direct evidence of the efficacy of anhydrous sulfur since the oxygen which oxidizes it is thus denied to the wine. The decrease depends on the aging conditions. In 225 liter barrels (about 60 gallons), the mean loss of free SO_2 is about 10 mg per month; that of total SO_2 about 15 mg, which corresponds to an annual disappearance of 180 mg per liter. The formation of sulfuric acid which results from this latter decrease is one of the causes of flavor deterioration of wines held too long in barrels. The decrease of SO_2 is 2 to 3 times less for wines aged in large casks or tanks. In bottles the loss does not exceed a few mg per year.

The preservation doses indicated in the following table may appear exorbitant. It is certain that at such amounts white wines would smell of SO_2. They are recommended so high in order that the wines might stay 4 to 6 months between two rackings and not fall to an insufficient level. These values have been fixed after long experience with the conditions pertaining in the commerce of wines of Bordeaux. The doses can be appreciably lowered for wines of lower pH or for wines kept under cold conditions, and on the same premises, where they avoid transportation and handling imposed by their commercialization. Higher doses are called for if the wines will travel long distances or if smaller barrels are used.

The amount of free SO_2 necessary to prevent the fermentation of a sweet wine is largely independent of the amount of residual sugar it contains. A refermentation will take place as readily with 5 gm as with 50 gm of reducing sugars per liter. The stability of such wines is in reality a

Levels of Free SO2 to Maintain in Wines According to Different Conditions and Practices
(in mg per liter)

Aging Requirements	Fine red wines	— 0 to 20
	Ordinary red wines	— 20 to 30
	Dry White wines	— 30 to 40
	Sweet white wines	— 80 to 100
Bottling Requirements	Red wines	— 0 to 20
	Dry white wines	— 20 to 30
	Sweet white wines	— 50 to 60
Requirements for Transport in Barrel or other Containers	Red wines	— 20 to 30
	Dry white wines	— 30 to 40
	Sweet white wines	— 100

function of the alcoholic degree. More SO_2 is required to prevent refermentation of a wine with 10% alcohol than for a wine with 13% alcohol.

Methods of Use

One of the greatest advantages of sulfur dioxide is its availability under a variety of forms. It can, at the choice of the winemaker, be obtained in the gaseous state, the liquid state or as a solid. In all cases, it is easy to measure by volume or by weight. The following paragraphs outline the uses of the various forms. The effectiveness of these different sulfurous products is exactly the same for an equal dose of free anhydrous sulfur, for the same reason that they do not remain in the wine under the form that they had at the moment of addition. They all form salts and combine in exactly the same way.

The use of burned sulfur (called mechage by the French). This method of adding SO_2 to wines is acidifying, limited, irregular from one barrel to another and is not convenient for large volumes.

While sulfur in the form of SO_2 can be useful and beneficial in the wine making process, it is important to realize that there are other oxidation-reduction states for sulfur which can cause grief. The following diagram may serve to illustrate this point:

Oxidation

$$H_2S \rightleftharpoons S \rightleftharpoons SO_2 \rightleftharpoons SO_3$$

Hydrogen Sulfide   Sulfur   Sulfur Dioxide   Sulfur Trioxide

Reduction

It should be evident from this that in the case where sulfur cannot exercise its reducing action, it can itself be reduced to form hydrogen sulfide (H_2S) whose presence the nose is quick to detect as the foul smelling odor of rotten eggs. Thus wine deprived of oxygen in the presence of sulfur can be as bad as or worse than when over-oxidized. There is a remedy, and the key to it appears in the preceding diagram. Oxidation of the affected wine by aeration and with the addition of SO_2 will in most cases affect a cure.

Sulfuring of wine by mechage is imprecise and irregular. According to the barrels, the quantity of SO_2 produced and its absorption by the wine at the time of racking can vary considerably. The combustion of sulfur is different from one barrel to another; it is disturbed in humid barrels but the absorption of sulfur dioxide in the wine which at racking flows into the barrel is more irregular still. According to the speed of filling and the pressure of the fall, the loss of SO_2 escaping through the bung-hole can be 10% or 50%.

Liquid — Sulfur dioxide liquifies at -15° C under a pressure of 3 atmospheres. It is sold in metallic cylinders. In this form it is used for significant additions, measured by weight by placing the cylinder on a scale.

In Solution — For precise additions and for small volumes an aqueous solution of SO_2 is used. The solution may be a 3%, 5%, or 6%, with the latter being the most common. Whichever is used, the proportion must be known and exact.

Potassium Meta-Bisulfite — Can be obtained in powdered or crystalline form, both of which are easy to dissolve in water, and should be. Do not use in pure form. It can also be obtained in tablet form of various strengths.

The Use of Sorbic Acid

For a long time, methods or products to replace anhydrous sulfur have been sought. It is certainly possible to discover products endowed with an antiseptic action more forceful or with a better anti-oxidative power. Up until now the only products found have been those that complement the action of anhydrous sulfur so that some SO_2 remains indispensable. Sorbic acid exercises such a complementary action particularly on yeast and as an anti-oxidant. But, to be effective, it must be associated with SO_2.

Sorbic acid is a non-toxic, non-saturated fatty acid that is perfectly digestible by higher animals. It possesses a specific anti-yeast action. It opposes the multiplication of yeasts in wine and alters their power to referment sugar, but does not destroy them.

Its use in France has been authorized since 1959 at a dose limited to 200 mg per liter. Analytical methods are available that can detect its presence in wine and determine the quantity added. Some countries do not permit the importation of wines treated with sorbic acid.

The activity of sorbic acid against yeasts is strongly reinforced by the presence of alcohol. The following doses are recommended for wines cleared of yeasts.

Wine % Alcohol	Sorbic Acid (mg/liter)
10	150
11	125
12	100
13	75
14	50

The activity of sorbic acid depends otherwise on pH. Its effectiveness is halved between pH of 3.1 and 3.5. Above a pH of 3.5 the legal limit of 200 mg/liter is insufficient. The use of sorbic acid by American wineries is authorized if no more than 0.1% remains in the wine.

Finally, the action of sorbic acid on yeasts is considerably reinforced by the simultaneous presence of small quantities of free SO_2.

At the doses indicated, sorbic acid displays no anti-bacterial properties. While it prevents the activation of fermentation in sweet wines, it prevents neither acetic bacteria growth nor the various bacterial actions on lactic acid. The danger of bacterial degradation of sorbic acid is ever present with the consequent appearance of a disagreeable odor akin to the smell of geraniums.

Sorbic acid is only effective when in association with a certain percentage of alcohol and some modest amount of SO_2. It reinforces the action of SO_2 but can not replace it.

Sorbic acid is relatively insoluble in water, so by preference , the more soluble potassium sorbate is the additive of choice. A solution of 270 grams of potassium sorbate per liter provides 200 gm of sorbic acid. Because of the poor solubility of sorbic acid, there are some necessary precautions to take when it is introduced into wine. It must be added slowly and with a vigorous agitation.

In recapitulation, sorbic acid aids in the yeast stabilization of wines if the following conditions are observed:

1. The size of the addition takes into account the level of true acidity (pH) of the wine.

2. The wine is carefully clarified (yeast populations below 1000 per cubic centimeter).

3. A rapid and thorough mixture is accomplished.

4. The wine is already protected by sufficient free SO_2 to prevent oxidation and bacterial development.

5. It is not used with red wines.

The Use of Ascorbic Acid

Ascorbic acid, or Vitamin C, exists in small quantities in grapes (about 50 mg/liter of juice), but it disappears in the course of fermentation or at the first aeration, and generally wines have none in them.

Ascorbic acid is a reducing agent, and thus inhibits oxidation. In wine, it rapidly fixes atmospheric oxygen and transforms to dehydroascorbic acid. 50 mg of ascorbic acid consumes about 3.5 cubic cm of oxygen. Its use has been authorized in France since 1962 with a dose limit of 100 mg per liter. Its use in America is practically unrestricted.

It has two different uses. First, it prevents the oxidation of iron and, in consequence, the development of iron casse. Second, in absorbing the oxygen from wine it prevents oxidation and conserves a fresh and fruity aroma.

When a wine that has just received an addition of ascorbic acid (50 to 100 mg/l) is aerated, the iron the wine contains, whatever its amount, remains entirely in the ferrous state. The same wine not so treated would soon develop ferric casse. Thus a wine susceptible to iron clouding would remain clear and limpid with the addition of ascorbic acid. If the addition of ascorbic acid follows the aeration and intervenes at the moment when the wine is showing signs of clouding, in only a few hours the process will be seen to reverse. After 24 hours all of the iron will have evolved to the ferrous state and a clear wine will result.

This reducing action of ascorbic acid has practical applications. The addition of ascorbic acid protects a wine rich in iron from the iron clouding that could occur following pumping, filtering, bottling or any other manipulation that exposed it to air. The great sensitivity of ascorbic acid to oxidation assures its practical efficacity only when the contact with air is limited. It protects well against the small, transient aerations but not against significant or continuous exposure. Its practical role is limited to protecting wine from the casual exposure due to bottling and not to preservation in barrels.

The addition of ascorbic acid to dry, white wines that are bottled young and that come from aromatic varieties, aids in preserving the

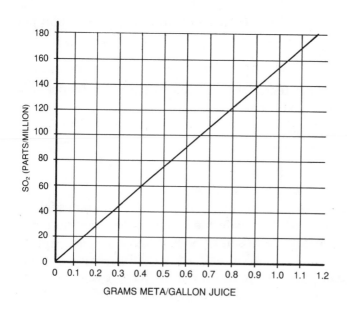

GRAPH 1

Grams of meta per gallon of juice as a function of total SO_2 in parts per million.

dominant fruitiness and floweriness of the aroma. For red wines, the duration of the period of bottle sickness, following bottling, is significantly reduced, and for sparkling wines, a little ascorbic acid added to the liqueur d'expedition improves the flavor.

Ascorbic acid exhibits its full potential only when the wine to which it is added contains a sufficient amount of free SO_2. It does not replace SO_2, it only acts in association with it.

Finally, ascorbic acid is best used as a preventive, to avoid the disturbing consequences of aeration rather than as a curative to reverse oxidation processes already well under way.

A Schedule For The Rational Use Of Sulfur In The Cellar Treatment Of Wines

For White Wine

1. At Crush — Calculate the expected yield of juice to be extracted from the total batch to be pressed. Conservatively expect 150 gallons for each 2000 lbs. of grapes. During crush, gradually add a previously prepared 6% solution of potassium meta-bisulfite dissolved in water (preferably distilled) calculated to achieve from 75–100 ppm of SO_2 in the pressed juice. Use the accompanying graphs to prepare the solution. The lower figure of 75 ppm can be used for cool, sound, very slightly under-ripe grapes while the higher might be used for warm, optimum maturity grapes with some rot or bird damage. For significantly over-ripe grapes with major amounts of rot a higher figure of 150 ppm SO_2 might be required

   If a malolactic fermentation is deemed desirable, do not exceed 60 ppm SO_2 at crush.

   Example: Batch of 500 lbs. of sound white grapes measuring 20.5% soluble solids with a total acidity of 0.79 g/100 ml expressed as tartaric.

   Juice yield = 500/2000 = x/150

   Cross multiply: 500 X 150 = 2000x, or

   2000x = 75,000; thus 37.5 gallons of expressed juice.

   Judging that 90 ppm SO_2 are desirable in this case, consult Graph 1 where it can be seen that 0.6 grams of sulfite per gallon of juice will be needed, or a total of 22.5 grams of sulfite for the entire batch.

Consulting Graph 2 you will see that a 6% solution can be achieved by dissolving 22.5 grams of sulfite in 350 ml of water.

2. Racking from gross lees and consolidation — No additions of SO_2 are needed if malolactic fermentation is desired. If, however, there is a detectable odor of H2S and the racking is going to be made into closed, glass containers, it might be desirable to rack with aeration and add 30 ppm SO_2. If the racking is to be done into oak barrels, no aeration is needed — and, of course, no additional SO_2.

3. Succeeding rackings — Check the level of free SO_2 from time to time and when it falls below 30 ppm, rack with the addition of SO_2 to maintain a level of 30–40 ppm SO_2.

4. Bottling — If the wine has been stabilized, fined and filtered or is otherwise ready for bottling, bottle when the level of free SO_2 is around 25 ppm.

For Rosé Wine

Treat exactly as a white wine.

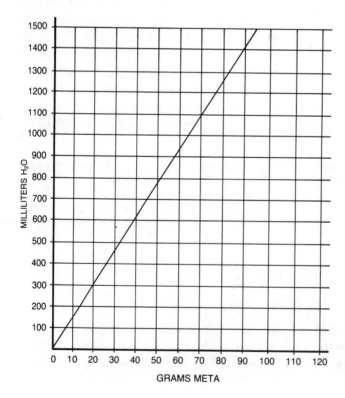

GRAPH 2
Grams of meta in milliliters of H_20 for 6% solution

For Red Wine

1. At crush — The eventual yield of juice from red grapes fermented on the skins is somewhat higher than for white grapes. Figure on 160 gallons from a ton of grapes, and calculate accordingly. Since it is often desirable to encourage malolactic fermentation in red wines, use no more than 60 ppm SO_2 at crush. However, when malolactic is not desired, as it often isn't with Foch, proceed as with a white grape.

2. Racking from gross lees and consolidation — Usually no addition of SO_2 required.

3. Succeeding rackings — Check the level of free SO_2 from time to time and when it falls below about 10 ppm, rack with the addition of SO_2 to maintain 10 to 20 ppm.

4. Bottling — The level of free SO_2 at bottling should range from a few parts per million to a maximum of 10 ppm.

Analytical Tests For SO_2

The evaluation of SO_2 is based on the oxidation of SO_2 by iodine. When all the SO_2 is oxidized, iodine in excess can be detected by using a starch solution which turns blue at the end point. This test is not easily done on red wines. Hazardous chemicals are involved in two different analyses, one determines the free SO_2 and the second the bound SO_2. Rather than outline the procedure here, those who have access to chemicals and laboratory equipment should refer to Chapter 7 for detailed instructions for these two analyses and many other advanced chemical tests.

Editor's Note: For readers who can not easily perform the SO_2 determination on a regular basis the arbitrary addition of 20 ppm of SO_2 at each racking and bottling will not result in excessive SO_2 levels in your wine.

CHAPTER 7

WINE ANALYSIS

Harold E. Applegate

T HIS CHAPTER is a brief compendium of chemical tests used in the field of enology but directed toward the home winemaker, beginner and sophisticate. While of use to the professional enologist, he would be better advised to consult a treatise on enology and thereby become acquainted with the strengths and weaknesses of each procedure as well as newer developments.

Basic Tests

The following two tests are the irreducible minimum. To fail to perform them would be like driving one's car with eyes closed.

A. Sugar content of fresh juice

1. Hydrometer — Strain freshly pressed juice through clean cheese cloth to remove larger particulate matter. Notice the calibration temperature of the Brix or Balling hydrometer and cool or warm the juice sample to this temperature. Hold a hydrometer cylinder at a 45 degree angle and nearly fill by pouring the juice down the side slowly to avoid bubble formation. Place the cylinder in upright position on a table and slowly lower the hydrometer into it until it floats free. Read the scale at the meniscus level as in Figure 1. The reading is the percent sugar in the juice.

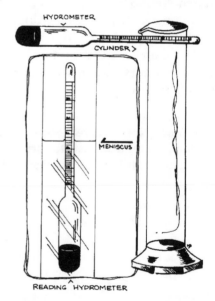

Figure 1

B. Total acidity as tartaric acid in juice or wine

Reagents:

0.1 Normal (N/10) sodium hydroxide (NaOH)
1% phenolphthalein in 95% ethyl alcohol

1. Juice or white wine — First clarify the juice or wine by filtration through Whatman #1 filter paper or by centrifugation. The latter method is a fast and most efficient method for those who have a small clinical centrifuge. Add 5 ml. of juice or wine to 75 ml of boiling distilled water followed by 5 drops of phenolphthalein indicator. Agitate well and continuously. Titrate with N/10 NaOH to the faint pink endpoint stable for at least 1 minute. Volume of NaOH used X 0.15 = grams of acid/100 ml juice or wine.

2. Red wine — Add 5 ml of red wine to 75 ml of boiling distilled water and, without adding indicator, titrate with N/10 NaOH until the solution is blue-green in color. Now add 5 drops of phenolphthalein indicator and complete the titration to the pink endpoint. This endpoint is very tricky and requires practice. One way to avoid the difficulty is to stir the red wine vigorously with a little bone charcoal and clarify as done initially. The resultant decolorized wine is then used as white wine. Use the same equation that was used for white wine to calculate the result.

Desirable Tests

C. Residual sugar in wine

1. Dextrocheck kit — Decolorize a small volume of wine with bone charcoal and Celite (an inert filter aid) and filter. To 0.5 ml of the wine add 1 reagent tablet; 15 seconds after boiling has ceased, read the color against the color scale furnished with the kit. If the color is dark brown, make a 1:5 dilution by adding 0.1 ml of wine to 0.4 ml water. Multiply the reading by 5. If the color is still off scale, dilute 1:10 by adding 0.1 ml of wine to 0.9 ml of water and use 0.5 ml of the resultant solution. Multiply the result by 10. The Clinitest kit for diabetics works in similar fashion with a different color scale and range. This kit is balanced for components present in urine. My suggestion is: stick to the kit made for wine.

D. Alcohol

1. The alcohol content of finished wine may be estimated by subtracting the residual sugar percentage in the wine from the percentage

of sugar in the original juice. The difference when multiplied by 0.57 gives the estimated alcohol content of the wine.

Example:

22% sugar in juice

2% residual sugar in wine

20 X 0.57 = 11.4% alcohol

2. Vinometer — Hold upright a clean, dry vinometer tube and fill with a few drops of wine. Invert the tube on a table and read the scale at the wine level. This method is very quick and inexpensive but only a rough estimate.

3. Ebulliometer — This instrument is expensive and fairly accurate. It utilizes the difference in the boiling points of water and dilute alcohol. With the condenser empty and 25 ml of distilled water in the boiling chamber, boil the water until the reading is constant. On the slide rule provided set the 0% alcohol index at the observed boiling point of w a t e r . Empty the chamber and rinse with wine. Fill the condenser with water, and add 50 ml of wine to the boiling chamber. Boil the wine until a constant boiling point is observed. On the slide rule read the percentage alcohol opposite the observed boiling point of the wine.

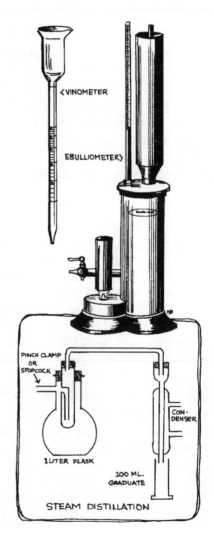

4. Distillation and hydrometer — This uses a highly accurate short range

hydrometer designed especially for wine. Add 50 ml of distilled water to 100 ml of wine and distill until approximately 95 ml of distillate is collected. Adjust the temperature to the calibration temperature of the hydrometer and dilute to 100 ml with water. Mix thoroughly. Insert the hydrometer and read the percent alcohol directly.

E. Volatile acid — This measures the state of health of the wine.

1. Rough method of Cruess and Bettoli — Decolorize 75 ml of wine (if red). Add 5 drops of phenolphthalein indicator to 20 ml of the wine and titrate to the endpoint with N/10 NaOH. The volume of NaOH used is designated "a". Place another 20 ml of the wine into a 250 ml Ehrlenmeyer flask, Add 2–3 grams of NaCl (sodium chloride) and boil until the salt precipitates heavily. Add 20 ml of water and repeat the procedure. Dilute with boiling, distilled water, add 5 drops of indicator and titrate with N/10 NaOH as before. The volume of NaOH is designated "b".

   (a - b) X 0.03 = grams of volatile acid/100 ml of wine.

2. Steam distillation — This uses the officially accepted Cash still or the homemade set up shown in Figure 2. Place 10 ml of wine in the inner chamber and 500 ml of distilled water in the outer one with the side arm open. Boil the water. When the steam is up, close the side arm to force the steam into the inner chamber. Distill slowly until 100 ml of distillate has been collected. Transfer it to a 250 ml Ehrlenmeyer flask, using a small volume of distilled water to rinse. Add 5 drops of phenolphthalein indicator and titrate with 0.025 N NaOH.

   Volume of NaOH used X 0.015 = grams of volatile acid/ 100 ml wine.

Advanced Tests

F. Sulfur Dioxide (Ripper method)

   Reagents needed:

   10% NaOH

   25% (by volume) aqueous sulfuric acid (H_2SO_4)

   0.02 N iodine made by diluting 100 ml of N/10 iodine with water to 500 ml.

1% starch solution made by boiling 1 gram powdered, soluble starch in 100 ml of distilled water for 3 minutes.

1. Total SO_2 — Add 50 ml of wine and 25 ml of 10% NaOH to a 250 ml Ehrlenmeyer flask. Stopper the flask and let stand for 15 minutes. Add 10 ml of 25% H_2SO_4 and 5 drops of the starch solution. Titrate with the 0.02N iodine just to the blue endpoint.

   Volume of iodine used X 0.02 X 32 X 20 = ppm or mg total SO_2/1000 ml of wine.

2. Free SO_2 — Add 50 ml wine to 10 ml 25% H_2SO_4 and add 5 drops of starch solution. Titrate with .02 N iodine as above.

   Volume of iodine X 0.02 X 32 X 20 = ppm or mg free SO_2/1000 ml of wine.

G. Tannin

If you do not own or have easy access to Nesler tubes and want to do tannin analysis, consider investing in a small colorimeter for your analysis.

Reagents needed:

Folin & Ciocalteau reagent — Purchase from a chemical supply house, or to make this reagent yourself consult "Wine & Must Analysis", Amerine & Ough, Wiley & Sons, NY, NY 1974, p. 66.

Saturated Sodium Carbonate (Na_2CO_3) solution — add 70 grams Na_2CO_3 to 200 ml of distilled water and heat until dissolved. Cool to room temperature, seed with a small crystal of Na_2CO_3, and let stand for 2 hours.

Tannic acid standard — Dissolve 100 mg of tannic acid in 100 ml water.

Standard series

To each of 11 Nessler tubes add 80 ml of distilled water, 5 ml of Folin-Denis reagent, and 10 ml of Na_2CO_3 solution. Add successively 0, 0.2, 0.4, 0.6, 0.8, 1.0, 1.2, 1.4, 1.6, 1.8, and 2.0 ml of the tannic acid standard. Add water up to the mark in each tube. Stopper and shake well. After 30 minutes the tubes are ready for comparison. The series represents 0, 2, 4, 6, 8, 10, 12, 14, 16, 18 and 20 mg of tannic acid/100 ml of wine and is for low tannic white wines.

Test

To a Nessler tube add 1 ml of wine, 80 ml of water, 5 ml of Folin-Denis reagent, and 10 ml of $NaCO_3$ solution. Dilute to the mark with distilled water, stopper, and shake. After 30 minutes compare color with standard series. Result will be in mg/100 ml of wine.

H. Residual sugar

Reagents needed:

Fehling's solution. Solution A and B can be purchased from a chemical supply house or prepared as follows:

(A) dissolve 34.639 grams of cupric sulfate pentahydrate ($CuSO_4$–$5H_2O$) in distilled water and dilute to 500 ml in a volumetric flask.

(B) dissolve 173.0 grams sodium potassium tartrate ($NaKC_4H_4O_6$) and 50.0 grams reagent grade sodium hydroxide (NaOH) in water and dilute to 500 ml in a volumetric flask.

Dextrose standard — dissolve 500 mg reagent grade dextrose in dis- tilled water and dilute to 100 ml.

Methylene blue indicator — dissolve 1 gram methylene blue in 100 ml distilled water.

Preliminary

Mix 50 ml of each of the Fehling's solutions A and B. Dilute 10 ml of this with 40 ml of water. From a burette add 5 ml of dextrose solution and boil 20 seconds. Add an additional 3 ml of dextrose and boil. Add 5 drops of the methylene blue indicator and with the solution kept boiling add dextrose dropwise until the color just changes to brick red. Repeat, adding 90% of the dextrose used initially. Then titrate to the endpoint.
Total volume of dextrose used is designated "a".

Test

Treat wine with charcoal and Hyflo Super-Cel and filter. It should be water white. Add 10 ml of the wine to 50 ml of the dilute Fehling's (A & B) solution above. Boil the solution, add 5 drops of indicator and titrate with the dextrose standard to the endpoint.

Total volume of dextose used is designated "b".

$$(a - b) \times 0.005 = \text{grams of sugar}/100 \text{ ml of wine.}$$

I. Detection of Malolactic Fermentation

This is a useful procedure for following the malolactic formation so necessary in the east.

Procedure

In a separatory funnel shake together 100 ml of n-butanol, 100 ml of distilled water, 10.7 ml of concentrated formic acid, and 15 ml of a solution of 1 gram of water soluble bromcresol green in 100 ml of water. Let the two phases separate well in the funnel (20–30 minutes). Draw off the lower layer and discard. Place 70 ml of the upper layer into a gallon mayonnaise jar and close. Next cut a 20 X 30 cm rectangle from a sheet of Whatman #1 chromatographic paper. Along a long side draw a pencil line 2.5 cm from the edge. Using 10 microliter pipettes spot 10 microliters of wine and let dry. Do this 4 times. Allowing 2.5 cm between spots along the line, spot in the same manner a 0.2% solution of tartaric acid in water and another spot of a 0.2% solution of L-malic acid in water. Draw the short sides of the paper together without overlapping and staple. Place the paper cylinder (with the spots on the bottom) in the jar and allow the solvent to flow up the paper by capillary action. This can be left overnight. Remove the paper and dry in air. When dry, there will be yellow spots and a blue-green background. Notice the yellow spot of malic acid. As the fermentation is finished the corresponding spot in the wine will vanish.

Conclusion

There are many other tests, iron and copper being among them. These are best left to the professionals. Keep your wine housekeeping clean with as little iron and copper contact as possible, and you will have no trouble.

CHAPTER 8

WINE ACIDITY: TASTE, MEASUREMENT & CONTROL

Robert A. Plane, PhD. and Leonard R. Mattick, PhD.

OF THE FOUR basic tastes (sweet, sour, salty, and bitter) only the sour taste is characteristic of all wines, and in dry, white (or other low tannin) wines it is the only taste of any consequence. The sour taste of wine is caused by natural fruit acids in the wine, such as tartaric, malic and a few other minor acids. Because of the importance of acidity in the overall taste of wines, winemakers require some methods of measuring acidity, some way of relating these measurements to the taste of wines, and some guiding principles that will help them adjust acidity when the sour taste is too high or low.

This chapter first discusses these topics in a general way, and in the last section outlines practical tips for home winemakers.

Acidity Measurement

All acids that are dissolved in water (or wine) tend to separate into two parts: a hydrogen ion (H+), which is characteristic of all acids, and an anion (A-), which is different for each particular acid. Many of the effects of acids depend on the concentration of the hydrogen ion. In wines these effects include inhibiting unwanted bacteria and molds from growing, and maintaining the color of red wine.

Chemists express the separation of hydrogen ion and anion by the following equation:

What this equation says is that an acid can separate (dissociate) into individual parts (hydrogen ion and anion) and these individual parts can recombine into an undissociated acid. Strong acids (such as the sulfuric acid found in automobile storage batteries) separate almost completely, while weak acids (such as the acetic acid found in vinegar) show relatively little separation. For this reason we can think of H+ as being associated with strong acidity and HA being associated with weak acidity.

What does pH and titration measure in a solution of weak acid which contains both the acid HA and H+? The pH measures only H+ and pH meters are calibrated to determine H+ concentration. On the other hand, when a solution is titrated with alkali, all of the acid, HA as well as H+, is neutralized and measured. In wine, about 1% of weak acid molecules are dissociated, thus HA is about 100 times as concentrated as H+. So it isn't too much of an oversimplification to think of titration as measuring the weak acid, and pH as determining the strong, or dissociated, acid.

Perception of Acid Taste

What stimulates the tongue to provide a sour taste? Is it the dissociated acid (H+) or the total acid (H+ + HA)? A related question: is the acid taste of wine predicted better by pH or by the titratable acidity? This question has been studied for years with only qualitative agreement that both pH and titratable acidity are involved. However, this fact alone indicates that the sensory response of the tongue is to both H+ and HA with unequal intensity. For wine it has been shown that the response is about ten times greater to H+ than to the undissociated acids. Remembering that the undissociated acids (HA) exceed the dissociated (H+) by about 100 times, the taste is mainly due to the undissociated acids. This can be understood by considering a specific wine in which the H+ contributes an acid taste equal to z. Each HA molecule contributes but 1/10 the taste of an H+, and so if H+ and HA were equal, the HA would contribute 0.1z and the total acid taste would be z from H+ plus 0.1z from HA or 1.1z total. However in a more typical wine there are 100 HA molecules for each H+. Therefore the 100 HA molecules will contribute 100 X 0.1z = 10z. The total acid taste is 11z, with 10z contributed by HA and 1z contributed by H+. If we simply measured H+, as by using a pH meter or pH paper, we would be determining but about 1/10 of the total effect. Titration comes much closer, measuring about 9/10 of the effect. It is generally true the taste relates more nearly to total acid (or titratable acid) than to pH.

The results of taste panels which evaluated acid taste in a series of wines and of distilled water containing wine acids give a quantitative measure of the relationship between acid taste, titratable acid, and pH. This relation, called the acidity index, is:

$$z = \text{total acid (grams/liter)} - pH$$

In the relation, the total acid (titratable acid) is expressed in the currently recommended units of grams per liter (which gives a number 10 times the commonly used percentage figure). For most table wines, total acidity lies between 5 and 10 grams/liter and the pH between 3 and 4. A mathematical definition of pH is given in the last section of this chapter which shows that the higher the H+, the lower the pH and hence the reason for the minus sign in the equation for the acidity index.

Calculation of the acidity index in 350 commercial wines, analyzed by John T. Williams, the California and New York winemaker, shows patterns of acidities which winemakers believe consumers prefer. For dry, red wines, the acidity index averages 2.50 with 60% of the values lying between 2 and 3. For white wines, the values run about 50% higher (average 3.80) and are more variable with grape variety and with residual sugar. For example, the Chardonnays average 3.20 and the Reislings average 4.35. In general, sweeter wines have higher acidity index values, but the relationship has not yet been worked out in detail.

Control of Wine and Must Acidity

The acidity index of an unfinished wine may lie below the desirable range, especially in the case of wine made from overripe grapes or grapes grown in a hot region. In such cases, acid can be added, usually to the wine, as opposed to the must. Frequently it is added as tartaric acid (H_2T), whose structure is shown in Figure 1.

There is a complication with adding tartaric acid, however. Wine is usually saturated with respect to potassium bitartrate (KHT), called cream of tartar or winestone, which is but slightly soluble in cold alcoholic solution. Consequently, much of the added tartaric acid precipitates with the K+ already present in the solution (Potassium is widely found in plant tissues, including grapes). To avoid this inefficiency and to avoid depleting a wine of beneficial K+, acid is sometimes added as citric acid. It is claimed by some that citric acid tastes different from tartaric acid.

The acid index of wine made from underripe grapes or those grown in cold climates, may lie above the desirable range. In such cases, acid may be either neutralized or removed. In general, neutralization by adding a base such as sodium carbonate (Na_2CO_3) is

$\begin{array}{c}\text{COOH}\\ \text{HCOH}\\ \text{HOCH}\\ \text{COOH}\end{array}$	$\begin{array}{c}\text{COO}^-\text{K}^+\\ \text{HCOH}\\ \text{HOCH}\\ \text{COOH}\end{array}$	$\begin{array}{c}\text{COOH}\\ \text{HCOH}\\ \text{HCH}\\ \text{COOH}\end{array}$	$\begin{array}{c}\text{COOH}\\ \text{HCOH}\\ \text{HCH}\\ \text{H}\end{array}$
tartaric acid (H_2T)	potassium bitartrate (KHT)	malic acid (H_2M)	lactic acid (HL)
Figure 1	**Figure 2**	**Figure 3**	**Figure 4**

less satisfactory than acid removal. The reason is that neutralization of the acid (conversion of HA to A-) raises the pH of the solution more than does the complete removal of HA. Although a small rise of pH from, say 3.0 to 3.5 makes little difference, a rise to higher pH, as will result from neutralization of very acid wines, is harmful. Near pH 4, wines may become bacteriologically unstable and red wines may change color.

Removal of acids is accomplished by several methods. The most common occurs automatically with the precipitation of potassium bitartrate (KHT). Grape must contains dissolved KHT. Alcohol lowers the solubility of KHT, and some often precipitates during the fermentation. Precipitation of KHT removes one of the most concentrated acid constituents present: HT-. To ensure maximum removal of acid in this manner, the temperature is lowered to near the freezing point of the wine (about 25° F) where the solubility of KHT is much lower than at room temperature. Wines so treated (any time between fermentation and bottling) are "cold stable", meaning that tartrate crystals will not form later in the bottle if it is refrigerated or chilled. However, at the low temperature used for cold stabilization, precipitation is slow and may require weeks. Introduction of seed crystals of KHT speeds precipitation.

A good method for lowering acidity is the addition of potassium bicarbonate ($KHCO_3$). Potassium bicarbonate acts in two ways. It neutralizes the acid by converting one of the hydrogen ions of tartaric acid to water and secondly it combines with the remaining tartrate ion to form the relatively insoluble KHT.

However, there is a practical limit to the amount of acid which can be removed in this way. For example, if after fermentation the total acid level remains above 10 grams/liter (1% acid expressed as tartaric), sufficient potassium bicarbonate to lower it to the desired level will raise the pH near 4 (where bacterial and color instability can occur). The only exception to this might occur in a wine that contained very little malic acid and much tartaric acid and therefore had a pH below 3- but such wines are very unlikely in cold climates where high acid levels are a problem. As grapes ripen, the ratio of malic acid to tartaric acid drops. However, the ratio is different for different grape varieties.

Wines which can not be satisfactorily de-acidified with potassium bicarbonate are those having both high acid and high pH. Wines made from Baco noir grapes are notorious in this regard. This condition indicates a high level of malic acid (see Figure 3). Malic acid (H2M) is a weaker acid than tartaric and gives solutions with higher pH (lower H+). High malic acid levels are troublesome for two reasons: 1) neutralization will raise the pH to unstable values and 2) potassium bimalate does not precipitate the way potassium bitartrate does. What can be done to remove excess malate? Two methods are commonly used in wineries around the world.

Malate can be precipitated with calcium. Consequently, calcium carbonate (precipitated chalk) is added to overly acid wines and musts.

There is, however, a complication. Calcium tartrate is less soluble (especially in acid solution) than calcium malate and little malate is removed until nearly all the tartrate is precipitated. This of itself is not harmful. However, high levels of calcium may be needed to finally precipitate the malate and calcium will remain in solution. Levels of calcium above 100 ppm give distilled water a salty taste and excessive calcium can contribute to off flavors in wine. To avoid this problem the Acidex procedure is sometimes used. It involves treating a fraction of the wine or must with calcium carbonate (containing appropriate seed crystals), removing the precipitated calcium tartrate and calcium malate, then mixing this partially deacidified wine with remaining untreated wine. In the final mixture the excess calcium will be largely precipitated by tartrate from the untreated fraction. The Acidex procedure is claimed to produce a double salt of calcium malate and calcium tartrate if the appropriate reagents and seed crystals are used.

The other method commonly employed for reducing excess acidity due to malic acid is the malolactic fermentation. This is a bacterial reaction which converts malic acid, with two acid groups, to carbon dioxide and to lactic acid (see Figure 4), which has only one acid group. This fermentation effectively cuts the acidity of the original malic acid in half. Its effectiveness and frequent utilization are shown by the previously noted 350 wines analyzed by John Williams. Of these, he checked by paper chromatography 293 for evidence of malolactic conversion and 56% showed significant conversion. It is important to note that 89% of the red wines checked had undergone malolactic transformation, while only 14% of the white wines (mostly Chardonnay) had. These are the wines which were probably aged in wooden barrels, which frequently host malolactic bacteria.

Two drawbacks of malolactic conversion are frequently pointed out. The first is the fact that its utilization requires bringing a bacterial strain into a winery and this may increase the likelihood of future malolactic fermentations when they are unwanted. A malolactic fermentation is undesirable when the conversion occurs either after bottling or in wines that have already achieved proper acidity. The second drawback is the fact that the bacterial reaction does not readily occur in wines where it would be most beneficial. Since the bacteria are sensitive to sulfur dioxide, the first drawback can be minimized. Raising the initial pH to 3.2 by the addition of potassium bicarbonate or calcium carbonate can remove the second drawback. There is some controversy as to whether the malolactic conversion is desirable. In some cases it seems to add desirable complexity and smoothness to wines, while in other cases it seems to decrease fruitiness and may add off flavors. The use of commercially available pure strains of malolactic bacteria can minimize off flavors and overwhelm some of the adventitious bacteria that would otherwise be at work in wines. There is a detailed discussion of when malolactic fermentation is not desired in Chapter 14.

Tips For Home Winemakers

The home winemaker frequently needs to adjust acidity and may not have the appropriate means for measuring and adjusting acidity. The following steps are recommended for such cases:

1. When possible, secure grapes of proper ripeness. If the acidity of the must measures between 8 and 10 grams/liter, in most cases little will need to be done to adjust the acidity. Values of the pH are of little direct help at this point since they reflect total acidity differently for different grape varieties. Instead, a grape juice sample should be titrated with tenth normal sodium hydroxide. The acidity, in grams/liter, will equal 7.5 X (ml base)/(ml juice). For red juice, a pH meter is helpful since phenolphthalein is masked by the color changes that occur in red juice near the neutral point

2. If the must lies just outside of the desirable acid range, the resulting wine should be carefully titrated after the first racking; if the wine does not have the proper acidity (6 to 8 grams/liter, depending upon wine type or style), adjustments can be made to the wine. If the must is more acid than 12 grams/liter, calcium carbonate should be added to the must. For each 1 gram/liter decrease desired, add 0.67 grams/liter (2.5 grams or 0.09 oz per gallon) of $CaCO_3$.

3. If the acid level must be raised, add citric acid to the wine at a rate of 0.85 grams/liter (3.3 grams or 0.12 oz. per gallon) for each 1 gram/liter of acidity increase desired. Tartaric acid may be added instead, at a rate of 1 gram/liter (3.8 grams or 0.14 oz. per gallon) for each 1 gram/liter acidity increase, but some of the added acid may precipitate after this addition.

4. If the wine acidity lies between 8 and 10 grams/liter, it may be lowered by the addition of potassium bicarbonate ($KHCO_3$). For each 1 gram/liter that the acidity must be lowered, add 0.9grams/liter of $KHCO_3$ (3.4 grams or 0.13 oz. per gallon). Note that this amount will both neutralize some of the acid and precipitate some of the bitartrate. After the addition, the wine should be chilled to aid the precipitation of the potassium bitartrate.

5. If the wine acidity lies above 10 grams/liter, it may be lowered by the addition of calcium carbonate ($CaCO_3$). For each 1 gram/liter decrease desired, use 0.67 grams/liter (2.5 grams or 0.09 oz. per gallon) of $CaCO_3$. To help avoid high calcium concentration in the final wine, divide the wine to be de-acidified into halves. Add all of the calculated amount of $CaCO_3$ to one half, with vigorous stirring. Or

better yet, slowly add wine to the $CaCO_3$ while vigorously stirring. Keep the treated wine as cold as possible for several days, then rack it into the untreated half. Avoid oxidation.

6. Alternatives to 4 and 5 for lowering acidity include introduction of a malolactic culture after raising pH somewhat above 3 where, at low SO_2 concentrations, the conversion readily occurs. Simpler, but less desirable in terms of wine quality, is the addition of water to dilute the acid by the desired amount. The acid is inversely proportional to the volume of the wine. To drop from 9 grams/liter to 8 grams/liter, for example, requires that the volume be increased by 1/8 by adding 1 pint of water to each gallon of wine.

SUMMARY

Must acidity:

	Titrate wine later	OK	Titrate wine later	Add CaCO3
		8 g/L	10 g/L	12 g/L

Wine acidity:

	Add Acid	OK	Add KHCO3	Add CaCO3 M-L culture, water
	6 g/L	8 g/L		10 g/L

APPENDIX

The pH is defined as the negative logarithm of the hydrogen ion (H+) concentration, expressed in gram-atoms per liter. Since the atomic weight of hydrogen is 1.008, then 1 gram-atom per liter is equal to 1.008 grams of hydrogen ion per liter of solution:

$$pH = -\log [H+]$$

If the [H+] is 0.001 (1 X 10-3) gram-atoms/liter, then the pH = 3. The pH increases one unit for each 10-fold decrease in hydrogen ion concentration, so a wine with a pH of 4 has only 1/10 of the hydrogen ion of a wine with a pH of 3.

When an acid, HA, is in solution in water or wine, it dissociates and reaches an equilibrium.

The extent of the dissociation can be defined in terms of K, the dissociation constant:

$$[H+] [A-]/[HA] = K$$

For the principal acids in wines, the values of K lie between about 10^{-3} and 10^{-5}.

The equilibrium expression can be rearranged:

$$[H+] = K [HA]/[A-]$$

By taking logs of both sides of this equation we get:

$$pH = pK + \log [A-]/[HA]$$

This is the so-called buffer equation. It shows that wine will be buffered (meaning that pH is relatively constant as total solution concentrations are changed) at pH values in the range of 3 to 5. But the higher the ratio of the concentration of the anion, A-, to the undissociated acid, HA, the higher the pH. It is for this reason that excess acids should be removed from wine rather than just being neutralized. In the later case, HA is converted to A- leading to an excessive rise in pH which can cause wine instability.

CHAPTER 9

THE RELATIONSHIP OF PH & ACIDITY IN WINE

Douglas P. Moorhead

GRAPE WINE or juice contains several dissociated organic acids, mainly tartaric and malic (along with their half neutralized anions) with very small amounts of several other acids. At least 95% of the acidity in grape wines will be derived from tartaric and malic acids. They commonly occur in roughly equal amounts, but the ratio of tartaric to malic will vary from about .75 to 1 to as high as 6 to 1. As grapes ripen the total acidity declines, mainly because of the reduction in malic acid; therefore the ratio of tartaric to malic acid will increase as the grapes ripen. Tartaric acid is specific to grapes while malic acid is the predominate acid in most other fruits, except citrus fruits.

Several changes in acidity take place during fermentation. Between 10 and 30% of the malic acid and virtually all of the citric acid disappear. Succinic, lactic and pyruvic acids are produced by fermentation. Carbonic acid, in the form of dissolved CO_2 gas, is produced in fermentation and remains in the wine for varying periods of time, but declines once fermentation is over. It does help protect wine from the effects of oxygen. Lactic acid is produced in small quantities during fermentation and in large quantities when a malolactic bacterial fermentation occurs. Acetic acid is produced in very small quantities, except under aerobic conditions, when it occurs as the final oxidation product of alcohol in spoiled wines.

Total acidity or "titratable acidity" in grape wines is calculated on the basis of tartaric acid in the U.S. Fruit wines are calculated on the basis of malic acid or citric acid, depending on which is characteristic of that fruit. France uses sulfuric acid for its standard, so you always need to know what standard is being used when interpreting acidity figures. The vast majority of wines will have between 0.5% and 1.0% titratable acidity by weight, but I have seen extremes of 0.25% in Muscat of Alexandria grapes from California and 2.3% in a batch of Vignoles (Ravat 51) from the Lake Erie Viticultural Area. Some of the other fruits will have even higher levels; lemons and limes may have as much as 8 or 9% total acidity!

Total acidity is a measure of the potential acidity in a wine and includes both the dissociated hydronium ions (those capable of transmitting electrical impulses) and the undissociated acid molecules. pH is a measure of the active acidity; it measures only the dissociated hydronium ions. pH can be defined as the logarithm of the reciprocal of the hydronium ion concentration. Water is very weakly dissociated; about 1 in 10,000,000 atoms are dissociated. This can be written as a concentration of 10^{-7}. The reciprocal of the logarithm of that number is 7. A pH of 6 would be 10 times as acidic as pH 7; pH 5 would be 100 times as acidic as pH 7. Grape wines will have pH levels between 3 and 4; hence are 1,000 to 10,000 times as acidic as water.

Although the taste effect of dissociated ions is about 10 times that of the undissociated acid molecules, you can practically ignore the taste effect of pH because only about 1% of the acidity in most wines consists of the dissociated ions. Total acidity relates much more closely to our sense of taste. The ideal total acidity in table wine, from the standpoint of taste, would be from about 0.6% to 0.85%. Most people will find wines with less than about 0.6% total acidity a bit flat and wines having more than about 0.9% too acidulous for enjoyable drinking.

The relationship of pH to total acidity is not a simple ratio because different wines will have different ratios of the various acids. Wines with higher ratios of tartaric acid will buffer to lower pH levels than those with higher levels of malic acid. In wines where the malic acid has been converted to lactic acid the pH will be even higher. It is therefore possible to have high acidity and high pH at the same time, or conversely low acidity and low pH.

While pH is not very important in the perception of acidity when tasting wine, it can have a profound effect on both health and stability. Low pH wines are not as subject to biological degradation because most spoilage organisms are inhibited by low pH. Further, sulfur dioxide (SO_2) is much more effective in inhibiting microorganisms at lower pH levels. The most effective form of free SO_2 is the undissociated dissolved SO_2 gas. The portion of the SO_2 in this form is quite pH dependent. It accounts for about 9% of the free SO_2 at a pH of 3.0, but less than 1% at a pH of 3.8. One study found that 16 ppm of free SO_2 was sufficient for biological stability at pH 3.02, but 47 ppm were required at pH 3.5 and 58 ppm were needed at pH 3.6. You probably can't add enough SO_2 at a pH of 4.0 or higher to confer stability on such a wine. Very low pH levels (below 3.0) may actually partially inhibit fermentation itself.

Fortunately most wines fall within normal pH and total acid ranges and therefore require only sound winemaking practices to assure sound wine. This chapter is concerned primarily with those wines which fall outside those ranges. I will admit to a bias toward as little intervention in altering acidity as is consistent with sound wine. A lot of wines, like people, may have a few warts but also have compensating virtues. I think that you really need to consider and weigh potential risk against potential gain when you plan to alter the acidity of your wine. There are many marginal wines where doing nothing is at least as good as trying for perfect pH and total acidity levels. With this caveat entered, what steps can we take when we have pH or total acidity level problems.

Wines with both high acidity and high pH

I have found that most of the wines with vitis riparia in their genetic background tend to have this problem. Foch, Leon Millot, Chelois and Baco noir are reds that commonly have this problem in cooler climates as do Vignoles (Ravat 51) and to a lesser extent both Villard Blanc and Vidal. Red wines made from grapes with vitis riparia in their parentage have commonly had the problem of turning to an undesirable brownish-red as they aged. I had long assumed that this was a problem specific to the species, but it now appears that it is merely an indication of high pH in the wine because of a higher ratio of malic to tartaric acid and that such browning is not inevitable if the wines are treated to lower the pH by the addition of tartaric acid followed by cold stabilization.

There are several treatments possible where you have both high total acidity and high pH:

1. Germanic style (fruity) whites can often be made quite acceptable by the addition of a small amount of sugar. This is very common with Reisling and other varieties such as Vidal, Seyval blanc and Catawba. We had a batch of Vidal one year with a total acidity of 0.93% to which the addition of 1.5% sugar proved a better treatment from taste standpoint than any of the acid reduction treatments. This approach might be considered aberrant in oak aged reds or Chardonnays, but it should not be dismissed out of hand with other wines.

2. Actual reduction of acidity with one of the carbonate compounds. Those approved for commercial wines are calcium carbonate, potassium carbonate, potassium bicarbonate and Acidex. Each of these materials raises the pH while lowering acidity. Above certain levels they will also impart a flavor from the metallic ions added. Further, they tend to react preferentially with tartaric acid over malic acid. Avoid using sodium carbonate or bicarbonate.

(a) Calcium carbonate — This material is best added to the juice or early in the fermentation because of the chalky taste imparted to the wine by the calcium ions, at least until the wine is cold stabilized. There is the further complication that cold stabilization takes longer and is more difficult than with wines treated with potassium salts because both calcium tartrate and calcium malate are relatively insoluble. 2.5 grams per gallon of calcium carbonate will lower acidity by 0.1% (1 gram per liter will lower acidity 0.15%). I would suggest the maximum safe rate for $CaCO_3$ would be about 10 grams per gallon which will give an approximate 0.4% reduction in acidity. Not all of the acid reduction occurs immediately; at least 20% of it occurs during cold stabilization. $CaCO_3$ does not raise pH as badly as potassium bicarbonate or potassium carbonate for a given reduction in total acidity.

There is also a way you can add it which permits a higher percentage of malic acid removal. You can add calcium carbonate to a fraction of your wine to allow almost complete acid removal and then add that treated portion back to the rest of the batch. I would recommend this method if you must drop more than 0.1 to 0.15% in acidity.

(b) Potassium bicarbonate — Has a practical limit of about 0.2% acid reduction because of a potassium (bitter-salty) taste imparted above that level and because of the increase in pH to the wine. About 1/3 of the reduction in acidity occurs later as tartrates are precipitated when the wine is chilled. It has the advantage of being able to be added immediately before consumption and having a quicker tartrate deposition than calcium carbonate. 3.4 grams of potassium bicarbonate per gallon will lower acidity by 0.1%. One gram per liter will lower acidity by 1.1%. You can not use maximum levels of calcium carbonate and then use potassium bicarbonate or carbonate for further acid reduction; nor use calcium carbonate after maximum use of either of the potassium salts.

(c) Potassium carbonate — This material may be used instead of potassium bicarbonate, but there is some evidence that you are more likely to pick up the "bitter-salty" ion taste, so the bicarbonate salt would be preferred. 2.4 grams per gallon will lower acidity by 0.1%)1 gram per liter will lower acidity by 0.16%).

(d) Where you have high pH along with the need to reduce acidity you may consider the addition of tartaric acid, preferably during or immediately before fermentation. Rates as high as 9.5 lbs per 1,000 gallons have been recommended. While you raise the acidity, which is undesirable, you also lower pH. After a good cold stabilization you will lower acidity without appreciably affecting the pH. With the wines I tested, 4 grams of tartaric acid per gallon increased acidity by 0.1%.

3. The time-honored method of reducing acidity has been by encouraging or inducing a malolactic bacterial fermentation. Typical acid reductions are 0.2 to 0.4% (with pH increases of 0.15 to 0.45 pH units). Malic acid is converted to the milder lactic acid and CO_2. Lactic acid has about half of the acidity of malic acid. Wines which undergo this fermentation are softer and more vinous and have less of the fruity, grapey character; they are also more stable microbiologically than non M-L wines. An M-L fermentation is desirable with almost any red. Chardonnay is a white which traditionally has gone through an M-L fermentation. Paradoxically the wines most in need of a malolactic fermentation may be the ones where it is most difficult to start. Inhibitory factors are free SO_2 levels above 5 ppm, temperatures below 55° F, alcohol levels above 12% and pH levels below 3.1. Leoconoctoc oenos strains such as PSU–1 are more tolerant of acidity than the Lactobacillus strains. On occasion you may have to perform a partial acid reduction with one of the carbonates in order to get the M-L started.

4. Another method of acid reduction which has been practiced a great deal in the east has been by amelioration with water and sugar. Many of the Vitis labrusca varieties such as Concord, Niagara (at least when picked before the grapes are fully ripe), Catawba, and Delaware have both high acidity and high flavor intensity. Dilution with water will help both problems. This would not be a satisfactory approach with most reds or with more delicately flavored varieties. A reduction from total acidity of 1.0 to 0.8% would require the addition of 25% ameliorating material.

5. One final method of lowering acidity is to blend a high acid wine with a low acid wine. Many amateurs in the east have done this by blending local Vitis labrusca varieties with warm region California grapes. This method is not always available because you tend to end up with either all high acid or low acid wines rather than a mix of the two.

Wines with high acidity and with low or normal pH levels

The discussion in the previous sections apply here, except that you have more freedom to raise pH and therefore acid reduction is easier and less critical to the health of the wine. Fortunately this is common in much of the east. Long Island appears to be unusual in the number of high pH grapes in a relatively cool climate.

Wines with low acidity

This is primarily a problem in the warmer areas of California and not very common in the east. However, it is important if you purchase either fresh grapes or concentrate from the warmer areas. Tartaric, DL-malic and citric acids are commonly used to increase acidity. If you use citric it is preferable to add it after fermentation because when added before fermentation some will be converted to acetic acid. The higher the temperature of fermentation the more acid must be added to get the same level in the finished wine. Because some of the tartaric acid will precipitate in the form of tartrates you must add more to get the same level of acid increase as you would from DL-malic or citric acids; however, this may be an advantage since you can get the pH lower without as much of an increase in acidity. Rates as high as 10 lbs. per 1,000 gallons (4.5 grams per gallon) are commonly used for tartaric acid additions.

During a demonstration at an American Wine Society Conference the wines presented for tasting consisted of a 1983 dry Catawba wine as a base wine and with several treatments:

The most preferred sample was the one to which 5.1 grams/gallon of potassium bicarbonate had been added. Nearly every taster found the 15.3 grams/gallon batch to have an unpleasant salty or bitter taste; close to half the tasters detected a taste in the 10.2 grams/gallon treatment.

A second group of samples were tasted in which the base wine was treated as follows:

Wine and treatment

Base wine (no treatment)

Base wine + 4% sucrose

Base wine + 3.8 grams/gallon calcium carbonate

Base wine + 4% sucrose + 5.1 grams/gallon potassium carbonate

The responses were very mixed with no majority preference.

Summary

1. Many acidity and pH problems can be avoided altogether if you follow good practices in the vineyard and harvest the grapes at the proper time. This will only be possible if you have some control over vineyard operations.

2. When the above isn't possible you should consider each of the alternative treatments, then pick the least drastic one which will give you sound wine. If you must err, do so on the side of doing too little, not too much.

3. If you make wines from grapes from other regions where you are not as sure how the wine will develop, it will pay you to invest in a pH meter in order to monitor the wines more closely. Better yet, cultivate the friendship of someone who has a pH meter! None of the pH paper strips are accurate enough for winemaking purposes.

4. Keep records on your winemaking practices. Historical perspective is very important in consistently making good wines.

This chapter is largely dependent on research work done by Robert A. Plane, Director of the New York Agricultural Experiment Station at Geneva, and Leonard R. Mattick, formerly Professor of Chemistry at the Geneva Station, now retired. I would like to acknowledge my debt to them as well as the debt we all owe them as winemakers; we should now be able to make good wines more consistently from grapes which have less than perfect acid and pH levels. Perhaps that will be reward enough for them.

CHAPTER 10

WINE BLENDING
Philip F. Jackisch

Introduction

MOST OF THE WORLD'S WINES are blended. Whether we buy an ordinary wine for everyday use or a fine wine for a special occasion, the chances are that it was made by mixing two or more distinct wines together. Although blending is a key step in making most wines, it is a subject on which little information is readily available. Because of this lack of information, many people don't know about all of the positive aspects of blending and some of them think that blending is only done to cheapen wines. In this brief survey we are going to look at why and how wines are blended. Winemakers (amateur and commercial), wine merchants, wine consumers, and wine educators should all be interested in the blending process.

It has only been in the past generation or so that blending has been questioned. Following the repeal of Prohibition in the U.S., many California winemakers — struggling to rebuild their shattered industry — offered wines with European names (chablis, burgundy, etc.). This practice had been followed in the eastern U.S. and elsewhere in the world for many years. Few American wine districts had any prestige to compare with the much older European districts and labeling a Catawba wine as a "champagne" probably did increase its appeal to the uninitiated wine consumer. But the Californians had an excellent climate in which to grow grapes and the fact that this major viticultural area was stooping to produce cheap and generally undistinguished imitations of European original wine types — usually by blending Central Valley grapes without much character — seemed to some people to be a tragic mistake.

Frank Schoonmaker was one of the first to urge California producers to avoid regional European names and to use varietal grape names for their wine. As producers began to follow this advice, and as more acres of premium grape varietals were planted in California in the 1950's and 1960's, varietally-labeled wines increased in number and began to compete with simple blended wines with generic designations. By the 1960's, a handful of dedicated winemakers were able to produce excellent wines without any blending. Wine writers, slowly becoming aware of the increased quality of California wines, focused attention on the new varietal wines. Cabernet Sauvignon, Pinot noir, Chardonnay, Reisling, and (eventually) Zinfandel, became the prestige wines of California.

By the 1970's, as new wineries opened up across the continent, it was natural for winemakers to feature unblended varietal wines at the top of their lists. Regional wine competitions began to proliferate and each offered many classes for varietal wines and few classes for blended wines. Winemakers played to the new audience for premium table wines and some claimed, with evident pride, that their varietal wines were made from 100% of the named variety. Before long, consumers were moved to believe that wines from one grape variety, grown in one vineyard, in one season, were superior to blended wines. With the prestige and marketing advantage of varietal wines firmly established, proposals were made to further limit by law the blending that could be done in making these types of wines.

The plain fact is that it wasn't the lack of blending that raised wine quality in this country in the past 20 years. In most cases it was the availability of better grapes grown in better locations. Some of the top wine producers recognized this fact and kept making blended wines, winning prizes, and selling wines as they always had. But many producers were lured into creating a new class of undistinguished wines — varietals without much character.

About the time that the detraction of wine blending was reaching a peak, more and more California winemakers rediscovered the advantages of blending. They found, as European winemakers had known for centuries, that most individual wines have imperfections which can generally best be overcome by judicious blending with other individual wines.

Now it is a curious fact that while the Europeans are masters at blending wines, some of their top spokesmen claim that wines are not made but rather "make themselves". Presumably they wish us all to believe that unless we happen to own a special plot of land in Bordeaux, Burgundy, or on the Rhine, we can never hope to make a really excellent wine no matter how hard we try. This is "do as I say rather than as I do" advice. If the Europeans had not used their blending skills for the past few hundred years it is very doubtful that their wines would have become so famous.

In the simplest terms, blending is a winemaker's attempt to make two plus two equal at least five. Blending can do this by diluting wine defects while increasing wine complexity. It is a rather rare wine that can not benefit from skillful blending, as we shall see.

The goals that winemakers have in blending can be grouped into four categories:

1. To give a wine that is better balanced or more attractive than the individual ingredients.

2. To give a standard wine that is reasonably constant in character and quality during repeated years of production.

3. To give a wine at lower cost than would otherwise be possible.

4. To give a new type of wine.

The tactics that a winemaker can use to achieve the above goals include:

1. Blending wines from two or more varieties of grapes.

2. Blending wines from one grape variety grown in different locations.

3. Blending wines from two or more vintages.

4. Blending wines that have received different vinifications.

5. Blending wines from various casks.

6. Blending non-grape ingredients together or with grape wines.

When combinations of the above practices are considered, the possibilities are almost endless.

Blending Strategies

For the commercial winemaker, blending practices are necessarily restricted by applicable laws and regulations, the availability of suitable blending stocks, consumer demands, economic considerations, and the skill of the winemaker or blender. Amateur winemakers don't face laws and regulations in making blends but many of the other restrictions apply. Yet within these restrictions a great deal of freedom exists and one needs some guiding principles to begin any rational blending program.

The following is a list of broad guidelines to blending:

1. Only sound wines should be blended. The blending of spoiled wines will only serve to spoil a larger quantity of wine (slight excess volatile acidity is a possible exception).

2. Grapes grown in warmer regions will generally be higher in sugar, potential wine alcohol, and body than the same grapes grown in cooler regions, while being lower in acidity, color, fragrance and flavor.

   Blending for balance of one or more of these characteristics usually involves a compromise. Rational blending demands that the quality that is lacking should be improved by blending more than other existing qualities are sacrificed.

3. Undesirably strong wine fragrances and flavors are often improved by blending with more neutral wines or with wines that have dissimilar types of fragrances and flavors. The strongest fragrances are possessed by the labrusca grape varieties of the northeastern U.S. and the muscats of Europe and California. Some people have learned to appreciate these strong and distinctive aromas and flavors, but broader consumer acceptability is often achieved by careful blending to tone down these assertive characteristics.

   As a general rule, the blending of two or more distinctive characteristics tends to reduce the prominence of each. This neutralization is sometimes more effective than the dilution obtained by blending in of neutral wines. Labrusca grapes, such as Niagara or Concord, can contribute their characteristic grapey aroma to a wine blend when present in as little as 2 to 5%. Scuppernong can have a rather one–dimensional floral odor — the smell of roses. But just over a generation ago a wine blend made from Scuppernong grapes, labrusca grapes, and some California grapes was the largest selling wine in America.

4. Premium grape varieties that possess distinctive but generally acceptable fragrances and flavors, such as Riesling, Chardonnay, Pinot noir, or Cabernet Sauvignon, can be dominated by those varieties that have noticeably stronger fragrances and flavors, such as muscats or labrusca varieties. On the other hand, blending of several of these premium grape varieties together can neutralize their characteristics to an unacceptably low level. For this reason one almost never finds commercial blends of Reisling with Chardonnay or Pinot noir with Cabernet Sauvignon. Nothing is accomplished by confusing the desirable characteristics of these premium varieties with each other. If blending with other varieties needs to be done to change color, acidity, or other secondary characteristics, this is best done by using relatively similar types of grapes or more neutral types (Merlot with Cabernet Sauvignon or Sauvignon blanc with Chardonnay, for example).

5. The blending of semi–distinctive grape varieties — including many of the French hybrids and such California varieties as Chenin blanc,

Pinot blanc, Grenache, and others — follows the same general rules as the blending of the distinctive premium varieties mentioned above. Undesirably strong aromas and flavors can be neutralized by different but equally strong aromas and flavors, while more neutral wines can be used to dilute these characteristics.

The special problem with these semi-distinctive grapes is that blending in more expensive grapes may not make enough improvement to pay and may actually lead to less distinctive wines. If varietal characteristics are carefully chosen, however, blending can often give good results.

Many generic commercial wines produced in this country contain more or less of these semi-distinctive grape varieties. Their value for blending depends on their availability, their lack of overly assertive qualities, and their relatively modest cost. In many cases blends of these varieties are more interesting than pure varietal wines. This seems to be true, for example, with many of the French hybrids which tend to be less complex than one would desire. Blends of two or more of these varieties are often more acceptable than one variety alone.

6. The blending together of neutral grapes, such as Thompson seedless and some others, is only feasible to prepare preblends, since such wines by themselves have no special wine quality. As noted above, however, these neutral grapes can sometimes provide balance to a blend with more expensive grapes while only moderately diluting the desirable fragrances and flavors. The main value of these neutral grapes lies in their low cost and ready availability.

7. The color and style of the wines blended should generally be similar. Thus, fruity red wines should be blended with other fruity reds, and austere white wines should be blended with other austere whites.

   Exceptions to this rule generally involve the most strongly odorous or flavored wines. When one is dealing with the assertive fragrances of the labrusca varieties the species' characteristics override individual varietal characteristics and reds, such as Concord, and whites, such as Niagara, can often be blended without producing a strangely flavored wine.

8. Blending wines produced by different vinification treatments often allows the winemaker more control than trying to stop a particular vinification step at a specific point. For example, it is extremely difficult to predict when a Chardonnay aged in new oak barrels will reach the desired level of wood flavor for the style of wine desired. One month in the barrels may be too little and two months may be too much. Even if the wines are tasted each day there is no assurance that

the winemaker will be able to transfer the wine at the proper moment. This is true because not all barrels will give identical amounts of aroma and flavor to a wine, and samples taken with a wine thief through a bung hole will not necessarily represent the average of the wine in that barrel. It is usually easier for the winemaker to allow some of the wine to pick up excess oak character and then blend this wine with other batches that have not received so much oak character.

The time that red grapes are allowed to remain on the skins is another area where blending can be useful. Especially with varieties new to the winemaker it is difficult to judge the optimum time to allow the must to ferment before pressing. Color pickup varies from variety to variety and does not necessarily parallel fragrance, flavor, and tannin pickup. Dividing the grapes into several batches, giving each a different skin contact time, then blending later can provide more information and control than trying to guess at the optimum contact time.

9. Blends should be made with a specific purpose in mind and no more ingredients should be used than the blender requires or has the skill to handle. Excessive blending can reduce any wine to mediocrity.

Planning the Wine Blend

Since the goal of blending is to produce a wine that is in some sense better than the average of the ingredients, it is necessary to have a definite ideal in mind and to consider the factors that influence the quality of a wine blend. The random mixing together of two or more wines will seldom accomplish the goal of improving wine quality.

Among the things that the wine blender must know are consumer preferences, the characteristics of wine ingredients, individual wine strengths and weaknesses, and the ways in which wines can be blended. There are multivintage blends (wines from one grape variety grown in several years), multilocation blends (wines from one grape variety grown in several locations), multivariety blends (wines from several varieties), and multiblends (combinations of the above).

Consumer preferences vary from region to region and the individual wine producer must have some idea of what these are for the people that will consume his wines. This is true whether the winemaker is an amateur producing for his family or is a small commercial producer in an area where wines have not been produced before. Too often the tendency of the small winemaker is to produce a wine, then wait and see if anyone likes it. This procedure is risky and in many instances gives unsatisfactory results.

As the first step in planning a new blend, the winemaker should try to find out as much as he can about the styles of wines that are acceptable to his potential consumers. The colors, aromas, and flavors of the existing commercial wines that appeal to them should be carefully noted and the limits of acceptability established, if this is possible. For example, a wine-maker planning to produce a completely dry sparkling wine for the first time would be foolish to do this if only sweet sparkling wines were locally popular.

In some areas white wines are preferred, possibly because of the local food specialties. In New Orleans, for example, where seafood and shellfish are specialties, some 85% of the wines sold in restaurants are white wines. Somewhat tannic red wines are popular where red meats are plentiful, such as in New York and Chicago.

In colder climates, such as the Scandinavian countries, sweet wines have long been preferred over dry wines. But sweetness may also be preferred due to cultural influences. A family used to Kosher wines with 20% sugar is not likely to instantly appreciate a totally dry red dinner wine. Relatively unsophisticated consumers often seem to prefer uncomplex wines with a pronounced aroma or flavor. In any area, the introduction of unfamiliar wine types will be met with some resistance.

Grapes (and to a lesser extent other fruits) vary considerably in their constituents from season to season and from variety to variety. It is not possible to go into these variations in detail here. But the winemaker should set himself the task of determining the characteristics of the grapes or other characteristics. As an example, in Michigan in one season Baco noir grapes grown in different vineyards varied from 14 Brix and over 2% acid to 22 Brix and under 1% acid. These differences appeared to be due to differing cultural practices — primarily cropping level. A winemaker planning to purchase fully ripe Baco noir grapes and only being able to purchase the underripe grape would definitely not be able to make the type of wine he originally had in mind.

In a vineyard in Indiana, Vignoles grapes were harvested three times from one vineyard at Brix 21, 24, and 26. The corresponding wines from these individual batches were: 1) fairly neutral in character, 2) having a muscat-like aromatic character, and 3) reminiscent of a German berrenauslese. Clearly, Vignoles changes radically in character with increasing ripeness. Riesling, on the other hand, is a variety that does not change radically as it ripens (in the absence of botrytis). These are the sorts of things that winemakers must know when assembling the wines that they plan to use in creating a blend.

The general strategy of a wine blending program is to accurately identify the strengths and weaknesses of the various wine blending stocks that are available. In many cases one wine stock is chosen as the main wine base and one or more other wine stocks are tentatively identified as secondary blending stocks. Either or both the primary and the secondary stocks may themselves be blends (in this case they will be referred to as preblends).

A preblend is prepared when no one wine stock has the desired characteristics to form the backbone of a blend or to be a secondary blending stock. We can illustrate the concept of the preblend by imagining that a particular white wine, chosen as the main wine base, has too strong a flavor. If other available blending stocks have certain imbalances — such as excessive acidity, too dark a color, or whatever — a preblend of several of these individual blending stocks may be prepared to balance out these unwanted secondary characteristics. Then, when this preblend is added to the main wine base, the blender will only be faced with one problem to solve — too strong a flavor in the wine base.

It is impossible to give a useful listing of all grape varieties that can be used in blends to accomplish a given purpose . The best guide to this might be the compositions of successful commercial blends, which are sometimes made known on back labels or elsewhere. Consumer-oriented wine magazines occasionally delve into the composition of particular blended wines. An increasing number of wineries issue free newsletters and in these winemakers sometimes discuss their new wine blends. Blends that have withstood the test of consumer acceptance represent a feasible solution to a particular blending problem. Other winemakers can benefit from knowledge of these blends.

Once acceptable wine stocks have been identified, the next step is to obtain as much knowledge about each stock as is required to solve the blending problem. No rational blending can begin before the blender knows what he is dealing with. To know his blending materials he requires careful tasting notes and physical and chemical analyses. Such analyses are often beyond the scope of the small winemaker but arrangements can be made to have these analyses done by outside labs, other wineries, or experienced friends if the winemaker can not do them himself.

The range of analyses required depends on the goal of the blending program. If the goal is to reduce excessive acidity and little more, the acidities of the various blending stocks need to be known while other analyses may be ignored. If, on the other hand, one is attempting to duplicate a successful complex blend from a previous year, many analyses will be required.

Some sources of information on grape characteristics, wine and must analyses, and sensory evaluation of wines are given at the end of this bulletin.

The wine blender should have some idea of the strengths and limitations of the various types of blending that he can do. Multivintage blending is usually done for one of two reasons: either to raise the quality of a particularly bad year or to combine fresh and aged characteristics in a single wine. Commercial wineries seldom get involved with the first of these reasons and amateur winemakers seldom get involved with the second (although perhaps they should).

Multilocation blends are usually used to adjust fairly subtle wine characteristics such as body or a particular shade or fragrance or flavor. Usually only the largest wineries, with multiple sources of grapes and sophisticated wine blenders, get involved in this. But it is something that smaller wineries that purchase grapes should probably pay more attention to.

Multivarietal blends are considerably more versatile than the other types of blends just mentioned for the obvious reason that there is usually more difference between varieties than between vintages or locations. Multivarietal blends can be used to stretch expensive varieties, to make a better balanced or more complex wine, or to create a style of wine that would be impossible from just one variety. Essentially all proprietary and generic wines are multi-varietal blends. In these wines the wine blender aims not only for a distinctive style of wine but for continuity in character from year-to-year.

Among the most expensive wines of Bordeaux multi-varietal wines are never multi-vintage or multi-location blends. Among fine non-vintage French Champagnes most wines are multi-varietal, multi-vintage, and multi-location blends. Part of the reason for this difference in approach probably lies in the climactic differences. About 2 years out of 3 in Bordeaux the weather is good enough to give very good wines, while in the more northern Champagne district the ratio is probably about 1 year out of 3. The Champagne producers therefore choose to blend for consistency in all but a few great years. The same thinking applies in the production of port wine in Portugal.

The time when wines are blended can have some influence on the end result. Some winemakers are experienced enough to be able to blend grapes in the fermenter rather than blend the wines later. This is only practical when grapes ripen at approximately the same time or can be held in cold storage until needed. Experiments by some larger eastern U.S. wine producers suggest that when Concord grapes are combined and fermented with California grapes (or juice) the resulting wine is better than if each type of grape is fermented separately and combined later.

While it is possible and sometimes desirable to blend grapes in the fermenter, the beginning wine blender should first become thoroughly familiar with the characteristics of the individual wines at his disposal before attempting any blending. The later in the maturity cycle that wines are blended, the fewer the changes that will occur. It takes a great deal of skill and experience to predict what a single wine will taste like when sampling a fermentation or a very immature wine. The added complications of trying to assess a blend at this point are beyond the abilities of most beginning wine blenders.

Blending Tactics

Once a specific blending goal has been identified and a specific wine base and tentative secondary blending stocks selected, the wine blending can begin. This blending should be done under conditions most conducive to accurate evaluation of the blends. It is best to work in a quiet room with light colored walls and a minimum of distractions. The wine cellar is generally a poor place for evaluating blends since the lighting is usually poor and there are often smells present which make objective evaluation very difficult. A laboratory or, for the home winemaker, a kitchen (not being used for cooking at the moment) are suitable rooms in which to prepare and evaluate wine blends.

One or more tasters should be assembled to evaluate the various wine blends. Larger wineries often use several staff members and may bring in outside experts for an important blending session. The qualifications of the tasters should include:

1. Some competence in evaluating wines

2. Familiarity with the types of wines to be blended

3. A reflection of the tastes of the consumers of the wines.

It is a mistake for a winemaker — even a home winemaker — to place too much reliance on his own personal preferences when blending a wine. A winemaker who acts as his own sole judge is much like the proverbial man who acts as his own lawyer — he has a fool for a client. At the very least, other family members or friends should be invited to sit in judgement of the blends if these people will be involved in consuming the wines later. The winemaker or wine blender need not take all advice — to do so might well cripple his artistic talent — but if he never takes advice he may end up producing wines that only he can appreciate.

Since consumers are much more definite about their dislikes than about their likes, the wine blender should take pains to establish what these dislikes are for his consumers. Sometimes a winemaker will build up a tolerance for certain flaws in his own wines — high acidity, excess sulfur dioxide, mercaptan smells, high volatile acidity — and he doesn't realize that others find these things objectionable.

Among the various factors that influence odor and flavor preference, age and experience seem to be most important. If the winemaker is attempting to produce a wine with general appeal he should be aware of the likes and dislikes of both young and old consumers and those with varying degrees of experience in tasting wines. Since it is unlikely that everyone will like the same wine, the winemaker should try to please those in the age and experience group that he considers most important. It is often very difficult for a winemaker to recognize that his own preferences are not necessarily the same as that of many consumers, but if he wants to gain wide acceptance for his wines he will have to make an effort to learn about what others like in a wine.

For the tasters assembled to evaluate the various blends, there should be a suitable number of clean wine glasses, water for rinsing the mouth, and a receptacle in which to spit tasted wines. If at all possible, the tasters should be presented with code-numbered glasses in which the blends have been put by another person. What we are talking about is duplicating as much as possible the conditions used in formal wine competitions where trained judges seriously consider which wines are better than average and how these wines rank.

To start, one or more blends should be prepared. These may include a 1:1 blend, and possibly a 1:3 blend and a 3:1 blend of the base wine and a secondary blending stock. (With practice the wine blender will have a good idea of suitable starting proportions and can save time at this step.) The blends should be tasted along with the unblended components and each glass of wine should be carefully evaluated and scored on items of interest. Particular attention should be paid to possible improvements that could be made in each sample. After the evaluation, when the identity of each sample is made known, the tasters can decide if any of the blends has been shown to be equal to or superior to the unblended components.

If a blend is poorer than either component, the notes that were taken should shed light on why this is so. Some wines just do not go well together and learning about these incompatibilities is part of learning to be a competent wine blender. It is not unknown for certain good wines to mutually cancel out the desirable qualities that each has. Some excellent wine stocks may have to be rejected because they do not fit into the particular blend that is being worked on at the moment.

If a blend is equal to or superior to the blending components, but falls short of the blending goal, a second round of blending should be held. This may involve fine adjustments in the proportion of the base wine and the secondary wine stock, or the introduction of new blending stocks. Further blending can proceed until no more blending stocks are available or until no further improvement in the blended wine can be noted.

If at all possible, the best blend should be tasted blind in competition with a standard wine that represents the blending goal. This may be a commercial wine with the desired characteristics, a wine from a previous successful vintage, or any other wine that approximates the goal of the blending program. Without a "benchmark" wine of this type, it is difficult to know if the blending goal has been met. Memory is a key component in successful blending, but this memory should be refreshed whenever possible.

If the blending goal proves to be beyond reach with the available blending materials, then the goal must be changed. If the goal was to produce a very fruity red wine and no blend can give this type of wine, then perhaps a mellow red or a hearty red can be made. Accurate information on the qualities of the various blending stocks, combined with some blending experience, can reduce the number of such false starts to a minimum. If a given style of blended wine is produced from similar stocks in succeeding years, it should then be possible to simplify the blending process and eliminate from consideration any stocks that have proven unworkable in this particular type of blend.

Certain commercial wineries often prepare blends from dozens of different wines. While it is undoubtedly true that a skilled wine blender can continue to improve a blend after many rounds, such large numbers of wines are more often than not a result of obtaining grapes from many different small parcels of vineyards. This is especially true in Europe where individual vineyard holdings often average just an acre or two. The beginning blender in the U.S. will seldom have wines made from grapes from many vineyards and will usually be faced with simpler blending tasks.

Wine blending skill is not something that can be learned in one or two sessions. The beginning wine blender should take every opportunity to practice wine blending in order to develop and sharpen his blending skills. One place to begin this practice is with sound commercial wines, especially those that haven't already been extensively blended. These wines will not usually have major flaws but by using them the novice wine blender can learn about the subtleties of blending. He can blend, for example, a relatively high acid German white wine with a lower acid Spanish white wine and see what happens to the individual fragrances and flavors in the blend. Careful notes taken during such practice sessions can prove invaluable later when serious blending is attempted on the winemaker's own wines of related type.

Many of us have certain "blindnesses" in wine evaluations and we should become aware of them. Odor and taste thresholds vary from person to person. Some people have a high tolerance for over-sulfited wines, others for oxidized wines or wines with high volatile acidity, still others for wine containing high levels of sorbates sometimes used to stabilize sweet wines. Some of these tolerances are inherited, others are learned, and some may be the result of ignorance. Persons, for example, who can not recognize a mercaptan smell in a wine may not find it objectionable on this account. The same inability to recognize certain characteristics may also apply to positive wine attributes, but this is more difficult to document.

The beginning wine blender should strive to test his own evaluations against those of other people. In this manner he can learn how his typical responses differ from the norm. When tasting in the presence of more experienced tasters he may learn to identify more wine characteristics and nuances. The wide divergence in wine ratings that usually occurs among a group of beginning wine tasters is less evident among more experienced tasters. While the elimination of all conflicting evaluations is impossible, and probably not desirable, the aspiring wine blender should take pains to ensure that when his wine evaluations differ from the norm he is not alone because of ignorance or some personal shortcoming.

Pearson Square

One of the tools that the wine blender can use to simplify calculations during the planning of wine blends is the Pearson square. This is usually presented in winemaking books in conjunction with alcohol fortification to produce dessert wines, but can be used for any wine constituent whose amount can be quantified. The square appears in this form:

A and B represent the amount of some component in two different wines, C represents the desired amount of that component in a blend, and D and E represent the proportion of wines A and B in the blend. (D = C - B and E = A - C.) We can use a simple example of blending to achieve proper acidity to illustrate the use of the Pearson square.

Suppose that you have a wine with 0.95% acid (which is placed at A in the Pearson square) and a second wine with 0.55% acid (which is placed at B). If you desire to blend to 0.70% acid (which is placed at C), the incomplete square will look like this:

D is then the difference between 0.70 and 0.55 (0.15) and E is the difference between 0.95 and 0.70 (0.25). Putting these values in place gives the completed square:

The proportion of the wine with 0.95% acid to the proportion of the wine with 0.55% acid should be 0.15 to 0.25 (or 3 to 5) in order to get the desired 0.70% acid in the blend.

Those that remember enough high school algebra can work the same problem out by solving the equation:

$$0.95 \, D + 0.55 \, E = 0.70 \, (D + E)$$
This is :
$$0.95 \, D + 0.55 \, E = 0.70 \, D + 0.70 \, E$$
Subtracting we get:
$$0.95 \, D - 0.70 \, D = 0.70 \, E - 0.55 \, E$$
Or:
$$0.25 \, D = 0.15 \, E$$
Which rearranges to:
$$D/E = 0.15/0.25 = 3/5$$

With blends of two or more wines it is possible to optimize several constituents at once. The mathematical technique that is used is called linear programming. It is beyond the scope of this chapter to go into the details of this technique, but the interested reader can refer to the mathematical literature for information. (Blends of up to 4 wines can be handled on a programmable calculator and larger blends can be handled on a computer.)

After a desirable wine blend has been identified, it is a good practice to prepare a slightly larger quantity of this blend, perhaps a few gallons, and to store this blend for a month or two before re-evaluating it. Instabilities in the blend (such as can occur when a wine that has undergone a malolactic fermentation is blended with one that has not) can be detected, as well as possible improvements in the blend as the various fragrances and flavors merge. If this intermediate blend is stable and holds or improves its quality, the final blend can then be prepared.

Examples of Commercial Wine Blending

Wine blending is practiced in every wine region. We are going to look at a few representative examples to view the scope of the problems that can be corrected by blending. Although most of these examples focus on one problem at a time, winemakers usually work to solve as many problems as possible when they blend.

Color

Grapes come in many colors and the wines from them range from almost colorless to very deep red. When a winemaker has a color problem, this is usually with a red wine.

Grenache is a very important variety in the warmer districts of southern Europe, California and Australia. When it isn't overcropped it is a premium variety, but it has a weak red color. Without blending, about all that it can make is a rose' wine. The French use it in red wines by blending in Carignane and other varieties. The Spaniards and Australians also blend it to good advantage.

When a winemaker adds a grape variety to a blend to modify the color, he may also change the acids or other components of the wine. This is the case with Cabernet Franc, used in some of the fine wines of Bordeaux. While it adds color to blends of Cabernet Sauvignon and Merlot — which is desirable — it also adds acidity, which is less desirable. For this reason one seldom finds wines containing more than a third of Cabernet Franc.

There is a way that a winemaker can add color to a red wine without upsetting its balance and that is by blending in a few percent of a wine made from a teinturier variety. These varieties are so strongly colored that a winemaker can use them essentially as dyes. Alicante Bouschet is one of these teinturiers. It is grown in the Midi in France and in California. (Only one California producer makes it into a varietal wine.) Colobel (Seibel 8357) is a French hybrid grown widely in France and to a limited extent in the eastern U.S. It gives a wine with up to ten times the color of a normal red wine and never more than 5% is used in wine blends. Almost the sole use of teinturiers is in wine blends.

One potential use of blending to correct a color problem does not seem to have received much attention so far. That is blending to offset color changes due to unstable grape pigments. Pinot noir is one variety that often lacks color, especially when grown in the U.S., and when it is aged its color tends to brown and fade faster than that of many other varieties. In the East, Baco noir is a fairly popular French hybrid that starts with a deep color but has the same type of color instability as Pinot noir. Baco noir ages well but a five year old wine from this variety does not have a very appealing color. Producers of wines with unstable pigments of this sort might do better by blending in varieties with more stable pigments so that the wine's appearance will not deteriorate so quickly.

Although dark red was once the dominant color in wines, that situation is changing. Many people believe that in the near future there will be an increasing market for light red wines. If this demand develops we will probably see at least some red wines lightened in color by having white wines blended in. Light red and rose' wines have been produced this way in various parts of the world for many years.

Fragrance

Turning to the subject of wine fragrance, we can find some parallels to the situation of blending for color. Just as a winemaker can dilute a red color by adding a wine without color, he can dilute an overly fragrant wine by adding one without much fragrance. This type of blending to control fragrance occurs in the eastern U.S. where some of the larger producers blend fairly neutral California wines with the assertive native American varieties, such as Concord. The resulting wines have greater consumer acceptance than would be the case with unblended wines.

Some blending for fragrance is a bit like using a teinturier. In France the variety Muscadelle is sometimes used in minor amounts in the famous wines of Graves, Barsac and Sauternes. Muscadelle gives a wine with a marked fragrance reminiscent of the muscat varieties and only a small portion is needed to give the desired degree of this floral character to blends.

The fragrances of wines are so complex that despite the best efforts of thousands of research workers we really don't know why some wines smell better than others. What researchers do tell us is that hundreds of minor components, many present at such low levels that we could not smell them by themselves, combine to give us an overall impression. When one particular group of components is present in enough quantity, we can identify fragrances that remind us of fruits, flowers, vegetation, fungi, and other things. The very best wines seem to have subtle and interesting combinations of these fragrance groups. Cabernet Sauvignon, for example, reminds some people of berries, green peppers, and cigar smoke. This crude description doesn't sound appealing, but when we smell such a wine we are aware of many fleeting impressions that combine to give us pleasure.

While some premium grape varieties reveal pleasing mixtures of identifiable fragrances, other varieties present a one-dimensional smell. Certain of the French hybrids, for example, have a strong weedy smell; others have a strong berry smell. When these individual varieties are made into pure varietal wines they generally are disappointing. The best winemakers have learned how to combine two or more of these varieties to produce a more interesting wine.

Acidity

In contrast to the blending of wines to produce a desirable fragrance (a most subjective task), the blending of wines to produce a balanced taste is easier. For one thing, the winemaker can use laboratory analyses to guide him. For another thing, the principles involved are much more straightforward since only three basic tastes are found in most wines: sour, sweet and bitter.

The natural acidity of grapes varies and with the temperature of the growing season. In cool climates or seasons, the acids in grapes stay at a high level; In hot climates or seasons, they decrease. Since these factors of variety and climate are reasonably constant, it has proven feasible for winemakers in the hot Central Valley of California to make long-term commitments to purchase and blend in grapes from the cooler coastal counties in order to produce wines having the desired acidity. In a like manner, major winemakers in the northeastern U.S. have purchased Central Valley wines for many years in order to lower the acidity of their local wines. Since few of the world's grape growing areas have an ideal climate, the blending of wines from hot and cool regions is widely practiced.

Sweetness

While the acid in grapes depends, to a large extent, on the temperature, the sugar in grapes depends on sunshine and the length of the growing season. Blending is seldom used to reduce the sugar content of table wines since it is fairly easy to pick grapes before the sugar gets too high or to ferment the wine until the sugar content reaches the desired level. Wine districts with long, sunny growing seasons usually specialize in sweet dessert wines and have no need to lower sugar contents in their wines.

It is in some of the cooler wine districts that blending to adjust sweetness is used. In Germany, for example, the cool climate gives wines of fairly high acidity. A certain amount of sugar in these wines counteracts the high acidity and has proven to be desirable. Many German winemakers have adopted the procedure of fermenting the main bulk of their wines to dryness, then blending in with these dry wines a "sweet reserve" of unfermented or only slightly fermented grape juice. This same type of blending is also practiced in France. Some larger winemakers, with modern equipment, can avoid this type of blending since they are able to stop the fermentation at the desired sugar level and stabilize their wines with a sterile filtration.

Tannin

The tannin content of wines is of concern to the winemaker. Different varieties of grapes have different tannin levels and when red wines are made by fermenting the musts in contact with the red grape skins, tannins are dissolved and enter the wines. Tannins are natural antioxidants and provide longevity to a wine that is to receive extensive aging, but they are bitter and when present in excess make a wine taste harsh.

The classic example of adjusting the tannin level via blending is provided by Bordeaux wines. Cabernet Sauvignon is a grape variety known for its fine varietal fragrance and flavor, but it produces wines that are often tannic and slow maturing. Merlot is a variety that is less tannic and faster maturing, but it is often considered to give a flat wine when used alone. Many of the finest Bordeaux wines are a careful blend of Cabernet Sauvignon and Merlot (along with Cabernet Franc and Petit Verdot in some cases). In California, after many years of making pure Cabernet Sauvignon wines, some winemakers have now turned to blending Merlot with their Cabernet Sauvignon wines and a few winemakers are going the other way and blending Cabernet Sauvignon with their Merlot wines.

Alcohol

It will come as no surprise that the alcohol content of wines can also be adjusted by blending. The fermentation converts sugar to alcohol and we have already looked at the factors that control sugar levels. Wines from cool climates have greater color, fragrance, flavor, and acidity than wines from hot climates. But wines from hot, sunny climates often do have higher alcohol levels.

In the production of the finest table wines in the cooler districts, winemakers usually achieve an adequate alcohol level by reducing the size of the grape crop. With more leaves per grape berry, the vine is able to ripen the berries even when sunshine is limited or the growing season is not extremely long. But in countries, such as France, where there is a very large demand for ordinary wines and growers frequently overcrop their vines, many of the resulting wines are thin and low in alcohol. In such circumstances, the practice of blending in wines from hot, sunny climates is routinely practiced.

The producers of ordinary French wines have long used the wine of the Midi and, until recently, the wines of Algeria to increase the alcohol in their blends. Up to a point, higher alcohol makes a better wine. The alcohol adds a bit of body, reduces the chances of the wine spoiling, and adds a slight sweetness that can balance an otherwise acidic or harsh wine. But with modern winemaking techniques there is less excuse than there once was for producing high alcohol wines. The continued sale of these wines in France seems to be more a cultural matter than an aesthetic or a technical matter.

Body

The body of a wine, as we have suggested above, is partially related to the alcohol content. Alcohol increases the viscosity or feel of fullness in the mouth. But no one really understands all of the factors that go into making up the thing we call body. What we do know from experience is that some wines have more body than others. A winemaker in the Napa Valley of California may find, for example, that a Barbera wine from one location is low in body while another Barbera wine from a second location is higher in body. By blending these wines he can achieve the amount of body that he desires. This may be an empirical process, but if the final wine is improved, the winemaker and his consumers both benefit.

Different grape varieties seem to vary in the amount of body they provide in wines. In the eastern U.S., Chambourcin, a French hybrid grape, has found favor with some wine producers because of its ability to enhance the body of blends.

Wood

Blending can also be used to adjust the level of wood extractives in wines. When wines are aged in small barrels the amount of wood character picked up by the wine varies greatly during the life of the barrel. A Chardonnay wine in a new oak barrel may take on a noticeable oak flavor in one month, while the same wine in a used barrel may not pick up much oak flavor in two years. In a case like this, a winemaker might choose to age the bulk of his wine in older barrels and store only a small portion of wine in new barrels. He can then blend the wine from old and new barrels to get just the amount of oak flavor and fragrance he wants. A winemaker can also use granular oak to flavor a small batch of wine in much the same way that he would use new barrels.

When the amount of wood character in a new wine is adequate, a winemaker usually blends together wine from all of the barrels before bottling. This is called "equalizing the vintage" in France. Most people do not consider this to be blending in the sense we have been talking about. But without this equalizing there can be significant bottle-to-bottle variation. Some small winemakers have been known to bottle wines of one vintage out of individual barrels over a period of years. A consumer who buys two bottles of such a wine can never be sure that the second will be similar to the first.

Oxidation and Maturity

Oxidation and maturity of wines is sometimes adjusted by blending. This is one of the purposes of the traditional Spanish sherry method of fractional blending. In the solera system, young wines are blended with older, more oxidized wines. This blending not only provides year-to-year consistency in the sherry, but also gives a more complex wine than would otherwise be possible, one containing both fresh and aged components.

French Champagne producers often blend wines of several vintages together to achieve the amount of maturity that they desire in their non-vintage wines. As we have just pointed out for sherries, this type of blending can give a desirable mixture of fresh and mature character to a wine. Some sophisticated California wine producers also do multivintage blending to achieve complexity in their wines.

Blending a sound wine with a spoiled wine is usually just a way to make a larger batch of spoiled wine. But there is at least one circumstance in which the blended wine can be an improvement over both the sound and the spoiled wine. Volatile acidity is a component of all wine (and consists of acetic acid and some ethyl acetate). When volatile acidity exceeds low levels (about 0.1%), it becomes objectionable, giving a wine with the smell of vinegar. Government regulations in the U.S. and abroad place upper limits on the amount of volatile acidity permitted in wines. If a batch of wine develops excess volatile acidity, the winemaker has a choice of either discarding that wine or blending it with wines low in volatile acidity, thus diluting the defect. The interesting thing is that small amounts of volatile acidity are recognized to sometimes provide a certain fruitiness or other character to wines and the federal government actually permits the addition of small amounts of acetic acid to commercial wines for this reason. So if a winemaker is lucky, when he blends a wine with excess volatile acidity to get rid of a flaw, he may actually produce a better wine than the sound wine component he started out with.

Not only can blending correct flaws and deficiencies in wines, but in many cases it appears that blending can improve the quality of wines lacking in noticeable defects. Some 20 years ago Singleton and Ough, at the University of California at Davis, showed that mixing two commercially acceptable wines of similar quality never gave a blend that was poorer in sensory scoring than the poorer of the pair, but frequently gave a wine that was at least as good as the better of the individual wines. These researchers suggested that this improvement might have been because of an increase in complexity of the components. At any rate, they decided that much blending as now commercially practiced is probably of more value than was previously suspected. If so, it may be true that the popularity of unblended vintage varietal wines in the U.S. has reduced the average wine quality below what it could be with careful blending. To some knowledgeable observers this certainly appears to be true in the eastern U.S. where many French hybrid wines are produced as unblended varietals. After all, if simply mixing two wines in equal proportions can raise wine quality on an average, skillful blending should be able to do much better.

In the Champagne district of France, where blending has reached a very high level of expertise, wine producers blend to a particular style of wine which they attempt to maintain year after year. This style is sometimes called, for lack of a better name, the "house style". The people blending the wine are sophisticated enough so that they blend not only for the usual factors of balance and complexity, but they adjust the components of the blend to give a flavor that will peak at the time that the wine will be consumed.

Three grape varieties are used in Champagne. In most vintaged Champagne wines only Pinot noir and Chardonnay are used, with Pinot noir predominating. But in non-vintage Champagne wines, which are meant to be consumed earlier, up to about 1/3 Pinot Meunier is included in the blend. This variety matures more rapidly in the bottle than the other two and peaks in about three years, corresponding approximately to the time of consumption of these wines. In the early years of aging, Pinot Meunier enhances the character of the blend and that is why it is included. In the case of a vintage Champagne that will not be consumed for 8 or 10 years, Pinot noir would so overwhelm the Pinot Meunier that there is little reason to include the latter variety.

It is interesting to note that when one tastes a non-vintage Champagne wine, during the first few seconds the Pinot Meunier forms the first impression, while Pinot noir and Chardonnay give a longer lasting impression. This facet of wine blending probably deserves more study.

We have already mentioned the fact that in the sherry and Champagne districts producers usually strive for year-to-year consistency in their wines. Since these two districts pretty much represent the northern and southern limits of premium wine production in Europe, we might ask why both groups of winemakers aim for this consistency. In Spain there are seldom any years that are exceptionally bad; in Champagne there are seldom any years that are exceptionally good. In such circumstances winemakers prefer not to gamble and use blending to achieve the most interesting wines that they can without waiting for the weather to take matters out of their hands.

The Bordeaux region of France seems to be the model for the vintage-year gamble. This is a gamble for wine producers and wine consumers, since both invest their money without knowing exactly what they are going to get. Fortunately, in most of the world's wine regions winemakers produce standard wines. These are wines that are blended to minimize year-to-year variations and surprises. Variable quality in a standard wine is probably a negative quality factor for many consumers. The gambling that occurs in Bordeaux lends excitement to the wine scene and the lore of wines would probably be lessened without it. There is little reason to doubt that judicious multi-vintage, multi-vineyard, and multi-variety blending could raise the average quality of Bordeaux wines, but what true wine lover would want to see this bastion of uncertainty levelled merely to provide good wines every year?

The people who can afford the "best" vintages of the "best" wines would argue that blending for consistency would only deprive the world of truly great wine experiences. In some cases they might be right, but the weight of evidence suggests that careful blending almost always improves quality. What is perhaps unfortunate is that skillful wine blenders don't always get the best ingredients to work with.

In the U.S., as elsewhere, high quality grape varieties are sometimes diluted with more neutral and less expensive varieties. This is usually done in order to provide a wine of reasonably high quality at a lower price than would otherwise be possible. The range in grape prices from the top varieties in California to the bottom varieties is often greater than a factor of ten.

Some people object to this dilution of the better quality grape varieties, apparently believing that consumers would benefit by buying the pure varietal wines and paying a higher price. There is some evidence to suggest, however, that diluting a very characteristic variety does not dilute the odor and taste impressions as much as might be expected. Careful studies have shown that our senses of sight and hearing do not respond in a linear manner, but rather respond in a logarithmic manner. Concert attendees in the 10th row do not expect to pay half as much as attendees in the 5th row. Although our senses of smell and taste are harder to quantify than our senses of sight and hearing, the same principles may well apply. With careful blending, the increased complexity of a wine might actually enhance the overall quality impression even when less of a premium variety was present. Proponents of truth in wine labeling, who seek to have the varietal content of varietally-labeled wines raised as high as possible, do not seem to understand this fact.

Consumer Blending

Wine consumers can do blending, just as wine producers do. The principles are the same. Wines from a cool region with low alcohol and body can be blended with wines from a hot region with low fragrance and flavor. Wines with a desirable, but overly strong, fragrance can be blended with more neutral wines. The possibilities are almost endless.

The consumer who attempts wine blending should start with inexpensive wines and try to make them more to his liking. All that is required is a few wine remnants — glasses or bottles of wines that were not finished during a meal. If the consumer saves some of these small portions of wines and later blends them together, he will be on his way to learning about the possibilities of wine blending. Small amounts of wines should be rebottled in containers that they will fill so that oxidation will be minimized. Most table wines will keep for a few days — especially if they are refrigerated — without losing too much of their original quality. These wines should be warmed to room temperature before blending is attempted.

Wine tasting events are almost the ideal situation in which the wine blender can practice. Most tastings feature a number of wines of similar type from different regions. It is a rare tasting when a skilled blender can not make a more pleasing (to himself) wine from the various offered wines than any of the individual wines served. By practicing in this way, anyone can gain proficiency in wine blending.

There are two major advantages of this sort of blending practice to the consumer. The first is that he will become much more familiar with the characteristics of individual wines and what they can contribute to a blend. The second is that he will be able to purchase inexpensive wines and blend them himself to obtain a wine that is more to his liking than the winemakers of these wines are able to do.

The temperature at which a wine is served also influences its fragrance and flavor. Low temperatures generally reduce the fragrance and apparent sweetness of a wine. High temperatures increase the fragrance, but also the perception of alcohol, while reducing the apparent bitterness of a wine. Acidity of wine seems to be little influenced by temperature.

By using insulated glasses, or by working rapidly, it is possible to blend a wine at various temperatures in the same manner that one blends different wines. In this way the best temperature for serving a wine can be determined.

CHAPTER 11

RED WINE BLENDING

Douglas Moorhead

U NLIKE WHITE WINES, where varietals are very common, most commercial red wines are blends of two or more varieties. With the exception of red Burgundy, which is made from the single variety Pinot noir and the Nebbiolos of the Italian Piedmont, virtually all of the great reds of the world are blends of two or more varieties. It is therefore axiomatic that we learn about the practice of blending if we hope to make really good red wines.

1. Of the 73 classified growths of Graves and Medoc in Bordeaux, all contain Cabernet Sauvignon and Merlot. Cabernet Franc is found in 62 of them, Petite Verdot in 46 and Malbec in 10. A composite blend (not weighted) would be about 60% Cabernet Sauvignon (range = 20 to 85%), 25% Merlot (range = 5 to 60%), 10% Cabernet Franc (range = 0 to 31%), 3% Petite Verdot (range = 0 to 15%) and less than 1% Malbec (range = 0 to 5%). The First Growths of St. Emillion show a range of 0 to 35% (average 13%) for Cabernet Sauvignon, 20 to 66% for Cabernet Franc (average 33%) and 33 to 80% for Merlot (average 54%) with two wines which also include Malbec. Cabernet Sauvignon is not included in four of the 12 wines. The other classified growths of St. Emilion show similar ratios. Chateau Petrus in Pomerol which commands the highest prices of any red Bordeaux contains no Cabernet Sauvignon, but is 95% Merlot and 5% Cabernet Franc. That is as close to a varietal as you will find among the reds of Bordeaux.

2. The red wines of the southern Rhone may use as many as 13 varieties. Even the famous vineyards of the northern Rhone utilize other varieties in addition to the dominant Syrah.

3. The reds of Rioja (Spain) are all blended. The predominant varieties are Garnacha (Grenache), Tempranillo, Graciano and Mazuelo. Blending is critical in producing quality wines in this region.

4. California has achieved fame with its varietal Cabernet Sauvignons, but recent trends show that the practice of blending with Merlot and, to a lesser extent, with Cabernet Franc is definitely on the increase. Another sign of this trend are the "Meritage" wines.

The above examples are used to reinforce the conventional wisdom that blending offers opportunities to improve any wine. There are exceptions, but not many. Those who praise red Burgundy may wish to counter this argument. While these wines are made from a single variety, it is a variety with a great deal of variability. Most European vineyards have many clones planted in their vineyards.

Rationale

There are many reasons for blending in producing red wines; some good, some not so good:

1. To mask or dilute the flavor and aroma of a bad wine (one with volatile acidity, sulfides or other off bacterial or moldy odors) — This is not a good reason for blending because you often end up with greater volume of a faulted wine. Even working off small amounts in other wine is detrimental to overall quality.

2. To improve color in a wine, either because it is too light or too dark, or because it shows some off hues because of high pH.

   (a) The use of a teinturier variety such as Colobel, Alicante Bouschet, Rubired or Royalty will darken a wine lacking depth of color, but bench tests are necessary.

   (b) The addition of a white to a red which is too deep in color may correct the problem, but it may be advisable to use a fining agent such as PVPP (Polyvinylpolypyrrolidone) or, gelatin to reduce color. Again, bench tests are advised.

   (c) Blending with a low pH wine or the addition of tartaric or phosphoric acids to correct the too-purple color of a young wine or the brownish-red color of an older wine with a high pH.

3. To raise or lower the alcohol level of a wine because it is out of balance. It is a time-honored practice to add hot climate wines with lots of body to some of the acidic low alcohol wines produced in cool climates, especially in less favorable years; both wines are generally improved by the marriage.

4. It may be advisable to lower pH in a wine, not because of color considerations, but to increase its longevity. Some of the French hybrids with Vitis riparia parentage can be high in titratable acidity and in pH at the same time. A wine of pH 3.8 or higher should be corrected or drunk quickly. One way to correct for high pH without at the same

time greatly increasing acidity is to add a strong mineral acid which is highly ionized. Marvin Yiengst, a longtime American Wine Society member from Baltimore, has done much experimentation in this area. His recommendation is to use 30% phosphoric acid because it affects flavor less than hydrochloric or sulfuric acids. The other way to correct this problem is to blend with a wine of lower pH.

5. To raise or lower titratable acidity — While pH is very important in considering a wine's longevity, titratable acidity is more important to our sense of taste. While good reds can cover a range of 0.55 to 0.85% titratable acidity (as tartaric), the normal optimum range from the standpoint of taste is about 0.6 to 0.7%. Wines can be blended to balance for acidity, provided they have the proper characteristics.

6. To accent or diminish a flavor or aroma component — This covers a wide spectrum of taste considerations such as raising or lowering the bitterness or astringency profile, muting an aroma component which is not in itself unpleasant, but out of balance, or trying to increase or decrease its body.

7. To duplicate a prior bottling — This is practiced more by large wineries where it is more important to have consistency of flavor.

Philosophy

There are several philosophical approaches to the practice of blending; perhaps we approach blending differently because we have either left or right brain dominance. Another theory is that our level of experience is more important. I suspect that almost any approach will work well if practiced with some consistency. Some of the philosophies of blending are listed below; few of us fall into neat categories.

1. Analytical — Approach blending based upon technical components of the wines such as pH, titratable acidity, residual sugar, tannin levels, alcohol levels, etc. (Left brained).

2. A gestalt approach — Examining the overall effect of the resulting wine in all of its ramifications, without necessarily being able to describe component parts.

3. Pragmatic approach — This may entail more than just tasting wine samples. It may be a very long process and may include examining the effects of variety and soil, among other things. There may also be considerations other than the best possible blend from the available components; you may be limited by the actual amount available of

one or more component. A commercial winery may also have to consider label limitations such as the 75% minimum requirement to label it as a varietal.

4. Tabula rasa — You just sit down and blend and record sensations until you get what you want preferably before the blending materials are used up.

Each of us will develop a philosophy of blending over time as we practice this craft. You need not be in a great hurry to establish which one. I find it useful to picture in my mind the expected result of blending different wines before actually trying them. The result is often about what I would expect, but I have learned that it is necessary to actually blend and taste to be sure. One can not a priori know what the result will be. Let me illustrate this with a couple of examples:

(a) A few years ago we were attempting to make a blended red from several batches of French hybrids, among which were Chambourcin, Chancellor, Leon Millot and Foch. We had blended from among these varieties in prior years with good effect. We had arrived at the conclusion that we would utilize Chancellor as the base wine and had found it improved with the addition of either Chambourcin or Leon Millot, but only in small amounts before the resulting blends turned dramatically worse. Further the Chambourcin and the Leon Millot weren't very compatible with each other. We wrestled with these wines for the better part of two days without coming up with a suitable blend. This was a very frustrating experience, but an unusual one fortunately.

(b) I once was tasting informally a Cabernet Sauvignon, a Baco Noir and a Fredonia (a Vitis labrusca). The Baco dominated when blended with the Cabernet and the Fredonia flavor dominated when blended with the Baco. Logic and prior experience would indicate that the Fredonia would be even more dominant over the Cabernet. This was not the case!

I hope that these will help illustrate the need to actually blend and taste before you dump different things together. Philosophy must be supplemented by experience.

Mechanics of Blending

There are several ways to practice blending. Through experience you can work out methods which will work for you. For me the following exercises are helpful:

1. Taste each of the potential components and make notes on impressions. Also note the volumes of each available.

2. Consider strong and weak points of each wine and consider what might improve them or take off some of the rough edges.

3. Take any pair of wines and make up 75–25, 50–50 and 25–75% blends. Taste and record your impressions. Compare these impressions with the straight components.

4. Repeat this procedure with the other possible pairings.

5. Once you have done the above you can refine pairings if there is reason to look at ratios between any of the above.

6. Next you will work on three or four way pairings with additional varieties.

7. If you have qualified tasters available it is helpful to do the above independently and then compare results.

We produce a Cabernet Sauvignon wine at our winery. Because we can make better wine by so doing we almost always blend it with Cabernet Franc and Merlot. We have called upon some friends whose tasting skills we have come to respect to help us make up our yearly blend for this wine. We weighed the risks of clashing egos and widely divergent ratios. Fortunately our tasters have, in each case, independently arrived at fairly similar blends.

CHAPTER 12

WOOD & WINE: THE LASTING MARRIAGE

Vernon L. Singleton, PhD.

Wooden containers are undoubtedly prehistoric and the first approximation of a barrel probably was a section of a hollow tree trunk with drum-like ends added. Barrels of roughly the same form used today were in use and may have originated in Roman Gaul. A famous stone bas-relief from Caesar Augustus' time (63 B.C.–14 A.D.) shows two barrels in a boat. The staves, wooden hoops, heads, and bilge are quite recognizable. For convenience a few English terms are useful: staves, bung stave, heads, hoops (now riveted steel, often galvanized, sometimes covered with wooden hoops), chime (the beveled extensions of the staves beyond the heads), the croze (the grooves in which the heads fit), and the bilge (the widest part of the barrel).

Until quite recently, at least in areas where good wood was plentiful, the barrel was a widely used general container. In early America, an itinerant or resident cooper was often called upon to produce a couple of barrels as a day's work with simple but specialized tools from timber produced on the spot. Barrels were primary holding and shipping containers for everything from beer, flour, salt pork, and tobacco to whiskey. Tight barrels were, of course, necessary for liquids but slack barrels and kegs would do for nails and, especially if lined, for flour, etc. The maximum production of tight barrels in the United States was reached in 1929 with an estimated 20 million barrels produced (Repeal of Prohibition was impending). Cooperage was the main consumer of white oak in the early 1900s and by 1908 white oak was used for 90% of tight cooperage. By 1952 the production of barrels was less than one fourth of that in 1929 and is still less today. There are, however, still cooperages in the United States capable of turning out as many as 2400 barrels a day. Contrary to casual opinion and owing to the bourbon whiskey business, there are many more barrels made in U.S. cooperages than in any other country.

Much of what made the barrel such a popular container was general and practical and had nothing to do with wine. To make the barrel strong, durable and convenient, the shape and nature of the wood are crucial. The barrel is a double arch and approximates the shape of an egg. You may have proved to yourself how strong an uncracked egg is when squeezed in the palms of your clenched hands. The barrel is similarly and for the same reason strong against external pressure. I have seen movies of full whiskey barrels being dropped 10 feet onto concrete. They bounce and spurt a few drops between the staves at impact, but remain intact.

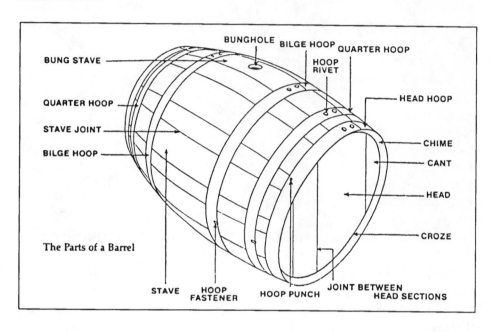

The Parts of a Barrel

The design of the barrel is admirable and its construction with hand tools daunting, but it is relatively easily understood in its simple circular form. The staves are cut or trimmed to a curvature for the bilge arch of the barrel. They are also tapered on a slow curve so that when drawn together at the ends they fit the head's circumference and the joints between them are snug. A snug fit for the full thickness of the staves requires the jointing of each stave edge on an angle to lie on a radius of the finished barrel. To prevent cracking when the ends are drawn in it is necessary to control the moisture content of the wood and to heat the wood to relieve the strain and set the longitudinal arch.

Properly cut or split, the width of the stave parallels a radius of the tree trunk. This places the rays of the wood at right angles opposing the diffusive loss of liquid from the barrel and also moderates the shrinkage of the wood as it dries. If the maximum shrinkage occurred from a full well-soaked barrel to dry wood, the total gap between the staves of a

Redwood aging casks at Paul Masson's Pinnacle Vineyard

properly made 200 liter barrel would be over 3 inches. If flat-sawed staves were used, it could be six inches. No wonder a wine barrel leaks if it is allowed to dry appreciably before refilling, and no wonder the cooper uses staves from quartered bolts. If the staves and heads are properly shaped, the wedging of the driven hoops plus the swelling of the wood makes the vessel liquid tight. Since they are flat, the heading pieces are much more subject to leakage. These joints are therefore filled with cooper's flag (cattail stems) and doweled.

The barrel has been called the package on wheels. I have seen old movies showing one expert freight handler "walking" barrels easily into place even though full they weighed 500 pounds. This helps explain why barrels of different sizes were "standard" for different products (convenient portions for weight and use). For spirits and wine they are generally in the 200–500 liter range, with the larger for more delicate or lighter products.

Heartwood of oak with tyloses blocking the springwood pores (white oak, as opposed to red oak which is not native in Europe and lacks tyloses), is the wood of choice for tight barrels even though at least 30 other woods have been used. White oak is not only suitable because it has tyloses, but also because it is tough, resilient (bendable), and decay resis-

Old German barrel resting in ornamental cradle

tant (high tannin content). It has the widest rays of any suitable wood and is therefore relatively retentive. It does not contribute peculiar flavors as do many other woods.

It seems clear, then, that the barrel was brought to perfection as an utilitarian container. The tight barrel was designed to hold liquids and keep them without taint. A great deal of thought, skill and fit-and-try research obviously contributed to its development. However, the development of methods more practical under modern conditions have replaced the barrel almost completely, except for wines and spirits aging. Obviously the barrel has special value for these products or it would have been replaced for them as well. In fact it has, for many of the lighter, modestly priced "picnic" styles of wine and for white spirits like vodka and gin.

Perhaps these points are being belabored, but I am trying to make clear that the white oak barrel was developed as a practical container for liquids and not for its special effects on wine. Coopers and winemakers were mutually concerned with a leak-free container, but otherwise had little appreciation for each other's concerns. The cooper said slow-growing trees were best for cooperage, I suspect, because it dulled his tools less and cracked less often. The winemaker might or might not agree, depending whether extraction or permeability was uppermost in his concerns.

A Barrel's Effects on Wine

Barrels and other wooden cooperage have, of course, some "atmospheric", public relations value to wineries. They also still have some convenience value. It is usually more practical and economical for a winery to use small stainless steel containers to enable segregation of small lots of wine and yet keep the containers all full to prevent acetification or oxidation. The main reason, however, for retention of barrel maturation for wines, particularly prestigious red wines and sherries, is the special effects on the wines. These are mainly two direct and one indirect effects: contribution of oak flavor, evaporative exchange through the staves, and (by ullage make-up or transfer) oxygen exposure. Three factors govern all of these effects: the nature and condition of the barrel, the time, and the surface to volume ratio. As far as the wine alone is concerned, the effect of time (at a given storage temperature and oxygen exposure) would be the same whatever the container. The barrels of a given type and condition the intensity of their effect depends almost entirely on the surface to volume ratios, roughly 90 cm^2/L for a 200 liter barrel, 190 cm^2/L for a 20 liter barrel, and 9 for a 2000 hectliter cask. Of course, stave thickness and previous treatment would have modifying effects.

The extractants from oak are still under study, but include vanillin and other substances with desirable odors, lignin fragments, hydrolyzable tannins, and "bodying" factors which affect the flavor impression of the wine. Flavor extraction from oak appears to be more important than oxidation. The evaporative changes lead to ullage, topping, and oxygen exposure during topping or transfer (but not otherwise, or at most very little in a good barrel). They also lead to slow concentration of the nonvolatiles in the wine, and, depending upon the relative humidity, change in the ethanol concentration (dry it rises, humid it falls).

Variables Among Barrels

The source of the barrel oak, Europe or North America where different species are used, makes a considerable difference in the extractives and relative flavors of the stored wine, if the barrel is fairly new. European oak is generally about double American oak in extractable solids and tannins. American oak, on the other hand, has more odorants. The overall flavor effect is similarly intense (but qualitatively different) so that the flavor from about 0.5 grams of dry oak of either sort will detectably flavor a liter of wine in a short time. Assuming 90 cm^2/L surface, 0.85 g/cm^3 bulk density for oak, and 3 mm penetration of the wine into the wood, wine in a new 200 liter barrel would be exposed to more than 40 times this amount of oak. It would be no surprise if the wine became excessively oaky, but with timely replacement and judicious blending, a very pleasing effect is produced.

Specific details of where the stave came from in a given tree (low and outside heartwood has more extractives) and of how the tree grew affect the permeability and the extractives. These are difficult for the cooper, much less the winemaker, to control in any practical way. It is only broadly possible to define and replicate a given order of barrels even if the same cooper and the same general area of tree production are patronized.

Wood seasoning practices differ and some opinions are strong as to which is better. Certainly, slow even drying requiring a considerable period or special management is necessary to prevent checking and mechanical damage to the stavewood. It is usual to stack the fresh staves outside for nine months or more. Chemical changes during this period seem minimal and remember that the center heartwood of a stave tree has probably been moist and dead for 100 years. Surely most reactions would have taken place. A number one grade bourbon stave is a minimum of three inches wide. This means the tree must have been at least 10 inches in diameter and probably 30 years old. For staves, at least 18 inches DBH (diameter at breast height) is preferred and is likely to take the tree more than 70 years.

Cooperage practices of importance in modifying the flavor the barrel contributes include whether the staves were bent and set by steaming or by exposure to fire. If fire was used, was the wood only heated, or toasted, or charred? These and other variables can be used to produce different cachets and nuances in wine as a result of barrel maturation. A major fascination of wine is its diversity.

Editor's Note:

Instructions for barrel use by home winemakers.

1. Fill the barrel completely with cold water. Allow the wood to soak up the water for 48 hours.

2. Pour the water out. Refill with very hot water and soda ash (2 lbs. of soda ash per 5 gallons of water).

3. After 12–24 hours pour out the water/soda ash solution. Rinse several times.

4. Fill with very hot water and allow to set overnight. Pour out and repeat 2 or 3 times, or until the water emerging is colorless or very pale. Rinse with cold water.

5. Fill with water and a weak sulfite solution. Pour out and rinse well after 1 hour.

6. Fill with sound but mediocre wine. After 1 hour pour out the wine. It will likely be undrinkable, but the barrel is now prepared for your good wines.

7. Never leave your barrel empty for more than an hour or two.

CHAPTER 13

REMEDIES FOR WINEMAKING MISTAKES

Jacques Recht

W E SHALL EXAMINE how to repair winemaking mistakes after they have occurred. Before going through each sickness a wine can have and establishing a treatment for it, we will first review the different special treatments and see how they can be applied to repair the mistakes.

Usually, sickness overcomes a wine in the bottle. The first thing to do is to undress the patient and dump it (the wine) into a barrel or tank. One exception to this rule is the wine which has undergone a malolactic fermentation. In such a case, bottles are placed upright to allow the corks to dry and let the CO_2 escape for a month through the dried cork. Capsules should be punctured or removed to allow gas to escape. A mechanical corker that clamps on a bench is useful for uncorking large numbers of bottles.

There are numerous tricks and tools available to the winemaker for correcting defects. These include heat, cold, air, SO_2, filtration, use of various additives as well as fining which will be discussed in this article. Professional winemakers are not attracted by ready-made fining mixes because each wine requiring clarification or each sickness requiring treatment is different and may require different proportions of constituents.

When fining, the expected results are not always obvious. Fining has been defined as the filtration of the poor. This infuriates me because there is more to fining than just clarification. A good fining may be less traumatic to a quality wine than filtration. The most used fining agents are:

Bentonite only — Ca, Na

Tannin, gelatin

Tannin, bentonite, gelatin

Bentonite, Kieselsol, gelatin

Casein

Egg

Isinglass

Blood

Mustard meal

Milk

Na alginates (sparkaloids)

Yeast

Yeast rinds

Polyvinyl polypirrolidon (PVPP)–Polyclar AT

Nylon (Polyamides)

Methyl-cellulose

Ferrocyanide, Cufex-blue fining

Specific clays

Besides fining, the simple addition of certain elements will suffice to correct a mistake or deficiency. The good "wine doctor" will choose the treatment which will be least traumatic to the wine. For example, there is no point in making a blue fining when the addition of 25g/100 liters of citric acid will suffice to remove a slight excess of iron. One must never forget that the wine is a living substance. We should not kill it on the operating table!

The additives useful for curing or stabilizing wines are:

SO_2

Citric acid, tartaric acid, malic acid

Tannin

Sorbic acid

Vitamin C

Arabic gum (acacia gum)

CO_2, N, O_2

Ca Phytate or Sodium Hexametaphosphate or polyphosphates

Active carbon (with a fining) — yeast rinds

Metatartaric acid

Potassium tartrate neutral

Ion exchange resins

Caramel

Glycerin (not ethylene glycol)

These products are authorized in most countries. In commercial winemaking the use of some of them is regulated.

Physical treatment includes cold, heat, filtration, ultra-filtration or lateral filtration, reverse osmosis, centrifuging, pasteurization, and hot packing. Some of these procedures are out of reach for home winemakers.

Biological treatments are in the future. Pectolytic enzymes have been used for some time, but down the road we may expect some enzymes to perform special tasks such as catalyzing malolactic fermentation in the absence of bacteria. Enzymes may be used also to break down undesirable polyphenols or large undesirable proteins without adjusting the wine's pH.

With all of these chemicals and methods available, one might think that all wine problems can be solved. It is not so. An excess of volatile acidity and certain off-tastes, like geranium, can not be cured.

Proper winemaking and vinting techniques should produce a healthy, clean, but not necessarily outstanding wine that will not require remedies. "A stitch in time saves nine" is also true in winemaking. The most frequent "accident" is bottle fermentation of residual sugar. There is a fair chance that by uncorking and dumping the wine, thereby aerating it, the fermentation of residual sugar will be completed. The addition of SO_2 is the remedy. There are two alternatives:

1. Add SO_2 to stop the fermentation and retain some sugar.

2. Wait for all of the sugar to be fermented, let the yeast settle, rack and filter, add SO_2 and adjust the sugar.

The latter method is best for nearly dry or semi-dry wines.

Potassium sorbate is an effective yeast controller, providing SO_2 is used to keep the wine in a reduced form. The sorbate allows one to use less SO_2. Only very sophisticated wineries will be able to do sterile bottling. Another alternative for using less SO_2 and no sorbate is hot packing (pasteurization). The wine is heated to 150° F. Bottles are rinsed with water at 160° F and the wine is bottled, corked and inverted immediately to pasteurize the cork. This should not be done with very fine wines. The dosage of free SO_2 at bottling without sorbate and after sterile filtration on 0.45 micron pads should be:

Dry whites: 30–40 ppm

Above 0.3% sugar white: 50–55 ppm

Red dry: 25–30 ppm

With 150 ppm Sorbate:

Dry: 20–30 ppm

Above 0.3% sugar white: 30–40 ppm

Above 3.0% sugar white: 50 ppm

These are practical figures. Winemakers may adjust these figures by taking pH and residual yeast population counts into consideration. In the future, there may be legal antiseptics allowing the use of less SO_2.

Oxidized-rancid wine seems to be the second most common problem for the home winemaker. This sickness can be caused by negligence or the use of overripe grapes containing bunch rot or botrytised grapes. Before starting a treatment, the addition of SO_2 and vitamin C should be attempted. The madeira taste in these wines is due to an excess of aldehyde. Sulfur dioxide should cure that problem. The brownish hue is due to oxidized polyphenols. If oxidation has occurred, the addition of SO_2 and vitamin C may suffice. If a casein fining test proves insufficient, a fining with PVPP may be necessary. The last recourse is decolorizing with active carbon in conjunction with a tannin gelatin fining. In this latter case, the resulting wine should be kept for blending purposes only.

Excess SO_2 is not a sickness but an accident frequently seen in wines made by winemakers divorced from the decimal and metric systems. Violent aeration at five hour intervals will get rid of some free SO_2. Checks on free SO_2 at each interval will show when no further progress is achieved in eliminating SO_2. In case free SO_2 is still too high after this treatment, it may be possible to reduce free and total SO_2 by oxygenation with O_2 gas. Home winemakers may prefer to use hydrogen peroxide (H_2O_2), the legality of which is contested in some countries. The hydrogen peroxide will oxidize the different forms of free and combined SO_2 to form sulfates. This treatment is brutal but efficient: 26.5 ml/100 liters of 3% .10 volume H_2O_2 takes away 15 ppm total of which 10 ppm is free. Wine should be treated for shock afterwards by adding some vitamin C.

Bacterial infections: Vinegar bacteria. Here we are dealing with acetic acid bacteria or lactic acid bacteria. In both cases, these bacteria need air to produce volatile acids. Volatile acidity can be prevented by keeping containers full and using SO_2. Volatile acidity in itself is not very perceptible to the nose. What is usually referred to incorrectly as volatile acidity is, in fact, the small quantity of ethyl-acetate which forms by esterification of ethanol with acetic acid. This is the unmistakable smell of nail polish.

Aeration and SO_2 addition will remedy a low level of volatile acidity only for a time. The ethyl-acetate will recur. The technique is to bottle small quantities of treated wine at a time which will be consumed within two weeks. There are no remedies to heal wines with volatile acidity contents above 0.1%. The wine is lost. Adding small quantities of this wine to a healthy wine is a poor practice.

Bacterial infections: lactic types. These bacteria may produce acetic acid and lactic acids from miscellaneous substrates including sugar. They are dangerous. Sulfur dioxide, free and combined, may be effective treatment particularly in the lower pH range. Some of the bacteria will produce by-products like dextrans and off-flavors. If such is the case, it becomes necessary to recondition the wine by proper fining.

Agitation i.e., churning through a pump, will break the long molecules responsible for any silky or oily appearance of wine hit by "graisse" or "tourne". Off-flavors may be eliminated or reduced with a yeast fining. The use of yeast rinds is promising in such cases. Whatever the treatment, it should entail reducing the pH and raising the SO_2 level to 30 ppm.

Hydrogen sulfide and organic sulfides are frequently a winemaker's misfortune and may be due to several causes: excess molecular residual sulfur on grapes, H_2S producing yeasts, poor balance in certain yeast nutrients during fermentation or poor fermentation monitoring. During fermentation, H_2S build-up is controllable. If any hint of H_2S occurs, a "remontage" (pump over with air) will take care of it. A late racking from the lees may also be responsible for the formation of H_2S or mercaptan. Like oxidation, when discovered early, the remedy is simple. Hydrogen sulfide and mercaptans may be oxidized. However, if discovered too late, some thiol complexes may form which will not lend themselves to a reversible reaction. These will have to be removed from the wine.

The use of copper sulfate is a poor answer to removal of sulfides. There is no point in adding a sulfate ion to all those already formed. Further, recent studies prove that yeast will produce more sulfides in the presence of a sulfate ion. The first step is to aerate the wine. Any H_2S will be oxidized. If a foul rotten egg odor is apparent, the next step is to pour the wine over copper flashing. If this proves insufficient, a fining with egg white or blood meal may prove satisfactory. The last recourse would be a tannin-gelatin, active-carbon fining (deodorizing) carbon not, as before, decolorizing carbon.

Tartrates — Red wine amorphous polyphenols. The treatment is to eliminate the excess potassium bi-tartrate and/or calcium tartrate first, and then make sure that all of the highly condensible tannins are removed. The wine is scheduled for cold stabilization. For the small operator, the treatment goes as follows: after clarification, i.e., tight filtration, fining and addition of SO_2 if metabisulfite is used, (SO_2 may be added after cold stabilization if SO_2 gas or solution is used), bring the wine to a temperature equal to:

$$C = [-(\% \text{ alcohol}) - 1]/2$$
Example: wine at 12% alcohol by volume
$$C = (-12 - 1)/2 = -5.5° \text{ C } (22° \text{ F})$$

Leave the wine at that temperature for 8 days. Check after 5 days with a shelf test by adding to 3 ounces of wine 2.0 ml of vodka. Leave sample at 0° C (32° F) for 3 days. If sample is clear, decant or filter the wine to a clean vessel. To prevent further tartrate formation or amorphous precipitations, add 5 grams/100 liters of Arabic gum. Add the gum after filtration. If used before filtration, Arabic gum will prematurely clog the filter pads.

Metal contamination. Metal "casse" may occur in white wines with as little as 10 ppm of iron or 0.5 ppm of copper.

In Europe, a blue fining would be the responsibility of a graduate enologist. Blue fining is not allowed in the U.S. An alternative is to use the ferro-cyanide complex called Cufex. Before going to these extremes, many other procedures are possible to remove a metal casse. For mild iron contamination citric acid at a rate of 50 grams/100 liters will suffice. Iron can also be eliminated by adding tannin and aerating the wine. Ferric tannate is then removed by a casein fining. The use of calcium phytate, $Ca_6 (C_6H_{12}O_{27})$, after aeration will also bind iron. Use of calcium phytate (5.0 ppm) will remove 1.0 ppm iron. The natural or organic route to achieve this result is to use wheat bran which contains Phytic acid. Use 100 grams of wheat bran per 100 liters of wine. Also, hexametaphosphate at a rate of 15 to 25 grams/100 liters is effective in removing iron when used along with a fining agent.

In some countries the sodium salt of Ethylenediaminetetracetic acid (EDTA) (10 to 30 grams/100 liters) is allowed. In this case fining is unnecessary since the metal is chelated in a soluble form. Copper can be eliminated with sodium sulfide (NaS), however, fining is necessary. Copper "casse" is usually due to the binding of copper to protein in the wine. Addition of 50 to 100 grams/100 liters of sodium bentonite will eliminate proteins and thus prevent the copper "casse" from occurring.

Protein. The best way to eliminate protein is by using beutonite, preferably calcium bentonite rather than sodium bentonite.

Pectin. Use of pectinase.

Off-odors of Butyric, oil types. Any odors due to the presence of an oil soluble substance can be eliminated by a milk fining — 100 to 200 ml/100 liters of a 2.0% fat milk.

Scratchy wines are cured by adding what fermentation has not produced i.e., glycerin. Adding a few drops of glycerin is a practice used by some winemakers to improve wines. Ethylene glycol is not a substitute and is highly toxic.

Overfining. Overfining usually affects the protein fining. For this, we must go back to the theory of fining. The principle is that a negatively charged particle in colloid state, such as tannin, Kieselsol or Bentonite, will neutralize a protein which, at the wine's pH, is positively charged. The overfining may be due to a lack of negatively charged particles to bind the protein (Gelatin, Isinglass, Blood). Adding tannin will clear the wine. It may also be that at a higher pH the protein used does not have sufficient positive charges. In this case, the best way to fine is the use of an extra dose of alginate salt such as agar or a commercial mix such as Sparkolloid.

Colloid state Polysaccharides, such as Arabinose, gums and mucilageneous substances are more difficult to get rid of. Multiple filtration is one way to go. Start with pads at 2.0 microns, ending at 0.45 microns.

Color adjustment. Severe treatment may cause a color change. A sweet white wine is not expected to look as pale as water. An addition of a small amount of caramel coloring will take care of that.

Commercial wineries usually hold, in bulk, small quantities of what are called "medicine wines" from previous harvests. One of those wines could be a heavy colored Foch, Chambourcin or Colubel. A small part of that wine can give back some hue to weakly colored wines.

CHAPTER 14

WHEN MALOLACTIC FERMENTATION ISN'T DESIRED

Phillip E. DeVore

IN THE PAST DECADE or so, malolactic fermentation has come into its own. Many winemakers and wine connoisseurs are aware of malolactic fermentation, and the term has become a buzzword among the cognoscenti. Some winemakers think that all red wines should go through malolactic fermentation. In reality, some wines don't benefit, or may be adversely affected. This chapter addresses the question of which wines should go through malolactic fermentation, and how this fermentation can be prevented when it is not desired.

In malolactic fermentation, lactic bacteria metabolize malic acid. Lactic acid is the primary product. Gaseous carbon dioxide is also produced, but is readily lost to the atmosphere. There are two primary effects on wines' sensory quality. First, titratable acidity is lowered, softening the wine. With white wines, the effect of lower acidity is straightforward. With red wines, the effect is more subtle. Both acids and tannins account for red wines' harshness and astringency. A lower acid level makes red wine approachable in spite of tannins. Young red wines are more drinkable while older ones are more likely to mature before all the fruit dissipates. The second sensory effect of malolactic fermentation is a reduction in fruitiness, offset by new tastes and aromas. These new elements contribute to the wine's complexity.

Another important effect of malolactic fermentation is a rise in pH. A change in pH has a subtle effect on sensory quality, but can have a major effect on aging potential. Wines with high pH don't age well, as they oxidize more rapidly. High pH wines are also more prone to bacterial infection.

How a wine will fare with malolactic fermentation is determined by several trade-offs. Will the softening and added complexity more than offset the loss in fruitiness and longevity? Generally, red vinifera wines from noble grapes (Cabernet Sauvignon, Merlot, Pinot noir, etc.) benefit greatly from malolactic fermentation. These wines tend to have adequate acid, are tannic, and have more fruit than they need. Also, the pH is generally low enough (especially when from cool climates) so that even after malolactic fermentation they have good aging potential. The benefits of malolactic fermentation for white wines are much more questionable. Chardonnays from cool growing areas (white Burgundies and California North Coast, for example) generally benefit from malolactic fermentation. The benefits to other white wines are less certain. Some great white wines are harmed by malolactic fermentation. Johannisberg Riesling, for example, derives much of its charm from fruitiness and hard acid moderated by sugars.

Some red wines do not benefit from malolactic fermentation. Wines not helped have low acid levels, high pH, and are enhanced by fruitiness. They are generally shorter lived wines. Most vinifera grapes shipped east in boxcars and trucks produce wines fitting this category. Some red wines produced from French hybrid grapes have high acid levels and high pH. In this case, the winemaker has a dilemma. Which is more important- softening the wine by lowering acid level or retaining aging quality and bacterial resistance?

My reservations regarding malolactic fermentation are based on the last five years' experience. A number of boxcar Zinfandels and one boxcar Cabernet Sauvignon have gone through malolactic fermentation. All have had at least some problem with bacterial attack. In earlier years, none of my wines went through malolactic fermentation, and none had any problems with surface yeasts or other micro-organisms.

Perhaps the greatest danger of malolactic fermentation is that it may set the stage for further bacterial attack. As the wine goes through malolactic fermentation, pH rises. As long as the pH does not go above 3.3 to 3.4, little harm is done. If the pH gets to 3.6 or above, the wine becomes subject to attack by undesirable strains of bacteria. The wine may spoil, becoming unfit for anything but the sink. At least when the wine goes to vinegar there is still a use for it! Vinegar formation is readily prevented by keeping containers topped up and minimizing contact with oxygen. The ravages on a high pH wine are much more insidious, and bacteria can spoil the wine with little advance warning. Bacteria thrive in a high pH environment. No doubt many spoiled wines in bygone days owed their fate to bacterial attack. This type of spoilage probably explains why one year grandpa made a great wine, and the next year it was a disaster.

Should a wine go through malolactic fermentation? Ultimately, the winemaker must make this decision. Some experimentation can provide the answer. Induce malolactic fermentation in half the batch. Avoid malolactic fermentation in the other half. Compare the resultant wines and decide for yourself. Should the two wines be commingled, the batch that did not go through malolactic fermentation probably will also go through malolactic fermentation. From this experiment you will learn how to handle future vintages with similar grapes.

The winemaker has various tools available to inhibit malolactic fermentation. Those that are more easily implemented are discussed first. Judicious use of sulfur dioxide is often effective. At the time of fermentation use 75–100 parts per million SO_2. Use another 50 ppm at the first racking. Higher acid levels often result in greater resistance to malolactic fermentation. This is because higher acid wines tend to have a lower pH. The lower the pH, the higher the effective acidity. It is the pH, not the titratable acidity, that gives wine resistance to bacterial attack. Lower pH retards malolactic fermentation in several ways. Bacterial action is discouraged by lower pH. Also, sulfur dioxide is more effective at lower pH. For red wines, titratable acidity should be at least 0.6 percent by weight. Since white wines benefit even more from higher acid levels, keep titratable acidity at 0.7% by weight or higher.

High pH wines (whether they went through malolactic fermentation or not) generally benefit from acid addition. The upper level of acid addition is limited by taste. Generally, acid additions of 0.1% by weight or more are possible. Tartaric acid is the best organic acid to use. It is the primary acid of the grape, and lowers pH slightly more than either malic or citric acids. Other considerations favoring tartaric acid include a less harsh taste than malic, and it is less inclined to bacterial attack then either malic or citric.

Several recent sources discuss use of hydrochloric acid for pH control. While hydrochloric acid is more effective than organic acids for lowering pH, there are a few cautions. Only food-grade acid should be used. Some hydrochloric acid has high concentrations of chlorinated hydrocarbons, which are potential carcinogens. Some wines treated with hydrochloric acid may acquire a salty taste. Potassium chloride, a common salt, is formed as hydrochloric acid is added to the wine.

All the problems dealing with high pH wines can be avoided by picking grapes with a low pH to begin with. As might be expected, pH has joined total solids and titratable acidity as primary picking criteria.

Several more tricks are available to control malolactic fermentation. Prompt racking of the crude lees also discourages malolactic fermentation as dying yeasts release nutrients to the wine. These nutrients aid in lactic bacteria growth. Fining also discourages lactic bacteria growth by lowering lactic bacteria population. Lactic bacteria seem to be a sociable species and are less active at lower population levels.

Lactic bacteria are often transferred from one wine to another. Keeping equipment sterile, or at least clean, minimizes the chance bacteria will be transferred from one wine to another. Barrels are an especially good breeding ground for lactic bacteria. Burn a sulfur wick before placing another wine in the barrel. Allow several hours for the SO_2 fumes to permeate the barrel. Rinse the barrel to minimize sulfur dioxide carry-over to the next wine. Keep the cellar temperature as cool as possible. Admittedly this may be difficult. Lactic bacteria growth is slowed by lower temperature.

Advanced methods are available to control malolactic fermentation. More precise measurement of effective (molecular) SO_2 level is one of the most important. Sulfur dioxide is most potent when in the molecular form. Molecular SO_2 should be at least 0.8 ppm. The amount of molecular sulfur dioxide depends on the free sulfur dioxide and pH. Combinations of pH and free SO_2 that give 0.8 ppm molecular SO_2 are:

pH	SO_2 (ppm)
3.0	12
3.2	20
3.4	32
3.6	50
3.8	76

Fumaric acid is very effective in preventing malolactic fermentation. Unfortunately, fumaric acid is not very soluble in wine, so some effort is required in getting the acid dissolved. Filtration is effective as it removes bacteria from wine. By filtering, lactic bacteria levels may drop below the level necessary for sustained growth.

How do you know if a wine is going through malolactic fermentation? A scant quantity of small bubbles is often a telltale sign. The bubbles are readily apparent by placing a bright flashlight behind the neck of the carboy in a darkened cellar. During or just after malolactic fermentation the wine is often gassy, and may have a faint sauerkraut aroma which rapidly passes after aeration. Paper chromatography is probably the most positive test. A rise in pH and drop in titratable acidity are also telltale signs.

What can be done if a wine is going through an unwanted malolactic fermentation? The answer depends on the controls available to the winemaker. With good testing procedures and the means discussed above, malolactic fermentation can probably be brought under control. With limited technology, two things can be done. Tartaric acid may be added until the wine reaches the maximum desired tartness. Then add 40–50 ppm sulfur dioxide. If this doesn't stop the fermentation, consider adding another shot of sulfur dioxide.

In conclusion, malolactic fermentation presents many perils. If the wine's pH, sulfur dioxide level, titratable acidity, and sensory quality can be determined, the benefits and hazards of malolactic fermentation can be weighed. Without some qualitative control, the hazards of malolactic fermentation are substantial.

CHAPTER 15

SIMPLE, FAST CHROMATOGRAPHY FOR OBSERVING THE PROGRESS OF A MALOLACTIC FERMENTATION

Chester H. Page, PhD.

MALOLACTIC FERMENTATION can be very desirable in some wines. It is important for the winemaker to know if a malolactic fermentation has taken place, or if it is still ongoing, before deciding to bottle the wine. This chapter explains how to monitor malolactic fermentation at home.

General Comments

I use radial, rather than linear, chromatography for two excellent reasons. First, a development time of an hour is sufficient, instead of the overnight development of ascending linear chromatography. Second, the applied sample spots can be much larger because in radial chromatography the spots become sharper as they travel on the paper. For example, a spot spread over a 1 cm radial distance (running from 5 mm from the center of the paper to 15 mm from the center) develops as a line of only 3 mm width. This sharpening property allows much faster (and sloppier) application of the wine samples.

Technique

1. Basic technique

    A piece of 15 cm diameter #1 filter paper is marked with circles of 1 cm and 2 cm radii, divided into 6 or 8 sectors as shown in Figure 1. The paper is laid on a piece of window glass under the hot draft from a hair dryer. When the paper has been warmed up (to speed drying of the spots) the wine samples (one or two drops total for each sample) are applied (still under the dryer) with a tiny pipette, to the inner and outer radius marks alternately (just outside the inner radius and just inside the outer radius). This allows fast spotting without excessive angular spreading which would lengthen and thereby lighten the lines.

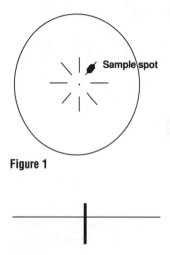

Figure 1

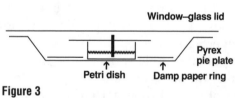

Figure 2

The center hole pricked by the compass used for drawing the circles is enlarged to about 2.5 mm with an 8d (2 1/2") finishing nail. A piece of filter paper is cut into 1 inch strips for making inch-long wicks. About 3/4" of strip is rolled tightly onto a 1 1/2" 17-gauge brad and "screwed" into the hole, and the brad is then withdrawn (Figure 2). 10–20 ml of solvent is poured into a petri dish (100 mm diameter) placed in the development chamber (Figure 3).

The pipette is made from a piece of 0.5 mm or 1 mm bore glass capillary by drawing a tip with about 0.1 mm bore.

Using the top of the wick as a handle, the paper disk is set on the solvent dish with the bottom of the wick resting on the bottom of the dish. The solvent flows up the wick by capillary action, then radially outward, transporting components of the sample at different speeds. Development is continued until the wetness reaches about 1/2" from the edge of the paper. The paper is removed, and dried with the hair dryer. There are several techniques for displaying the component spots on the paper, discussed below. The solvent remaining in the petri dish may be returned to its bottle for later use.

Figure 3

2. Detecting (displaying)

The classical method for making the separated acid spots visible was to spray the dried chromatogram (the filter paper) with a mist of a solution of a pH indicator, being careful not to get the paper wet enough for the indicator solution to run and blur the spots. This is a cumbersome technique in a non-laboratory environment. A later development, usually recommended in modern suggestions, is to include an appropriate amount of indicator in the solvent. Not all indicators are suitable; some cause "tailing" of the spots, reducing the resolution. In all cases, the residual volatile "swamping" acid in the solvent must be driven out of the paper (usually by a hot draft) so that the whole paper won't appear to be a huge acid spot.

My own preference is a third technique, not requiring any special laboratory indicator reagents; infrared "toasting". I have a hotplate with an exposed heater which looks like a standard electric stove heating element (it probably is); I set this hotplate on its side to make the heater vertical.

Figure 4

I can "toast" chromatograms by holding them an inch or two from the red hot heater with a pair of tongs. (If the setup were horizontal instead of vertical, the paper would always droop onto the burner.) In a few minutes, the areas holding the residues of tartaric acid, malic acid, lactic acid, etc. turn toasty brown. The colors can be intensified (repeatedly) by exposing the chromatogram to the vapors of (clear) household ammonia, for example by replacing the petri dish with a plastic ring support and pouring some ammonia into the pie-plate developing chamber, and again covering it with a piece of window glass. In a half-hour or so, the ammonia fumes will convert the acid residues to their ammonium salts which brown very nicely while the heat decomposes them back into the acid residues and free ammonia. This cycle can be repeated, providing considerable sensitivity for the detection of small residues. (Figure 4)

Solvent

In principle, the solvent is "dilute water", to move the samples along gently. It is prepared by saturating n-butanol (normal butyl alcohol) with water. To get proper behavior of the acids being separated, the solvent must hold a "swamping" acid to repress the dissociation of the sample acid into ions, instead of being molecular. Common swamping acids are hydrochloric, acetic, and formic. Formic acid is the conventional choice for malolactic separation, but I find that acetic, although slower running, gives sharper lines (perhaps because of the slower transport). As a bonus, glacial acetic acid is available in photographic supply stores.

The solvent is prepared by mixing 10 parts (by volume) of n-butanol with 1 part of acid, then adding about 2 parts of water and shaking. You will find that about 2 parts of water will be dissolved — a slight excess will make the solvent cloudy (no harm) but too much excess will cause a separation into two layers, water below. These layers can be separated with a separatory funnel or by careful decanting from a properly shaped vessel.

For including the indicator in the developing solvent, use a 1% aqueous solution of the indicator (e.g., bromocresol green) as the source of water.

Since the solvent is a dilute solution of water, evaporation of water from the developing chromatogram can affect the operation, making the travel speeds vary, etc. It is good practice to keep the development chamber atmosphere saturated with water, e.g., by laying a ring of wet paper towel around the petri dish.

Advanced Spotting Technique

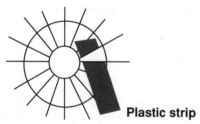

Figure 5

The angular spread of the sample spots can be reduced, and up to 24 samples used per disk, by a special technique. Of course, you will seldom have many samples needing to be tested at the same time, but the extra sample spaces provide for calibration samples of tartaric, malic and lactic acids, separately or in combination. The extra spaces also allow comparing different spotting techniques, for example, amount of sample.

Draw circles of 1 and 2 cm radius and mark the outer circle with evenly spaced marks for the desired number of sectors. With a straight-edge and a razor blade, make radial cuts from the inner circle to beyond the outer circle. Slip a thin plastic strip (through adjacent cuts) under one sector (Figure 5) and apply the sample to wet that sector completely between the two circles; about 1 drop needed. After it is dry, a second drop can be added.

Reference Samples

A solution of 1 gram tartaric acid plus 1 gram malic acid in 200 ml of water is a reasonable imitation wine to provide tartaric and malic markers for position comparison with the wines being tested. A lactic acid line can be obtained with the use of calcium lactate pills, available at the drugstore. Formic acid will give a good line from calcium lactate, but acetic will not (formic is about ten times as strong an acid as acetic). A lactic acid sample can be prepared by using oxalic acid (sometimes available in paint stores for wood bleaching). Two 650-mg (10-grain) calcium lactate pills are dissolved along with 1/2 gram of oxalic acid. This precipitates calcium oxalate and converts most of the lactate to free lactic acid. This solution is very milky from the suspended calcium oxalate, but filters readily. Using too much oxalic acid will leave some free oxalic acid which makes a line on the inner edge of the lactic acid line.

CHAPTER 16

MAKING WINE VINEGAR

Phillip E. DeVore

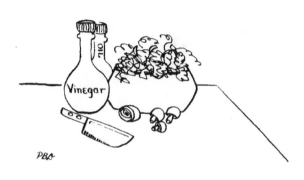

H IGH QUALITY vinegar can be made at home which can equal or surpass most gourmet vinegars and be far better than common cider vinegar. Little equipment is required to make vinegar at surprisingly low cost. No previous experience is necessary, so non-winemakers can succeed along with those accustomed to conducting fermentations.

We have made a number of disappointing wines, but never a poor vinegar. Here are the lessons gleaned from 10 years of vinegar making and experimentation.

A good wine for vinegar production should be hearty, vinous and free from major flaws. Defects in the wine will carry over to the vinegar. The best wines do make the best vinegar. We have used the dregs from decanting old red wines for red wine vinegar. Most of these bottles have been red Bordeaux and California Cabernet Sauvignon, which helps explain why we have been so happy with our red wine vinegar. Since the dregs can only be used for cooking or thrown away, our vinegar cost has been quite low. Our white wine vinegar, made from lesser wines, is also quite good.

Preferably the starting wine should be dry (sugar free) so that there will be less chance of off-fermentations. However, good results can probably also be achieved with a slightly sweet wine, since the sugar will largely be converted to acetic acid.

White wines are more difficult than reds to convert into vinegar because they tend to have less nutrients, which are necessary for bacterial growth. White wines are usually heavily fined in order to gain and retain clarity. Fining removes proteins and other nutrients that bacteria can metabolize. Tight filtering of white wines removes even more nutrients and also spoilage bacteria which could help in the conversion process.

Lastly, white wines tend to have higher levels of sulfur dioxide to check oxidation and browning, but sulfur dioxide also retards microorganism growth. The result is that whites are slower to acetify (turn to vinegar) than reds because there are fewer nutrients to support bacterial growth. Jug wines are often difficult to turn into vinegar since they are technically well made and resist microbiological attack. We recommend that your first batch be made from red wine.

For those interested in the chemistry of vinegar production:

$$CH_3CH_2OH + O_2 \text{------} CH_3COOH + H_2O$$
(Ethyl Alcohol) (Oxygen) (Acetic Acid) (Water)

Theoretically, 1% alcohol by volume will produce 1% acetic acid by weight. Actual yields will be slightly less. Starting with 2/3 wine at 12% alcohol and 1/3 water, the vinegar will average about 7% acetic acid. Many commercial vinegars are in the 5% range. Our vinegars will be strong but not overpowering.

Vinegar is best made in a warm (70–85° F) dark place, preferably free from disturbances. Bacterial growth seems to be retarded by bright light. Temperatures somewhat above 85° F will hasten the process, but quality will suffer. Good vinegar making, like winemaking, can't be rushed. Time is necessary for aging, which smooths out harsh flavors. Esters form, enhancing complexity. Temperatures below 70° F will prolong the process. In fact, low temperatures are responsible for many slow conversions.

An adequate air supply is necessary. Place a double layer of cheesecloth over the jug's neck, fastening the cheesecloth with a rubber band. Cheesecloth keeps vinegar flies and other insects out, while permitting air to pass freely.

The vinegar batch must have an adequate, but not excessive alcohol level. Too little alcohol makes weak vinegar, less resistant to attack by undesirable bacteria. Too much alcohol retards bacterial action and ultimately produces an excessively strong vinegar. An alcohol level of around 8% is ideal. This is achieved by adding one part water to two parts wine. For the first batch, procedures will be a little different.

A final, but very important, property of the vinegar base is its effective acidity as measured by the pH. The lower the pH, the more acid the solution. At a pH of 3.0 or lower, most microorganisms that could harm the vinegar (surface yeast and lactic bacteria being the most common) are rendered ineffective. Fortunately, acetobacter (vinegar producing bacteria) can work well at pH 3.0 or lower. An important safeguard is to keep the solution very acidic.

Winemakers should, if possible, avoid making vinegar in the winery in order to reduce the chance of wine being contaminated by acetobacter.

If vinegar is to be made in the winery, choose an isolated location. We have made vinegar in an out-of-the-way corner in the winery with no adverse results.

The best size container for your first batch is a 3 to 4 liter wine jug, which will ultimately yield about a gallon of vinegar per year, enough to supply most households. Should you desire more, production is easily expanded.

To make one gallon of vinegar which will fit nicely into a 4 liter jug and allow enough head space to provide good air contact, put into the jug:

1 quart homemade or commercial vinegar

2 quarts wine

1 quart water

Ideally, a quart of homemade vinegar should be used, but it is seldom available. If a smaller quantity of homemade vinegar or culture is used, make up the remaining volume with commercial 5% vinegar to maintain acidity. Commercial vinegar has probably been sterilized so it will not provide a source of vinegar bacteria.

An active vinegar culture will reduce the time until the first batch is ready, and reduces the chance of off-fermentations. A friend making vinegar may be able to supply you with a pint or so, or you may be able to get a culture from a wine making supply shop. A cultured starter is helpful, but not essential. Winemakers strive to prevent spontaneous vinegar formation.

There are several ways to monitor the conversion to vinegar. Smelling or tasting are the easiest. Those with facilities for titration may follow the conversion to acetic acid more quantitatively.

For those interested in following the conversion by titration, use 1 N sodium hydroxide and a 5 ml sample. Part of the total acidity is due to natural wine acids and thus is not acetic acid. Total acidity, expressed as weight % of acetic acid (or grams acetic acid/100 ml) is given by:

$$1.2 \, (V) \, (N)$$

Where:

V= Volume of sodium hydroxide in ml

N= Normality of sodium hydroxide

As vinegar makers, we may be frustrated over how long it takes to get our first batch completed. But as wine lovers, we should be happy that this may be a lengthy process. If wine converted to vinegar that easily, it would be difficult to make an untainted alcoholic beverage.

If all goes well, your first batch could be ready in a few months. If conditions aren't ideal, the first batch could take a year or longer. Subsequent batches will go a lot faster, since half the battle is getting the vinegar bacteria population established.

Be alert to the formation of a thick, wrinkly film growing on the liquid surface. There may also be a sherry-like smell. This film is a flor, or surface yeast, and if left unchecked could destroy the vinegar. Skim off the surface growth and add some more vinegar. Once the batch really gets going, surface yeast should not be a problem.

Most likely vinegar formation will be accompanied by evidence of bacterial growth. Formation of sediment or loose strands are common signs, but don't be too concerned if there are no visible signs of bacterial growth. A lot of vinegar can be formed before the bacteria shows its presence. When the alcohol content drops to 4% or below, a new vinegar bacteria may take over. A thick, smooth, gummy, translucent layer may form just below the surface. This is often referred to as "mother of vinegar".

When the vinegar is deemed ready, pour or siphon off a quart or so. Less sediment will be carried over if the vinegar is siphoned. A good siphon tube is made from three feet of 1/4 inch I.D. surgical rubber hose. Should a winery racking hose or other winery equipment be used, sterilize everything before returning it to winery service.

Replace the lost volume with a water-wine mixture in the ratio of 1/3 water and 2/3 wine. Use this ratio for all subsequent batches. No more vinegar need be added because the necessary acid environment has been established.

Your freshly drawn vinegar should be stable and unlikely to spoil. Small amounts of sediment will continue to form. We have never found sterilization necessary, but you can sterilize the vinegar by heating to 150° F for five minutes or by adding 150 ppm sulfur dioxide.

Occasionally the vinegar jug will need a thorough cleaning. Washing soda works well as does chlorine bleach. A curved brush may be necessary to clean the jug's shoulders. Rinse thoroughly to ensure that the jug is odor-free before returning the vinegar. Discard the sediment.

A further extension of the art is making specialty vinegars. Two popular ones are tarragon and garlic. Both are usually made with white wine vinegar. For tarragon vinegar, add one sprig of tarragon to one pint of white wine vinegar and let soak for at least two weeks. The taragon may be left in the vinegar for visual effect. For garlic vinegar, add several chopped garlic cloves to one pint of white wine vinegar. After two to four weeks strain through a cheesecloth and bottle.

CHAPTER 17

ELEMENTS OF WINE TASTING

G. Hamilton Mowbray

Introduction

Enjoying Wines is one thing, and a very pleasant thing it is indeed, but judging wines requires long and arduous practice, discipline and concentration. Almost anyone can learn to judge wines simply by tasting enough of them, but the process is immeasurably speeded up if the learning is accomplished under the direction of competent tasters whose ability to express what they experience can light the magic lamp of understanding. Any subjective endeavor carries with it its own perils and any guide post, no matter how ill-defined, is infinitely better than none at all.

Wine judging ability, like any other skill, is based on repetition and practice. However, the repetition and practice must not be random and helter-skelter. It must be organized. First, the mechanics of tasting must be mastered, and then a concerted program of disciplined practice needs to be undertaken. What follows is a series of guidelines that may be expanded, contracted, or in other ways orchestrated to suit the needs of the individual.

Judging relies on memory and thoughtful application. Comparisons are constantly being made between current impressions and those registered earlier. If the concentration is not there at the time of tasting, neither will the memory be. All too often, we swill our wines giving little thought to the nuances and complexities they might combine. Each such occurrence is the loss of a learning experience and no degree of regret can bring it back again. Serious judges of wine can not afford many such experiences. Judging also relies on a normally developed sensory system. No hypersensitive qualities are necessary or even desired, no matter what the poseurs and wine snobs say.

Wine is not judged by using analytical balances, chromatographs or abstruse chemical determinations. These are aids for the winemaker. Sound wines of ordinary quality can not be differentiated from sound wines of extraordinary quality by chemistry alone. There is literally no way that the most clever wine chemist in the world can tell the difference between a well-made vin ordinaire and the most prestigious classified growth except by using his God-given sensory equipment. Thus, an understanding of the capabilities and the limits of the eye, the nose and the palate we were all born with is paramount. These we shall pursue in order.

The Physiology of Wine Tasting

We are endowed with exquisite sensory equipment. We have an eye capable of resolving detail that approaches the width of one microscopically small receptor element of the retina, and under the right conditions, of detecting the smallest known quantity of light energy — the photon. Some idea of the eye's color sensitivity will be indicated shortly. We inherited an ear so finely tuned that it can, again under the right conditions, just barely detect acoustic energies that are on the order of those produced by the collision of molecules in random movement. Greater sensitivity would, on the face of it, seem to be maladaptive. Further, we are endowed with a sense of smell so acute that we are able to identify some volatile substances when they are present in one part in ten the 14th power. Whether you are mathematically inclined or not, that is an unthinkable number. If my mathematics are right, it would be roughly analogous to picking out one face from the total world population if that population were multiplied by 250,000.

The Nature of Light and Color

Light, coming from a source said to be white, contains all of the colors (or more technically wavelengths that are subjectively translated to hues) that the human eye is capable of distinguishing. If an optical device called a prism is inserted between the light source and the eye, all of the wavelengths are separated in space, and the hues are separately discernable. Water droplets in the atmosphere can, under the right conditions, act as a prism with a resultant rainbow. These are pure hues; red, yellow, green, blue and purple, and the only hues the eye can see and recognize. Mixtures of these hues yield other color sensations that have been given various names — brown, magenta, turquoise, orange, and on and on almost ad infinitum. Pure hues are rare in human experience. They exist in rainbows, as the combustion products of certain elements and from light transmitted through finely-ruled diffraction gratings. They almost never exist in wine, so, when speaking of wine, we speak of its color — that is, its combination of hues which are contributed by the genetic character of the grape or grapes from which the wine was made. The color may be more or less intense, or, be more or less saturated, depending on the growing season, the varieties of grapes used in the blend or on the care and treatment the winemaker has given it in the cellar. To gain an appreciation of this rather subtle concept, take a red wine and dilute it with water in varying degrees — say, by 0%, 10%, 25% and 50%. In each of the four samples, the color is the same, only the saturation of the color is different.

The eye is amazingly good at detecting simultaneous or near simultaneous differences in hue and saturation. Thus in side-by-side comparisons infinitely small changes can be accurately perceived. However, it takes a great deal of training and experience to detect even gross differences when the periods of observation between one sample and another are widely separated in time. In side-by-side comparisons under controlled viewing conditions the normal, healthy eye can perform literally tens of thousands of accurate discriminations. Lacking a standard for comparison, only seven — or at most nine — correct identifications can be accomplished reliably either in hue or in saturation.

The wave length composition of the light by which a wine is viewed is important. A wine is seen as red because all of the wave lengths, or hues, represented in the light source are absorbed except those hues in the red range which are transmitted to the viewer. If the light source doesn't contain representative wave lengths (again translated hues), then it may change the apparent color of the wine. Sunlight is the source of choice, tungsten-filament lamps are good, but cool-white or cold-white fluorescent lamps are absolutely unacceptable. Their wave length composition is inadequate for revealing the true color of wines — and particularly red wines.

The Color Of Wines

The color of white wines

White wines, so called, have every color but the one commonly known as white. They may vary from almost absolutely water clear, through greenish yellow, strawish to mildly golden and finally amber to golden brown. It is all a matter of their age, their provenance, the way they were made, the grape involved, or the state of their health. In evaluating them it is necessary to know something about all of the above.

A young, dry, white table wine, no matter what its source — whether single variety or blended — should be very light straw with perhaps a hint of green or yellowish green in its make-up. Young means six months to a year of age. Any serious deviation indicates problems. These will be explained later. Premium, dry white table wines, whether single grape variety or blended, with a year of age on them may have a straw-yellow hue with or without a hint of green depending on the grape variety or varieties.

Sweet white wines that are sweet by reason of being late picked or by reason of having been infected by Botrytis cineria should be light yellow to amber depending on their age. The older they are the more amber they will be. A deep golden amber, tending to brownish is not uncommon in very old, well-kept Premier Grand Cru Sauternes and German Beerenauslesen.

The custom in some wine-making countries — Italy and Spain are examples — is to ferment white wines on the skins of the grapes for some amount of time. The result is a wine high in tannin and in color that requires then some relatively long time in barrel aging. The resultant wines are hardy and somewhat colored in spite of the fact that they are completely dry. This is a wine-making style and should not be confused with carelessness in technique.

The effect of cellar treatment on the color of white wines

Wines made from a white grape that is crushed, pressed, fermented and aged in no matter what containers will have color problems unless something other than grape juice is used in the process. That something is usually sulfur-dioxide in one form or another. Sulfur-dioxide is an antioxidant and an antiseptic. It prevents light-colored fruit juices from browning, and it also has an anti-bacterial action that discourages certain undesirable organisms from attacking the sugars of fresh fruit juices. Used judiciously, it is a great boon to winemakers. In excess, it is a curse. In minimum doses, it ensures a healthy fermentation and a lively colored wine true to its type. Overdone, the result is a wine with sulfur overtones in both taste and smell and a color that is bleached beyond recognition.

Evaluation hint — a white wine whose color belies its age should be carefully searched by nose and palate for traces of excess sulfur, or for attenuated fruitiness and varietal character both to smell and taste.

White wines aged in oak barrels or vats may become highly colored because of the leaching out of substances in the wood. Fining agents may remove the color, but they are less successful in removing the smell and taste of the wood products leached from the barrel.

Evaluation hint — white wines with correct color for their type but with excessive woody overtones have likely been strongly fined. This is a delicate evaluation because some grape varieties can tolerate more of a wood flavor than others.

Color indications of white wine deficiencies

Young white wines with amber or brownish colors are likely to be spoiled by reason of too much exposure to air. There will be an accompanying, distinctive smell and taste which will be described later. This sort of accelerated aging may be caused by a defective cork, overheated storage or poor winemaking technique. No matter what the cause, it is a wine to be rejected and returned to the wine merchant for a refund.

An old white wine may suffer the same deficiency but then all wines — and white wines are certainly no exception — have a finite lifetime. They are mortal, just like the rest of us. Many white wines bear their age gracefully, gradually fading away to a mere shadow of their former selves. They can still be enjoyable even though diminished. When they are finally beyond the pale, we can only bow our heads and regret that we didn't spend more time with them when they were in their prime.

Wine made from moldy grapes whether it is the noble mold, Botrytis cineria, or some other will show an abnormal amount of color. There will also be accompanying taste and smell characteristics. In the case of noble mold they will be pleasant and desirable, but in other cases not.

The Color of Red Wines

Color in most red wines comes from pigments in the skins of the grape. It is extracted during the fermentation process along with other alcohol soluble constituents. Many grape varieties give up their color grudgingly and various devices are used by winemakers to ensure adequate color in the finished wine. Heating is one such device. Another is to mix in a small quantity of grape varieties known as teinturiers — literally, "stainers". These latter have colored pulp and juice, as well as colored skins. As their name implies, their color-producing qualities are dramatic. Wines made from them leave tell-tale, purplish droplets on the sides of the glass and will turn the pearliest-white teeth to a macabre bluish-black. Fortunately it is not a permanent dye.

Besides being very dependent on the grape varieties involved, the color of red wines is also much influenced by the year and the soil in which the grapes are grown. Some soils, and particularly soils rich in iron, bring out colors, all things being equal, better than others. The vagaries of the growing season are also always to be reckoned with. Cool, rainy summers produce red wines with more unsaturated colors than dry, warm summers.

In general, however, young red wines contain more purple colors than wines with some age. As they grow older, the purple gives way to reds more on the ruby side and finally, as they approach middle age, a brickish red becomes evident. In their dotage, the brickishness is accentuated. There are corresponding changes in aroma, bouquet and flavor as might be expected. For wines of breed, the spriteliness of youth evolves to the concentrated power of maturity followed finally by the gentle dignity of old age.

Many years ago, the tendency to make wines with deep, opaque colors was more prevalent than it is today. The economics of wine production and a change in consumer eating patterns, have led to wines with less color intensity and shorter aging requirements. There are still dark, tannic wines being made in Italy and California, mainly from the Nebbiolo grape in the first case and the Cabernet Sauvignon and the Zinfandel in the latter. Whether this is entirely desirable is a matter of personal taste–both of the winemaker and the consumer.

As with white wines, young red wines, showing abnormal colors are suspect. Premature development of brickish red or brownish tints reveals undue exposure to oxygen or poor handling, with early demise to be expected.

The Color Of Rosé Wines

The color of rosé wines varies more than that of any other wine type. It may range from nearly red through a healthy pink, light strawberry to the barest blush of color. It all depends on the grape variety, the method of vinification and the intent of the winemaker. No matter how the color was derived, it should be pleasing. Purple, brown or orange tones are to be deplored.

The Clarity of Wines

The French have been known to say that a brilliantly clear wine is a wine for the Americans. They do not mean that Americans demand perfection, but rather that they are more fussy than is warranted. Frequently wines do not fall bright naturally, but require some assistance if total clarity is to be achieved. Knowing this, many wine–knowledgeable people are prepared to accept a wine au naturel rather than risk the sensory losses that may be associated with mechanical fining and filtering. That is a purist viewpoint which is not likely to appeal to most wine consumers wherever they may be.

For esthetic reasons if for no other — and there are others — perfect clarity in a finished wine is desirable. This is an easy determination to make with white wines and most rose's, simply by looking through them at a moderately bright source of illumination. For extremely precise evaluations, viewing a fine, illuminated gridpattern through a glass containing four ounces of wine is ideal. The curved surfaces of the glass act as a magnifying lens, so that the crisper the magnified grid lines, the clearer the wine. Red wines are less easy to evaluate for clarity. One expedient is to use a polished silver tate-vin as they do in Burgundy. An ounce or two of red wine in this cup-like container can be surveyed in good light for the appearance of brilliant highlights and sparkle from the raised portions of the bottom.

With the technology of winemaking as advanced as it is today, it is rare indeed that a bottle leaves the winery with anything but perfect clarity insofar as the unaided eye can tell. However, according to Emile Peynaud, the renowned French scientist, a wine that appears limpid may contain as many as 5000 yeast cells per cubic centimeter. Over a period of time, these could cause clarity problems to develop. Other constituents of bottled wine may also generate haze and turbidity under the proper conditions. Some of these troubles are associated with undesirable smell and taste characteristics. Being able to recognize them by sight can be a great aid in the overall evaluation of a wine.

Microbiological causes of haziness

As noted, yeast residues in bottled wine may not be visible for sometime after bottling, but with time, they may become visible as powdery deposits on the sides or on the bottoms of the bottles. Agitation caused by moving or pouring will distribute these particles throughout the wine as a slight haze. It may be particularly noticeable in white wines. While there may be no noticeable taste or smell deficiencies in the wine, the haze can be a psychological barrier to full enjoyment.

Heavy, flocculant deposits are sometimes seen in white and rosé wines that have been subjected to high temperatures or long storage at room temperatures. They are not microbiological changes in the purest sense. They were not present in the finished, bottled wine but developed because of excessive amounts of proteins which were subsequently precipitated due to abnormal storage conditions. They are more unsightly than the yeast hazes and thus even less desirable, although they do not detract from the olfactory quality of wine. Their contribution to the mechanical aspects of taste can, however, be alarming. Wines are spoken of as being "chewable", but that is hardly the sense in which the term is meant.

Various undesirable yeasts and bacteria may be present in wine that is bottled. In great enough numbers and under the right circumstances they may proliferate even though the conditions in a tightly corked bottle of wine might not be considered ideal for organic development. In every such case, the result is disastrous to smell and to taste. In advanced cases most of these invasions show visual deficiencies as well.

There are two other cases in which deposits may be observed in bottles of wine. Both are benign. White wines that have undergone a prolonged period of chilling at refrigerator temperatures may throw deposits of a clear, crystalline nature. These are tartrate crystals. Tartaric acid is a natural constituent of fruit juices and wines made from them. Below certain temperatures, the salts of this acid form crystals that precipitate to the bottom of the container. They do not cloud the wine when it is poured, but they may collect in some quantity in the last glass that is poured from the bottle. Their presence does not indicate spoilage, but only that the wine may have been over-chilled by you or by someone else before you acquired it. The second case concerns red wines of premium quality — that is, wines that are meant to be aged before consumption. After 4 or 5 years in the bottle such wines may throw a dense, blackish deposit. It may range from a trace to very considerable amounts. It is a natural component of red wines that have a high content of tannic acid when young. Part of the aging process consists of the shedding of these tannins. Aged red wines therefore, have to be handled gently and decanted carefully before serving. To shake them up and pour them is to destroy all of the pleasure that the years have built up for you.

Non-microbiological causes of haziness

Iron and copper are two metals which in excess are anathema to wines. Both can cause cloudiness. Iron casse, as it is known technically, may show up in bottled wines that were perfectly clear to the eye prior to bottling. Fortunately for the consumer, but not for the producer, it shows up within a few days after bottling, so it is not likely to reach the market in that condition except under unusual circumstances. Copper casse is a trifle more insidious. It may develop in an apparently stable white wine after some months of storage. First, a fine, powdery sediment develops in the shoulder of the bottle, followed in time by a brownish trace the whole length of the bottle. Direct sunlight accelerates the process. Neither of these two disorders is particularly harmful to the taste of the wines in which they are evident, but , again, they are unsightly.

Finally, it should be pointed out that many of the conditions described above affecting the visual aspects of wine may occur in combination, clouding not only the wine, but the diagnosis as well.

Visual Indications of Viscosity

One last visual inspection is in order before turning to the pleasures afforded by nose and palate. It can tell you something about the alcoholic content and the body of the wine as well as anticipate the feel of the wine in the mouth before you ever sniff or taste. The indication involves appreciation of the wine's viscosity.

In layman's terms viscosity is the resistance a fluid offers to flow — or to sheer stress in engineering terms. The greater the resistance, the higher the viscosity, so that to everyone's understanding, molasses has a higher viscosity than water. So does alcohol. Wine, being essentially a solution of water and alcohols, has a viscosity that is higher than water alone and is directly related to the percentage of alcohols in the solution. A fairly accurate appreciation of the viscosity of a wine can be had by swirling a glass that is one-third full of wine or by tilting it slightly and returning it to the upright position and then observing what happens as the wine on the sides of the glass returns. If the glass is clean, well rinsed and dry, some noticeable amount of time will elapse before beads of wine form on the sides of the glass and slowly descend. The time it takes for this to happen is a measure of the wine's viscosity. The longer it takes, the higher the viscosity, the higher the percentage of alcohols and, in general, the more weight the wine will appear to have in the mouth. An estimation of the "body" of the wine can thus be made just by careful observation.

Before closing this section, one further word needs to be said. Some works treating the subject of viscosity give great importance to the presence of glycerol in table wines. Glycerol, a natural product of fermentation, is present in varying degrees and it does have a high viscosity, but only in sweet wines made from grapes affected by "noble rot" is it likely to be in sufficient quantity to have any noticeable effect on viscosity.

The Physiology of Smell

There is a group of specially adapted sensory cells located in the approximate center of the head, which, when properly stimulated, evoke sensations that we know as smells. The stimulating agents are volatile chemicals contained in the inspired air.

There have been many attempts to classify the qualities of odors that we are able to detect, but none of them has been completely successful. The reason is no doubt due to the mind-boggling chemical complexity and the vast range of molecular substances that can excite our receptors differentially. The only classification that makes any sense, and it is crude enough, is one that attributes to us the ability to discriminate six basic qualities. They are spicy, flowery, fruity, resinous, burnt and foul. Since all of them can be found in wines, singly or in combination, I would be quite willing to declare the case closed, and go on from there, except for the fact that there are other odorous qualities also found in wine, which do not fit into any of those categories. There is, for instance, the vegetal quality — call it stemmy, grassy or what you will — that I find sometimes in wines from California. Then there are the medicinal smells (not necessarily foul) of doctored wines and the petro-chemical smells of some wines made from hybrid grape varieties that do not find a place in the classification. And there are others. It is not, as you may be beginning to agree, a simple matter.

Indeed, it is incredibly complex. Out of more than two million known chemical compounds, it is estimated that fully 20% have an odor that is more or less specific for each. Further, specialists can identify the substances from which those odors emanate. The qualitative diversity of odors is thus enormous, and that they can be discriminated with remarkable precision says something about the considerable sensitivity of our olfactory system. Without doubt, it is many times more sensitive in this respect than any of our other senses. Trained color specialists may be able to discriminate a few hundred nuances in the colors they work with and musicians considerably fewer tonal qualities, but there are hundreds of thousands of identifiable odors. Jacques Le Magnen, in his little classic entitled "Odeurs et Parfums" claims that wool specialists can, by using odor alone, discriminate Australian from American wool, and what's more, can identify the species of sheep from which the wool was taken. As unbelievable as that may sound, it has been established time and time again that trained wine tasters can, again by smell alone, tell all they need to know about a wine, including the alcoholic content, the year of production, the grape variety and the district in which it was grown.

Intelligent use of the olfactory system depends on the understanding that it is easily fatigued. We adapt quite rapidly to ambient smells, and what was noisome on first contact becomes, if we endure it long enough, bearable, if not completely benign. How else could we bear to live in close proximity to oil refineries, paper mills, tanneries or a whole host of other necessary, but air polluting industries? Adaptation occurs not only to objectionable odors, but to pleasurable ones as well, and as a general rule, adaptation is quicker the more subtle the smell. Since, also as a rule, the subtler odors are the more pleasurable ones, it behooves us to be patient and not hurry our olfactory examination of a glass of wine where subtlety and pleasure are the very name of the game.

Smells are emotionally evocative stimuli. There is not an experience of our lives that has not been associated in some way with smells. A particular odor or hint of an odor coming out of the blue from who knows where can start a train of memories that we hardly knew still existed. Often we are not aware of what it was that triggered the memories. Careful observation and close introspection may give the answer but, as likely as not, we just shrug it off and chalk it up to advancing age. The close association that exists between smells and memories is fortunate for those of us who wish to derive more than a passing pleasure from the wines we taste. For the professionals among us it is a god-send. Wine is ephemeral; it is constantly changing and it is not the same today as it was yesterday. Without a memory to rely on we could not hope to make sensible evaluations. How would we know whether 1973 Chateau X was maintaining its standards unless we had a very clear memory of past vintages at the same stage of development? It would be impossible. The fact that it can be done says something more about the most underrated of our senses — the sense of smell.

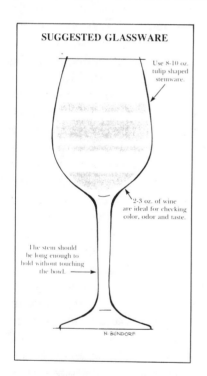

SUGGESTED GLASSWARE

Use 8-10 oz. tulip shaped stemware.

2-3 oz. of wine are ideal for checking color, odor and taste.

The stem should be long enough to hold without touching the bowl.

N. BUNDORF

The odors of wine

The odorous aspect of wines involves two separate and distinct concepts. They are the concepts of aroma and bouquet. Aroma is the odor or odors associated with young wines, while bouquet can only develop with age. By far the largest percentage of the wines of the world are enjoyed because of their aroma. When that dissipates, as it inevitably does with age, they hold no more interest. A tiny proportion of the world's wines made exclusively from the noble Vitis vinifera grapes, aged under the right conditions, develop bouquets that make them the most sought after wines in the world. They are rare and consequently they are expensive.

While we speak of aroma, there are in fact two types of aroma. The primary aroma is predominately fruit and is contributed by the particular grape variety involved. All of the best wine grape varieties — and some that are not so good — have their own distinctive odor-producing characteristics. Extreme examples are the Muscat, the Reisling, the Gewurtztraminer, the Pinot noir and the Cabernet Sauvignon from Europe and the Concord from America. The secondary aroma is exclusively a product of fermentation. The yeasts in converting the sugar of grapes into alcohol, also produce many odorous compounds as well. These are largely fruity but not necessarily the fruit of the vine. They may encompass such smells as are generally associated with plums, peaches, raspberries, cherries, strawberries, bananas, lemons, quince, apples, currants and nuts such as hazelnuts, walnuts, almonds and others. They may also be flowery (iris, honeysuckle), spicy, and many, many others. As was indicated earlier, these aromas dissipate early, and whether the wines displaying them are white, red or rosé, for maximum enjoyment, they should be drunk within two to three years of their production.

Bouquet is a term that is synonymous with fine wines. It develops slowly during long aging in barrels and becomes concentrated after further bottle storage where contact with air is denied the wine. The development of bouquet is a poorly understood process, chemically speaking. What is certain is that it can only attain its full development in what the chemists call a reducing situation — i.e., denied access to oxygen. A glass bottle with a 1 3/4 to 2 inch cork was discovered, empirically, to be ideal. The rate of aging and so, the rate of bouquet development is directly proportional to the size of the container. The smaller the container, the quicker the reaction, which is why magnums, standard 75 centiliter bottles and so-called half-bottles are all ready to drink at quite different ages, other things being equal. The odors associated with bottle bouquet are diverse. Most of them may be familiar to you in other experiential contexts. They are generally more earthy in origin and more pervading than the aromas, but they can also be spicy and perfumed. Some examples are cloves, cinnamon, bitter almond, peach kernel, vanilla, caramel, tobacco, coffee, cedarwood, licorice, musk, ambergris, venison and other game. The list does not begin to be exhaustive. The more carefully you search, the more odors are likely to be found. In the bouquet of a wine there is often one dominant odor. The agreeable character of this odor denotes a good wine, but the diversity and the complexity of the nuances found in the smells are the mark of the great wine.

Not all wines smell pleasant. Someone has written that the nose is the sentinel at the outpost that keeps the mouth from harm — and the stomach too, I might add. Developing problems in wines often advertise their presence in odorous form, sometimes so slight as to be barely detectable and perhaps not altogether unpleasantly. At other times, the smell can be thoroughly objectionable. The wine drinker should familiarize himself with these smells, and particularly the more subtle ones, so that he can evaluate properly the wine he has purchased — and return it if necessary. The winemaker must know them to avoid marketing an unpalatable product and to be able to take corrective action if such a course is possible.

There are a few simple procedures for getting the most out of a wine, aromatically speaking. They are simple, but they are important. The glass, and glass it must be (not plastic and not metal) should be the familiar, tulip-shaped stemware. That shape is specified because the tulip-shaped bowl traps the odors more efficiently than other configurations, and the stem or the foot provides a handle, keeping the bowl free of fingerprints and giving clear view of the contents. The glass should be poured no more than 1/3 full or about 2 ounces in a 6 ounce glass. Then, having completed the visual inspection, stick your nose in the bowl and take one good strong sniff. Remove it and take a few seconds to consider the sensation. Now, swirl the wine gently with a rotary movement of the hand and take a couple of more good sniffs. You should notice immediately an accentuation of the odors, with perhaps the appearance of some that were not detectable in the first sniff. You may want to repeat the swirling procedure a couple of times to be sure that you have exhausted the possibilities of bringing out new and different odors. Don't exhaust your smell receptors in doing it, but leave enough time between sniffs for them to recover. Finally, and especially if you think you detect some off-, foreign or objectionable odor, swirl the glass violently without spattering your neighbor or yourself and sniff carefully again. If anything is there that shouldn't be, violent swirling will bring it out. Your olfactory examination is now completed and all that remains is to record your impressions.

Odorous deficiencies of wines

Any personally objectionable smells in a wine are, for the beholder, a deficiency. They may come from poor winemaking practices, from seasonal variations in the quality of the grapes used or from a particular winemaking style that does not appeal to the judge. The two former cases are to be deplored, but the latter must be recognized as a matter of prejudice and dealt with accordingly. The good will learn to overcome his prejudice or will not judge such wines.

Following is a list of the most prevalent aromatic faults to be found in wine:

Caramel — common in some overbaked sherries and wines made from concentrates.

Geranium-like — caused by the bacterial decomposition of sorbitol.

Hot-alcoholic — the nose-burning sensation of out of balance highly alcoholic grapes.

Moldy — can be caused by contaminated barrels, corks or moldy grapes.

Mousy — a typically flat, rather dirty smell caused by bacterial invasion of high pH wines.

Oxidized — a sherry-like, somewhat metallic smell in wines that have been exposed to too much air or are simply over-the-hill by reason of being too old.

Raisiny — caused by the use of excess amounts of dried or over-ripe grapes.

Rancid — particularly rancid butter- associated with wines undergoing bacterial spoilage. Not to be confused with rancio, a style of winemaking that is appreciated in some quarters.

Rubber-boot — another indication of bacterial spoilage.

Sauerkraut — sometimes the result of a malolactic fermentation in the bottle.

Stemmy — just as it sounds; the smell of green stems acquired during fermentation.

Sulfide — the rotten-egg smell of hydrogen-sulfide or the barnyard odor of mercaptans.

Vegetal — not stemmy, but more like asparagus, alfalfa or ensilage. A regional characteristic of some California wines.

Vinegary — the smell of acetic bacterial spoilage and a combination of acetic acid and ethyl-acetate.

Woody — comes from too long storage in oak. Should not be obtrusive, but not to be confused with the cedar cigar-box smell of some outstanding Bordeaux wines.

Yeasty — comes from improperly stabilized wines or from wines that have been left on the lees too long in which latter case it can be most offensive.

The Physiology of Taste

Taste, in contrast to smell, is an adumbrated sense. Much of the sensation we normally attribute to taste is actually smell. A severe head cold with accompanying nasal congestion makes that uncomfortably clear. For those who have never experienced such an infirmity, try sipping some wine with the nostrils held closed. The attenuation of total sensation is dramatic.

the tongue

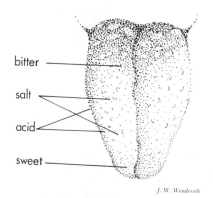

bitter

salt

acid

sweet

J. W. Wenderoth

Most authorities agree that there are only 4 basic taste qualities. They are sweet, sour, bitter and salt, and each quality has its own, specially adapted sensory cells located on the tongue to mediate a specific experience. Fortunately, for evaluative purposes, the different taste buds are not distributed randomly over the tongue's surface, but are more or less grouped together in slightly overlapping but generally different areas. Thus the receptors for sweetness are to found on the top surface of the tongue toward the tip, while those for sourness, acidity or tartness are located along both sides, bitterness on the middle portion in the back. The appreciation of saltiness, which is seldom, if ever, encountered in table wines, comes from receptors located on the tip and sides of the tongue.

Sweetness in wine is contributed by unfermented sugars, alcohol (ethanol) and in unusual cases by glycerol. Individual thresholds for and tolerance of sugar in wine vary so widely that hard and fast rules probably should not be made. Usually, however, if the sweetness is not allayed by a background acidity, it soon becomes cloying and tiresome and most would find it unsatisfactory for accompanying a meal. Even sweet dessert wines without supporting acidity leave much to be desired. Wines without detectable sweetness are termed "dry" and should appeal because of their mild tartness and palate-cleansing qualities. These are without question the wines to drink with the main courses of a meal.

Acidity, in balance with alcohol and sugar, if any, is what gives wine its structure. Without sufficient acid a wine is bland and insipid, but in too great a quantity the wine is sharp, acerbic, biting and altogether unpleasant. The acids involved are mainly the natural organic acids of fruits, i.e., tartaric, malic, citric and lactic. The last is not a normal fruit acid but appears in wine, especially red wine, through conversion of malic — a naturally strong acid — by a family of bacteria known as lactic bacteria. In the cooler regions of Europe and North America, this conversion is encouraged by winemakers because of the softening effect it has on the finished product. It is usually desirable only in red wines since its occurrence in white wines tends to destroy their natural fresh fruitiness. For grapes from warmer regions, such as most of California and the Mediterranean region of Europe, the malolactic conversion is avoided like the plague. Their problem is never too much acid, but, indeed, quite the reverse. Wines with detectable sugar may sustain higher amounts of measurable acidity than wines without sugar because sugar masks acid and the psychological effect is an altogether softer wine. Other, natural products of some wines exaggerate their apparent acidity. Tannin is one such substance, so young red wines, which are often quite high in tannic content, to be at all palatable require lower total acid levels than white wines whose tannic content is usually low.

A mild bitterness in wines can not only be tolerated, but actually enjoyed. Wines from some grape varieties have a natural bitter accompaniment that compliments a variety of dishes. It is all a matter of taste. The natural tannins of red wines have among other things, a bitter component. So do white wines fermented on their skins, as is the case with many an Italian white wine. This bitterness is to be distinguished from astringency which is technically a tactile sensation associated also with high tannin content. The distinction is difficult for some people. The key is to remember that bitterness is perceived only on the back portion of the tongue while astringency affects the whole of the buccal cavity — tongue, cheeks, gums, teeth and palate.

Excessive bitterness in wines is to be deplored. It can be found in wines that are too young to drink and in wines, young or old, that are undergoing changes caused by bacterial spoilage.

Saltiness is a taste experience that can be dispensed with in a few words. In wines, it shouldn't happen. Some few wines of the world grown on shore line soils may pick up salts from the medium in which the grapes were grown. They are rare and to be avoided. Succinic acid, an organic acid produced in the fermentation process, has a salty bitterness about it, but it is usually present in such small quantities as to be practically undetectable. Sodium salts can be added to wine by some cellar treatment methods designed to assure cold stability. These methods, while currently widespread in America, are not to be condoned even though the salts so induced may be perceptually undetectable.

The Other Components of Taste

Besides the chemical aspects of taste just described, there are other sensory qualities to be considered. The tongue, cheeks, palate and throat are host to receptors for touch, pain and temperature as well as to those for taste itself. They all play an important role in evaluation.

The touch, or technically, the tactile sense, is involved in judgements of a wine's body and its astringency. These are two of the most troublesome concepts for neophyte wine-tasters. The body of a wine can literally be reduced to a feeling of weight and substance in the mouth. A big or full-bodied wine asks to be chewed. The body is contributed by those substances in solution in the wine that are heavier than water. They are, in decreasing order of importance, alcohol, sugar and glycerol. As each of these substances, and particularly the first two, increase in proportion, the bigger and the fuller the body of a wine will be. They may also substitute for each other. If, for instance, alcohol is reduced and sugar increased, the perception of body may remain unchanged, and vice versa. Low alcohol, low sugar and low glycerol wines are thin, light bodied and watery and, if, simultaneously, the acid level is high, they are decidedly unpleasant. It is all a matter of balance.

Astringency, the other difficult concept which also involves the tactile sense, is encountered almost exclusively in red wines. It results from the tannin extracted from the skins of the grapes during primary fermentation. Young red wines often have it in excess, but as they age, the tannins combine with oxygen in the wine and precipitate as solids to the bottom of the bottle. They form unsightly deposits which gentle handling with decanting before consumption can eradicate. But consumed too young, red wines with high tannic content attack the whole buccal cavity, including the teeth, making it feel as though the whole were coated by a thin film of fuzz. Strong tea will do the same thing and for the same reason, too much tannic acid.

The pain sense comes into play when a wine is too high in alcohol. Perceptually it is hot, burning the nose when it is sniffed and when it is swallowed, the tongue, the cheeks, the throat and the esophagus and even the stomach on occasion. Masochists will appreciate this sensation and indulge themselves by consuming quantities of highproof spirits. For wine-lovers it is anathema. After dinner, perhaps, when the palate is satiated, high proof beverages in moderation — and I am thinking of Port or Brandy — may be in order as a final soporific. As a companion to good food, any beverage with more than 12 to 13 percent alcohol is barbaric. I can think of one exception — Maryland terrapin soup with Sherry. Perhaps my gourmet friends will say there are a few others.

As everyone knows who has ever had a clinical thermometer stuck into his mouth by a brusque, impersonal and starchily stiff nurse, the temperature of the firmly closed mouth is about 98.6° F. Anything taken into the mouth below that temperature will therefore be perceived as cool to cold or even frigid, depending on its temperature — and that's an ambiguous term — will in most circumstances appear to be cool. Their taste characteristics will be affected by the temperature at which they are drunk. The appreciation of taste and the appreciation of smell are affected by temperature. The cooler the beverage, the more attenuated the smell and the taste. In the case of smell, it is a matter of reduced volatility, while in the case of taste it is a matter of anaesthetization. The more distasteful a substance, the colder it should be when imbibed, which is why I suspect, all cola beverages are served at a temperature of 32° F. Incidentally, I might add that extreme heat is almost as effective an anaesthetic for taste as is extreme cold. What do you think of room temperature coffee?

White wines are usually served chilled because of their higher acidity which is attenuated by the anaesthetic effect of their lowered temperature. High alcohol white wines may also be improved by the same treatment. The custom of drinking white wines chilled and red wines at room or cellar temperatures probably arose long years ago when acidity reduction was little understood by winemakers. In the cool climates of northern Europe where wine customs originated, white wines were often acidic for reasons that we may attribute to fermentation processes. Red wines often were not acidic for the same reasons. Fermented on the skins in open vats as they were, malolactic fermentation was almost guaranteed. This process, little understood then, but better understood today, was a sure route to soft, low-acid, red wines. Paradoxically, slight chilling to 58–60° F can add interest to the taste of light, fruity, red wines such as Beaujolais. It gives them an apparent tartness which at warmer temperatures they appear to lack.

The Taste and Odorous Constituents of Wine

The taste, or what might in some circles be termed the gustatory character of wine, depends on its chemical composition. Wine may be considered to be a water-alcohol solution containing sugars, acids, salts, phenolic compounds and, indeed, other substances as well. Each constituent has its own taste and odor which it contributes to the whole. The quality of a wine is not bound to the amount of one substance alone which may be present, but instead to a harmonious rapport between all of them. Balance is the key word and the ideal, in fact the Holy Grail of winemakers, and often just as elusive. The flavor of wine should be considered as a result of an equilibrium between the odor-producing substances and the taste constituents.

A wine owes its quality to the harmony of these different flavors in combination. Neither one nor the other should dominate. It is as true for sweet, white wines as for dry white wines or for red wines that contain little or no residual sugar.

Alcohol is among the constituents of wine that provide a perception of sweetness. It is easy to show that a solution containing 4% alcohol (32 grams per liter) is as sweet as a solution containing 20 grams of glucose per liter. It is easier to show that alcohol reinforces the sweetness of sugar. On the other hand, as has been said, sweetness and acid are mutually masking in their effects. The addition of sugar or alcohol diminishes both the perception of acid and bitter flavors. Only a moments thought should be required to make that clear. Why else add sugar to grapefruit, coffee, tea or lemonade? In wines, the sweet substances serve to balance out the otherwise over-riding flavors of acid and bitter substances.

The Psychological Variables

Ambiance, as suggested earlier, plays an important role in the appreciation of a wine. Noise, smoke-filled rooms, highly perfumed bodies — male or female — are decided distractions. On the other hand, compatible friends, exotic surroundings, relaxation to the point of letdown or other unusual conditions can contribute to the momentary enjoyment of a wine far beyond its actual worth.

Certainly the heightened enjoyment of a wine, even though attributable to context, is to be applauded. May we all have many such occasions in our lifetimes. However, don't mistake those occasions for the more serious problem of evaluating wines for their worth in any context. Be wary of the special aura that may surround any wine at any given time. Be especially wary of the prestige of the label. It should not have to be said, but experience tells me that it must. In a recent tasting of 1975 Bordeaux red wines, the worst wine of all was a Premier Grand Cru Classe', at a price more than twice the next most expensive and some ten times more than others in the tasting. Yet people will buy it, and extol its virtues simply because the label is known to be expensive.

One's own physiological state at the time of tasting can not be ignored. Fatigue, lassitude, boredom or variations in body chemistry can play tricks with one's palate. And, of course, it goes without saying that any food or beverage taken prior to tasting or concomitant with it can have lasting after-effects, both negative and positive. If a wine known to be enjoyable on previous occasions suddenly appears to be markedly different, don't immediately damn the wine. Look to your own physiological state first, and try to determine if something in you has changed. Be suspicious also of the opposite effect — namely, a wine known to be of modest and humble origins that appears to assume a quality incommensurate with its background. Subtle, undetected changes in body chemistry are not rare, and not so subtle changes induced by medication can alter sensory perceptions, and particularly those of taste and smell which are based on chemical reactions.

Exercises to Improve Your Understanding of Wine

In this section, I will outline the bare-bones of a study course, which, if pursued diligently, should put you on the road to becoming a competent wine judge. Expansions and contractions can be made as needed for individual cases. Some small items of equipment and a source of certain chemical supplies will be needed, as will become clear. These should not prove to be a serious obstacle to anyone with the motivation, some will be in your own pantry, others can be purchased from home winemaking shops. Liter carafes are available at wine retailers or a quart bottle will do. An analytical balance is important but teaspoon measures are given where possible.

Getting acquainted with the four basic tastes

Make up the following solutions with tap water, unless your local water is heavily treated with chlorine and other so called purifying chemicals. If it is, use bottled, non-effervescent, spring water or distilled water.

For sweetness:

20 grams (5 tsp.) of sucrose (table sugar) / liter water

For acidity:

1 gram (1/4 tsp.) of tartaric acid / liter water

For saltiness:

4 grams (2/3 tsp.) table salt / liter water

For bitterness:

10 mg of quinine sulfate / liter water (Purchase capsules at a pharmacy and divide into 10 mg portions).

Taste each of these solutions attentively, paying attention to where the particular sensation from each is experienced in the mouth. No doubt everyone has experienced all of these tastes before, but the exercise of tasting them as pure solutions, without interfering sensations and with concentration, may be new to most.

People differ widely in their ability to detect small amounts of substances in solution. That is one reason there are such disparities in preferences, and it is just as well, for if we all liked the same things to the same degree, there wouldn't be enough to supply the demand. Because we do differ, each of us should know his strengths and weaknesses if he is going to judge wine. Some have a quicker appreciation of residual sugar than others, and where one might be slow to detect sugar, his perception of bitterness or acidity may be acute. There are some simple tests for determining the individual sensitivity to the basic taste qualities. A large part of success in wine evaluation is knowing yourself, so the following exercises are strongly recommended:

With someone to help you, prepare a series of three glasses, two of which will contain plain water, while the third will contain a solution of water and sugar. The strength of the sugar-water solution should be drawn from preparations ranging from 50 grams of sugar to a liter of water, through 30 grams, 20 grams, 10 grams and 5 grams/ liter. The person to be tested should be presented the three glasses arranged in a random order and be made to select the glass with the sugar-water solution in it. At least five series of presentations should be made at each of the also randomly ordered strengths. The solution that can be judged sweeter than plain water successfully three times out of five represents a near threshold judgement. Greater precision in locating the threshold can be obtained by locating a rough threshold first, then refining the sugar-water ratio and making more than five individual judgements per solution strength. As an example, if the first rough determination indicates that the threshold is around 20 grams of sugar/liter, then make up an equally graded series of five solutions centering on the 20 gram figure, and repeat the threshold measurement using ten judgements per mixture instead of the original five. Any mixture that can be picked correctly about half of the time may considered the threshold. Emile Peynaud in his delightful book called "Connaissance et Travail du Vin", states that about 25% of the population can detect as being sweet a solution containing 5 grams of sugar/liter, another 25% needs 10 grams/liter, whereas the rest of us need 20 grams/liter or more.

Similar thresholds can be established for acidity using from 0.05 to 0.5 grams of tartaric acid/liter of water, and for bitterness by using 1 to 5 mg of quinine sulfate/liter of water. Saltiness is a less important characteristic of wines and may be neglected.

Generally, it will be found that the range of thresholds for sugar and for bitterness are rather broad in the general population, while those for acidity are much narrower.

Wine is a complex beverage so no one aspect of it is tasted or otherwise experienced in complete isolation. The acid is always tasted against a background of alcohol, sugar, etc. The constituents interact with each other in various ways, and many of these interactions can be rather simply demonstrated, as Professor Peynaud has set forth in the work previously cited.

To show how acid and bitter tastes reinforce each other

Using water, as above, prepare three solutions, each with 0.75 grams of tartaric acid/liter. To one, add 10 mg of quinine sulfate, to another add 1.0 grams of tannic acid and keep the third as a control, or standard, for the basic acid taste. Now compare the taste of all three. The taste of the tartaric acid masks the bitterness of the quinine at first, but finally the bitterness will be perceived in the after-taste. The disagreeable nature of the acidity is reinforced by the presence of the bitter flavor.

When the bitterness is due to the tannic acid, the acid and bitter tastes tend to add to and the acidity reinforces the tannic astringency.

To show that alcohol has a sweet flavor

Make up a 4% solution of ethanol (ethyl alcohol) and water using 32 grams of alcohol/liter of water, and a 10% solution using 80 grams/liter. These solutions can also be prepared from 80 proof vodka which is 40% ethanol. One part 80 proof vodka + 3 parts water = 10% ethanol. One part 80 proof vodka + 9 parts water = 4% ethanol.

At 4%, the alcohol has a lightly sugared taste compared to plain water, but the taste of alcohol is not particularly apparent. This sweetness is indeed different from the sweetness obtained from sugar, but it obviously belongs to the same family. With 10% alcohol, you find the sweetness very strong, coupled with the sensation of heat. This solution demonstrates well the complex taste of alcohol, having both flavorful and tactile aspects.

Moreover, alcohol clearly reinforces the sweetness of sugar itself. You may experience this by making up three sugar-water solutions using sucrose (table sugar) at the rate of 20 grams/liter, with each of the solutions having a different alcoholic strength, namely, 0%, 4% and 10%. Tasting of these solutions will demonstrate clearly how the presence of alcohol can enhance the impression of sweetness. On the other hand, at this concentration, the sugar does not decrease the feeling of warmth contributed by the alcohol.

To show how sweetness modifies acidity

Prepare the three following solutions:

1. 20 grams (5 tsp.) of sucrose (table sugar)/liter water

2. 1 gram (1/4 tsp.) of tartaric acid/liter water

3. 20 grams of sucrose (table sugar) and 1 gram of tartaric acid/ liter water.

Compare the sweet and sour taste of solution (3) with the other two basic tastes. The third solution appears to be both sweet and sour at the same time, and the attention can be directed to first one and then the other. But their respective intensities are modified compared with either (1) or (2). The tartaric acid clearly diminishes the sweet taste of the sugar. On the other hand, at these concentrations, the effect of the sugar on the acid taste is less noticeable, the solution appearing to be stronger in acid than in sugar. For the acidity to be clearly diminished, it would take about 30 grams of sugar/liter. Because of individual variation, these effects will not at these solutions strengths, affect everyone the same.

Now, make up solutions with 1 gram of tartaric acid/ liter, but with alcoholic strengths of 0, 4%, 7% and 10%. At 4% alcohol the acidity is scarcely different from the one with no alcohol. At 7% alcohol, the acidity is clearly diminished. The 10% solution is more complex. The perceived sensation is of harshness, with the acidity reinforcing the burning feeling contributed by the alcohol.

To show how sweetness changes bitterness

This idea should not be new to most who sugar their coffee and their tea.

Prepare two series of bitter solutions, one with 10 mg of quinine sulfate/ liter and the other with 1.0 gram of tannic acid/ liter. Each series should be then arranged as follows:

Control solution (no additions)

20 grams sugar/liter

40 grams sugar/liter

4% alcohol

10% alcohol

Compare the tastes of these solutions. The sweetness softens the disagreeable nature of the bitter quinine, which is only perceived as an aftertaste. The quinine even adds some interest to the taste of the solution with 40 grams of sugar/liter. In somewhat the same way, the sugar delays the appearance of the bitter and astringent taste of the tannin. The perception of the tannic taste in the control solution is rapid, but with the solution containing 20 grams of sugar that perception is delayed by two or three seconds, and with the 40 gram solution it is delayed by five or six seconds.

The taste of the alcohol masks the taste of quinine. The effect on the taste of tannin is more complex, for the "hotness" of the alcohol at 10% accentuates the final disagreeable impression.

To demonstrate the balance between sweetness, acidity and bitterness in wine

The following test can not be made by everyone because it involves some equipment that is not usually found outside of chemistry laboratories. Most high school labs can satisfy the requirements. It is included for those who, by whatever means, have access to the equipment. It is highly recommended for those who can arrange it.

Distill 200 ml of a soft, well-balanced red wine. Collect 100 ml of distillate and bring to a volume of 200 ml with water. Cool the residue and bring it likewise to a volume of 200 ml with water. The distillate contains the alcohol of the wine but does contain any of the fixed acids or the phenolic compounds — the coloring substances. These latter are all in the residue from which the alcohol has been distilled.

Taste the two liquids separately comparing them with the original wine. The distillate has a soft, sweetish flavor combined with the alcoholic feeling of warmth, but, overall, a certain blandness. The residue, however, is extremely acid and bitter, practically untasteable. The wine from which these both were derived is pleasant only because, in combination, a certain equilibrium has been attained. The wine is in balance. It would be instructive to repeat these experiments with a wine that is out of balance on the side of too much acid and astringency and with one that is out of balance on the side of low acidity and high alcohol.

To show the differing strengths of the various sweet constituents of wine

The following solutions will be needed:

4% alcohol (32 grams/liter)

20 grams glycerol/liter

20 grams glucose/liter

20 grams sucrose/liter

20 grams fructose/liter

The alcohol, the glycerol and the glucose, with some nuances in sweetness, show practically the same flavor intensity. Sucrose is clearly sweeter; 20 grams of sucrose is equivalent to 30 or 35 grams of glucose. Fructose is sweeter still; 20 grams of fructose is equivalent to 40–45 grams of glucose.

To show the different qualities and strengths of wine acids

The six following solutions will be needed:

1 gram (1/4 tsp.) tartaric acid/liter

1 gram (1/4 tsp.) malic acid/liter

1 gram (1/4 tsp.) citric acid/liter

1 gram (1 ml) lactic acid/liter

1 gram (1 ml) acetic acid/liter or 20 ml of 5% white vinegar/liter

0.5 gram (1/8 tsp.) succinic acid/liter

The tartaric, malic and citric acids of the grape have the same, pure acid flavor. To be sure, tartaric acid can be characterized as harsher, malic acid as being greener, and citric acid as being fresher. If the solutions are adjusted to have the same pH, these differences become even more noticeable.

The acids created during fermentation, namely: succinic, acetic and lactic, have more complex tastes, reflecting their origin, and their flavors are less intense. Lactic acid has a very light acid taste — tart, but not sharp, acetic acid has an unpleasant sharpness, whereas succinic acid at this concentration seems hardly acidic at all. Instead, it has a strong flavor of salty bitterness which at this intensity is unpleasant, causing salivation. Of all of the wine acids, succinic acid is the richest in flavor, per unit of weight.

From the standpoint of wine evaluation you should note the strong acid flavor of tartaric acid and the very considerable difference between the acid tastes of malic and lactic acids. This latter explains in part the softening of a wine which has undergone malolactic fermentation. Finally, note the strong after-taste produced by acetic acid.

Analytical Taste Tests

A demonstration of the effect of alcohol on the taste of a wine

This test should be made with both a red and a white wine. White wine flavors are less complex because of the relative absence of phenolic compounds so that a change in their composition is more noticeable.

As a first exercise, the percentage of alcohol should be increased by 1% to 2% in a series of samples of wines. If possible use a neutral wine distillate, if not, neutral grain spirits may be used, but the effects will not be as desirable. In an exercise of the same kind, the alcohol may be diminished by the addition of water with adjustment of acidity by the addition of tartaric acid. In this case, not only will the reduction of alcohol be perceived but also a corresponding decrease in the body and the amount of flavor.

A change of 1% alcohol in a wine is not always perceived by untrained tasters. This test is not easy, for alcohol does not display its influence by its taste alone, but indirectly in modifying the balance of the other tastes. The taster must pay attention, above all, to the duration of the agreeable sensations as the wine first comes into the mouth (the "attack", as it is called), and on the moment when the impression of acidity appears, rather than on the final impression which is not always improved by an increased percentage.

The first tasting should be made knowing the order of the samples. This allows you to pin down the exact role that alcohol plays. Then you should taste the samples presented in a random order, trying to reconstruct the correct, increasing or decreasing order.

This tasting of "fortified" wines underlines well the indirect role played by alcohol because of its two-fold contribution of sweetness and warmth. Differences of the same degree in natural, unadulterated wines are more easily perceived, because other elements of the wine associated with a better maturity of the grape accompany the increased alcohol.

This test repeated over several weeks, progressively reducing the alcohol percentages, will improve the sensitivity of the taster. Trained tasters should be able to discriminate differences of 0.3%.

Other, easily constructed tests consist of classifying a series of wines of the same type according to their alcoholic degree, and then trying to give an estimation of their alcoholic content. In this regard, do not depend on the label on a bottle of wine to give you an accurate statement of its alcoholic content. Federal law permits a plus or minus 1.5% deviation from the figure quoted on the label.

To increase your sample by 1% alcohol, dilute 1 part of 80 proof vodka with 27 parts of wine.

To increase your sample by 2% alcohol, dilute 2 parts of 80 proof vodka with 26 parts of wine.

To show the effect of glycerol

Take a young, harsh, red wine and make up samples containing 3 to 6 grams/liter of glycerol. Compare them to the control wine in a blind tasting, or, if necessary, with knowledge of the respective order. Glycerol reinforces the sweet taste instantaneously, slightly increases the perceived body, improves the development of the wine in the mouth by masking the acid tastes, but it has little influence on the tannic after-taste. Glycerol acts through its own sweet flavor and not through its viscosity. This is another demonstration of the way the sweet constituents of wine moderate the acid tastes.

To show the effect of the addition of sugar

This test is to teach the recognition of small quantities of reducing sugars in wines which should be dry. Add, for example, 2 to 4 grams of sugar/liter to a dry wine and try to put the individual samples in their correct order of increasing sweetness. Use the unsugared wine as a comparison base. Make the test with both red and white wines.

To show the effect of the addition of different acids

To begin this exercise, use a red and a white wine of low to medium acidity. California jug wines with no-to-little background sweetness are ideal. To two samples of these wines, add the equivalent of 0.5 grams/liter of tartaric acid to one and 1.0 grams/liter to the other. Depending on the level of ability of the tasters, either more or less tartaric acid per sample may be used. Taste the treated samples against the untreated wines. Make the same trials with wines called "mellow" or "demi-sec", meaning that some residual sweetness can be expected. Taste the samples in either a known or a random order. The object here is not to discover individual threshold taste abilities, but rather to teach the understanding of the role of acidity, a basic quality, in the taste of wine. Because most of us are not sufficiently analytical in our approach to wine, this demonstration is important.

It has previously been noted that these differences are more easily perceived in white wines than in reds, largely due to the complexity contributed by the tannins in the latter.

For those who have the laboratory facilities available, and a good understanding of the techniques involved, these same tests can be made by de-acidifying high-acid wines to the extent required by the tasters involved. Other tests can be made comparing different wines and classifying them according to their total acidity. Obviously, white wines and red wines should be considered separately.

Finally, the addition to wine of the other organic acids which it contains naturally, helps the neophyte taster appreciate more easily the taste qualities these compounds contribute to the flavor of wine.

Into samples of the same red wine of average quality, put 0.5 grams/liter of the following acids: tartaric, citric, and lactic. You will notice that tartaric makes it harsher, citric acid produces a fresh, crisp, rather pleasant acidity, whereas the lactic acid is scarcely noticeable.

The experimental additions of malic and succinic acids at appropriate levels (see above) are instructive in other ways. Malic acid contributes a vegetal flavor whereas succinic acid provides complexity.

A demonstration of volatile acidity (ascescence)

The perception of volatile acidity in wines has both aromatic and taste components. The taste comes from acetic acid which contributes little in the way of smell whereas ethyl acetate, the ester of alcohol and acetic acid, provides the strong, characteristic odor.

Make up samples of the same wine adding 0.25 grams, 0.5 grams, 0.75 grams and 1 gram/liter of acetic acid and 50 mg and 200 mg of ethyl acetate. These samples should be prepared separately, tasted and then poured together for a final tasting.

The acetic acid will be perceived strongly in the aftertaste as a sharp harshness, but with very little odor component. The aroma associated with ethyl acetate is typical of wines that have been mishandled and have been attacked by acetic acid bacteria. It should be detectable at levels representing 160–180 mg/liter. Above that figure, it hardens the wine in a very disagreeable manner.

The role of sulfur dioxide in wine evaluation

A little bit of sulfur dioxide is a good and necessary thing, but, too, a little bit of it goes a long way. Necessary in all wines to some extent but in white wines more generally and in sweet wines from botrytized grapes particularly, as an anti-oxidant, it can have undesirable side-effects. Used in the form of anhydrous sulfur dioxide or dissolved crystals of potassium meta-bisulfite, it can perform its desired function without being obtrusive. Its overuse leads to dull, lack-luster wines whose fruit is smothered by the sharp, acrid odor it produces.

As a demonstration, prepare 24 hours in advance, examples of the same wines — dry white — brought to 0, 50, 200 and 300 mg/liter total SO_2.

Since 10–30 ppm free SO_2 are in the average dry white wine, the amount of SO_2 that must be added to increase the free SO_2 can only be estimated by the average person. For teaching purposes use the solution as follows on 750 ml portions of neutral white wine that has no discernible SO_2 smell.

A freshly made solution of 1/4 tsp. potassium metabisulfite ($K_2S_2O_5$) in 25 ml of water contains 1300 mg of the salt which will release about 750 mg of sulfur dioxide when added to wine.

The preceding exercises are largely elementary to understanding the nature of wine. With a little ingenuity and, it must be admitted, a certain amount of technical competence, many variations can be played on this same theme.

CHAPTER 18

SENSORY IDENTIFICATION
OF WINE CONSTITUENTS

Philip F. Jackisch

W INE can be appreciated by a person who knows little of the underlying composition of them, but such appreciation will be at a rather low level. Serious wine appreciation begins with a knowledge of the various desirable and undesirable sensory attributes of wines and what causes them. No one can reliably tell what is good or bad about a wine until he can put a name to it. When such names describe objective qualities of a wine it becomes possible for one person to communicate his experiences to another and the learning process is greatly speeded up.

One method of learning about the constituents of wines that give rise to sensory impressions is to isolate these one or two at a time before trying to find them in a mixture as complex as the average wine.

This chapter will describe some basic wine constituents and their sensory results. The individual can prepare most of these basic wine components in his own home and practice with them there. Teachers of wine appreciation classes may also find valuable suggestions to aid them in their teaching.

The Appearance of Wine

Clarity

Sound, well-made wines are generally sparkling bright or brilliant in appearance.

Wines that have a cloudy, hazy or dull appearance are usually spoiled with a bacterial infection or contain excess pectins, proteins or metal salts.

Wines whose appearance is between brilliant and dull are often described as being clear.

In order to gain experience in detecting these levels of clarity get out three perfectly clean wine glasses. In the first glass place 5 ounces of water and a drop of milk and mix well. This will represent a dull or hazy

HAZY   CLEAR   BRILLIANT

wine. Take one ounce of this mixture and dilute it with three ounces of water and place it in the second glass to represent a clear wine. Place four ounces of plain water in the third glass to represent a brilliant wine.

You will find that you can most easily detect the difference in clarity of these three samples by holding the glasses up so that you can look through the liquid into a light source. A candle flame, a bare light bulb, or sunlight reflected off of a metal surface will all serve as suitable light sources. The first glass should have a noticeably dull appearance through the whole liquid. The second glass will appear much clearer but the outline of the light source will not be as sharply defined as in the third glass.

Once you have performed this experiment and are certain that you can tell three glasses apart you can take samples of a white or light red wine and repeat the experiment. Depending on the depth of color in the wine you may have to use two or more drops of milk in the first glass in order to see the effect clearly.

Some wines, especially white wines that are chilled before being served, may contain small white crystals of potassium bitartrate (cream of tartar) in the bottom of the bottle or on the underside of the cork. This is a harmless, almost tasteless, natural substance that does not affect wine quality. Some older red wines may contain a precipitate or sludge of oxidized tannins and pigments in the bottom. This material has a bitter taste and it is best removed by standing the bottle upright for a day or two before serving, then carefully decanting the wine into a another container and leaving the sediment behind in the last ounce or so of wine in the bottle. This type of natural sediment can not be considered to be a wine defect.

Color

There are three aspects of color that are important in evaluating a wine. The first is the hue, such as red, yellow, or other pure color. The second is the shade or the strength of the color. A red wine, for example, can vary from a pale pink to an almost opaque dark red. The third aspect is the purity of the color, that is whether it contains orange, brown, or other tints in addition to the main color.

You can learn more about these aspects of color by filling several clean wine glasses with water and adding various amounts of pure food colors to the water. One of the first things that you will notice is that adding 8 drops of red color doesn't seem to make the color twice as dark as adding 4 drops. Our senses seem to work in a nonlinear manner and you can investigate this effect by mixing solutions of food colors or diluting dark wines with known amounts of water until you have found the ratio that makes one sample twice as dark as another.

To study color purity, try adding 5 drops of red food color to each of three wine glasses half full of water. Then add one drop of yellow food color to the second glass and a little bit of diluted blue color to the third glass. You will find that you can most easily tell the colors apart by looking down at the glasses at a diagonal to the surface of the liquid. You can get the same effect by tilting the glasses. In either case you should have a white table cloth or piece of paper underneath the glasses.

After some practice with these artificial mixtures you can work with actual wines and doctor the colors with small amounts of food colors or larger amounts of water. Your aim should be to learn how to most easily detect these differences between wine colors and to describe these differences in terms of the primary color, the depth of color, and the purity of the color.

An interesting experiment is to have someone else select one of the glasses and present it by itself, then have you try to tell which glass it is. Although our eyes are very sensitive to small changes in color intensity and purity, we find it much harder to make decisions based on memory alone. It is easier and more reliable to make judgements when we have several glasses of wine to compare side by side.

Young white wines will usually have a very pale yellow color, sometimes with a bit of green in it. As the wines are aged the color will darken and gradually turn to brown. Sometimes darkening occurs when very ripe grapes, partly affected by molds, are used to make the wine, as happens with some German wines and French sauternes. Table wines, such as some Chardonnays, that are aged in oak will pick up a brown color from the wood and from the oxidation attending the aging. Dessert wines, such as sherries, will often show the same darkening.

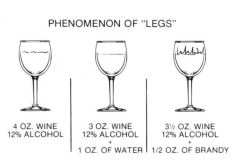

PHENOMENON OF "LEGS"

4 OZ. WINE
12% ALCOHOL

3 OZ. WINE
12% ALCOHOL
+
1 OZ. OF WATER

3½ OZ. WINE
12% ALCOHOL
+
1/2 OZ. OF BRANDY

Young red wines will usually be close to pure red but may have a slight orange or purple tint depending on the grape variety used. With aging the color will gradually lighten and turn toward brown. Careful observation of the color of wines can give useful clues as to their condition and age.

Other Appearances

Some young wines, especially white wines that are bottled young and chilled before being served, will show small bubbles in the bottom of the glass. This is usually due to dissolved carbon dioxide that is left from the fermentation and, if so, is a sign of youth. If a wine is red and slightly hazy, the appearance of bubbles often signals the presence of a bacterial fermentation in the bottle.

In most wines one can observe little rivulets of wine rising above the surface on the walls of the glass. This action is due to the alcohol surface tension, allowing some of the wine to rise until its weight pulls it down.

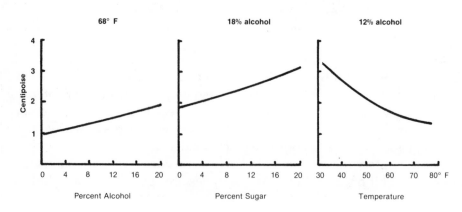

EFFECT ON VISCOSITY OF ALCOHOL, SUGAR, AND TEMPERATURE

68° F

18% alcohol

12% alcohol

Centipoise

Percent Alcohol

Percent Sugar

Temperature

You can observe the variation in this effect by putting 4 ounces of table wine with about 12% alcohol in one glass, putting 3 ounces of wine and 1 ounce of water in a second glass, and putting 3 1/2 ounces of wine and half an ounce of brandy or other distilled beverage in a third glass. If you then swirl the glasses and allow the wines to settle you should see distinct differences in the heights of these rivulets of wine — sometimes called legs — on the walls of each glass.

In table wines higher alcohol content is usually associated with riper grapes, which can be expected to provide more fragrance and flavor to the wine. Higher alcohol content also increases the viscosity of wines which results in greater body or a feeling of thickness in the mouth.

Body

The body of wines seems to be a greatly misunderstood concept. One rough definition is "the lack of watery character". Some people seem to confuse intensity of flavor with body. If we accept body as a feeling in the mouth apart from flavor, then viscosity is one way to objectively measure body. All of the dissolved substances in a wine contribute to body. But since alcohol is the major substance in most wines, next to water (which has less viscosity than wine), then alcohol is a major contributor to body. Sugars in sweet wines also contribute significantly to body. It is interesting that appearance can be used to estimate alcohol content and hence the body of a wine even before the wine is tasted. Careful attention to a wine's appearance should not be slighted in the overall evaluation of a wine.

The Taste of Wines

In the usual order of business we first look at wines, then smell them, and finally taste them. We are going to change this order a bit and consider taste next for two reasons. First of all, tastes are simpler than odors

and easier to identify and describe. Secondly, from the standpoint of wine quality, appearance is less important than taste, which is less important than odor. We are therefore going to save the most subtle and important sensory qualities for the last.

Acidity

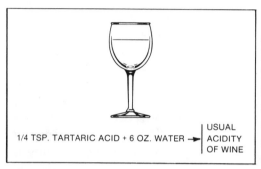

1/4 TSP. TARTARIC ACID + 6 OZ. WATER → | USUAL ACIDITY OF WINE

There are four primary tastes: sour, sweet, bitter, and salty. Few if any wines have a salty taste but all wines have some sourness, due to the presence of natural fruit acids. This natural sourness is one of wine's most distinctive qualities and sets it apart from most other beverages. The slight sourness of wines is sometimes a barrier to their enjoyment by young adults brought up on sweet and bland beverages drunk between meals. But when wines are consumed with meals, as most wines are meant to be, their slight sourness serves to moderate the greasiness of many main courses and makes wines a natural accompaniment to meals.

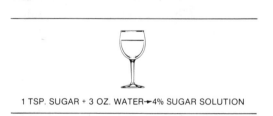

1 TSP. SUGAR + 3 OZ. WATER → 4% SUGAR SOLUTION

The major acid found in most grape wines is tartaric acid. Samples of this pure acid can be obtained at stores that sell supplies to home winemakers or in a spice called cream of tartar. If you can obtain this pure acid, you can prepare a solution of it that has the same acidity as most wines by dissolving 1/4 teaspoon in 6 ounces of water. When you taste this solution you will find that it is more sour than most wines. This is because the other constituents of wines partly hide or mask the sourness of the fruit acids. Adding a little sugar to the solution will decrease the apparent acidity or sourness. It is partly for this reason that many people start their wine experiences by drinking wines that are somewhat sweet.

If you can not obtain pure tartaric acid, you can approximate the acidity of the average wine by adding 1 ounce of reconstituted lemon juice to 9 ounces of water. The taste will not be exactly the same because the major acid in citrus fruits is citric acid, but the overall impression of sourness will be approximately the same.

Sweetness

The appreciation of sweetness is probably the only taste preference that we are born with. All children seem to like sweets and it is only later in life that we develop an appreciation of foods and beverages with sourness, bitterness, or saltiness. About half of the American public likes wines that are noticeably sweet. Sweetness in wines is not good or bad by itself, but it can hide other flavors if it is present at too high a level.

Sweet wines contain between about 2% and 20% sugar. Most people can taste sugar in a wine when it is above 0.5% or so. This is called the sweetness threshold or the level at which sweetness can just be detected.

You can learn about sweetness by dissolving a level teaspoon of table sugar in 3 ounces of water to give approximately a 4% sugar solution. Table sugar isn't the sugar found in wines, but it is related. Grapes contain the simpler sugars, glucose and fructose, which are combined as a double sugar in ordinary table sugar or sucrose. The 4% sugar solution is of interest because this marks the approximate dividing line between the sweetness that is acceptable in table wines and the sweetness that places wines in the dessert wine category.

You can investigate your sugar threshold in wines by setting up a series of glasses with three ounces of dry wine in each, then adding 1/8 teaspoon of sugar to the second (leaving the first glass unsweetened), 1/4 teaspoon to the third, and 3/8 teaspoonful to the fourth. This experiment will be more meaningful if you have someone else take the glasses away and make a little code mark on each of them, then present them to you so that you can try to tell which is which.

Assuming that the wine is actually dry — that is without any sugar — then the samples contain 0%, 0.5%, 1.0% and 1.5% sugar. If you can tell the unsweetened wine from the 0.5% sugar sample at least half of the time, then your sweetness threshold in that wine is 0.5% (or perhaps less). It will also be of interest to try and tell the 1.0% sample from the 1.5% sample in order to determine your difference threshold for sweetness, which may be different from the initial threshold.

If you repeat this process with several types of wines, both white and red, you will gain valuable insight into your ability to detect sweetness

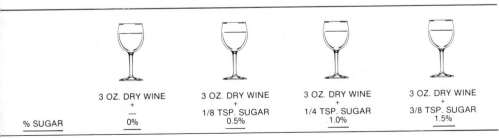

% SUGAR	3 OZ. DRY WINE + — 0%	3 OZ. DRY WINE + 1/8 TSP. SUGAR 0.5%	3 OZ. DRY WINE + 1/4 TSP. SUGAR 1.0%	3 OZ. DRY WINE + 3/8 TSP. SUGAR 1.5%

and your preference for sweetness in wines. If you find that the differences are too easy to detect you can mix intermediate samples by mixing equal quantities of adjacent samples. For example, if you mix one ounce of a sample with 0.5% sugar and one ounce of a sample with 1.0% sugar, you will have a new sample with 0.75% sugar.

Bitterness

Bitterness is detected more toward the back of the tongue than other tastes, so you will probably have to swallow the samples to find it. Bitterness also has a tendency to linger, so it will provide what is called an aftertaste. Most white wines have little or no bitterness, but some young red wines and a few special dessert or aperitif wines do have a noticeable bitterness.

Bitterness in wines generally is caused by the tannins extracted from the grape skins, stems, and seeds. You can obtain grape tannin as a light brown powder from most home winemaking supply stores. Dissolve 1/4 teaspoon of this powder in 3 ounces of water to produce a solution that will have approximately the bitterness of a young red wine.

Alternatively, you can brew up some tea using about 2–3 times the normal amount of tea leaves. Tea contains tannins that are similar to those found in wines and it also contains caffeine, another bitter substance. While this strong tea will not taste exactly like the bitterness found in red wines, it will give you a general impression of the bitterness caused by tannins.

If you want to learn to distinguish the three tastes found in wines, try mixing lemon juice and sugar in various proportions with your strong tea. After some practice in this way you should find it easier to detect bitterness in wines, even in the presence of sourness or sweetness. Sourness or sweetness will, however, mask the bitterness in certain cases, which probably explains why some people add sugar or lemon to tea and why some young red wines taste more mellow when they are slightly sweet.

Astringency

Astringency is not a taste, but rather a feeling. It gives the mouth a "dry" or "puckery" feel. Since it is often found in red wines that have bitterness, it is worth knowing about and worth learning to identify.

To experience the feeling of astringency, dissolve 1/4 teaspoonful of alum (available in most grocery stores in the spice section) in three ounces of water and taste this. Then compare this sensation to the bitterness of strong tea until you have the difference clearly in mind.

Remember, however, that bitterness and astringency are often found together in red wines and do not expect to be able to find one without at least some of the other.

Balance

Some wine evaluation forms have a special section for balance and this is a term that is frequently used to describe a wine. This is a complex, somewhat subjective concept, but at a simple level what it means is that a wine has a pleasing balance of acidity, sweetness and bitterness.

One way to gain an understanding of balance is to start with a wine that you like and add small amounts of acid (tartaric acid or lemon juice) until the wine is not as pleasant as the original wine. Repeat this process with the addition of sugar and later with the addition of tannin or strong tea, using a fresh wine sample each time.

Once you have a good idea of what an out of balance wine is like, whether that imbalance is caused by excessive acidity, sweetness, or bitterness, then you are in a position to go further.

You can investigate the effects of one taste component on another by starting with a white wine that is too sour (either naturally or because you added some acidity) and adding a little sugar until the overall taste seems improved. You can also go the other way and start with a wine that is too sweet and add acidity. With a red wine you can start with excessive bitterness and add some sugar. If this causes the wine to taste more mellow, but out of balance, try adding a little acidity.

It is no coincidence that some of the most popular table wines sold in this country have moderate levels of sweetness, since, as we mentioned earlier, many people prefer some sweetness in their wines. But it is also no coincidence that many such semi-sweet wines also contain higher than normal levels of acidity, and , in the case of red wines, higher than normal levels of bitterness. The winemakers have learned to balance the tastes of these wines. They have done this so successfully that at least one red wine of this type has been described by wine writers as being "too bland". This suggests that perfect balance in taste may not be as important as interest and at least some wines that are a bit out of balance may still be pleasant because they are interesting.

Balance can also refer to harmony between all of the sensory impressions of a wine. If you, for example, look at a Reisling wine and find a golden color you suspect that the grapes were very ripe and probably infected with the "noble rot". If you taste the wine and it has a fair amount of residual sugar your general impression hasn't been disturbed. But if the smell of the wine is typical of underripe grapes and there is no hint of the apricot smell that you would expect from the other clues, the wine will appear out of balance because, clearly, something is wrong with it. Using all of your sensory perceptions and checking them against each other will help you determine when wines are properly made, and when they are not, what is probably wrong with them.

The Flavor and Smell of Wines

The smell of anything is detected through the nose and in order for it to get there it must be a volatile material. Flavor, as ordinarily defined, is the combined sensation of taste and odor perceived in the mouth. Flavor is greatly influenced by odor for without odor an apple and an onion would have similar effects on the mouth.

In addition to the senses that we have mentioned, there is also the general chemical sense, detected by the trigeminal nerve system in the nose. This chemical sense is the sensation we experience when we smell something that is irritating and it reveals itself as a sharp, burning, or itching feeling in the nose. Anyone who has inadvertently smelled a container of household ammonia or bleach has experienced this sensation. There are a few components in wines that, when present in excess, can activate our chemical sense.

The odor of a wine is often divided into aroma — the portion of the smell that is derived from the grapes — and the bouquet — the portion of the smell that is derived from the chemical changes that occur during the winemaking and aging processes. In addition, there are a variety of smells that are caused by various chemical additives to wines or by defects in the

1/2 OZ. 100% PROOF VODKA + 4 OZ. WINE 12% ALCOHOL → | 4½ OZ. WINE 16% ALCOHOL

wine. Since we are concerned with basics in this chapter we can not go into great detail about all of these various smells, but we can touch upon some of the most important ones.

Alcohol

Alcohol is the major volatile component in wines. It also gives wines a slight sweetness, since it is chemically related to the sugars. When the odor of alcohol is too strong it seems hot or sharp and is detected by our chemical sense, referred to above. Some high alcohol wines give this sensation, especially when they are warm.

In order to experience the smell of alcohol, pour a little vodka into a wine glass and sniff it. Warming the vodka will increase the sharp chemical sensation.

To learn the effect of high alcohol in a wine add 1/2 ounce of 100 proof vodka to 4 ounces of a table wine having 12% alcohol. The alcohol content will now be about 16%. Smell and taste the wine and see if you don't find the result less pleasant than the original wine.

Volatile Acidity

The acids we mentioned earlier have no volatility and therefore no odor. But all wines contain small amounts of acetic acid and related compounds that do have some volatility and do contribute to the odor of the wine. In small quantities (about 0.05%) this volatile acidity can add something positive to the character of a wine, but in larger quantities it signals that the wine is turning to vinegar and is definitely a negative quality factor. Acetic bacteria plus air give rise to volatile acidity in wines.

You can learn to detect the odor of acetic acid by smelling ordinary distilled white vinegar. In wines that have excessive volatile acidity the acetic acid is accompanied by its ethyl ester and you can experience this more complex odor by smelling a typical wine vinegar. Wine vinegars have a volatile acidity that is about 5–8%. This is about 50 times higher than the limit permitted in wines sold in the U.S. Try adding 10 or 20 drops of wine vinegar to an ounce of good red wine and see if you can detect the volatile acidity in the mixture. Ten drops of wine vinegar should raise the volatile acidity to approximately the legal limit. Also try lesser additions and see if some of them improve the wine character.

Acetaldehyde

This is a volatile constituent that results from the direct air oxidation of the alcohol in wines. In most wines it indicates that the wine is spoiled and will often be accompanied by a somewhat brownish tinge in the wine's color. In certain wines, such as the fino sherries, it is a natural and desired component and contributes to the "nutty" flavor of these wines, but in table wines it is usually undesirable. For some reason, a few people seem not to mind moderate oxidation in table wines and actually seem to expect it in white French Rhone wines and Hungarian tokays.

The easiest way to learn to identify this particular odor is to obtain a fino sherry and smell it in contrast to an ordinary white wine in a stoppered bottle in a warm place for several weeks or months until the wine has become oxidized. Red wines are less suitable for this since they contain more tannins which are natural anti-oxidants and tend to protect the wine from such oxidation. You can mix small amounts of sherry or oxidized wine with a fresh white wine to learn to detect beginning oxidation.

Sulfur Dioxide

Sulfur dioxide is a gas that is widely used in the winemaking process to prevent oxidation and browning of wines and to stop bacterial spoilage. People vary greatly in their sensitivity to it. When it is present in too high a concentration it can activate the chemical sense and give a tingling sensation in the nose and can even, in some cases, cause sneezing. The smell is reminiscent of lighted stick matches. It can also affect the flavor of wines and give them a "musty" character, something like an old airless barroom. It is most noticeable in some white wines (in red wines the sulfur dioxide is largely chemically combined with the pigments and other components) especially slightly sweet wines where it helps to prevent further fermentation.

The easiest way to experience this odor is to go to a store that sells home winemaking supplies and get some sodium or potassium metabisulfite. Add a tiny pinch of one of these chemicals to a dilute solution of tartaric acid or to a white wine and carefully smell.

For many years some German wines contained rather high quantities of sulfur dioxide and it got to the point where a few people could not identify this odor separately from the wine and considered it a part of the "German character". Fortunately, sulfur dioxide is quite volatile and if you happen to open a bottle of white wine that contains a bit too much sulfur dioxide you can alleviate the problem by swirling the wine in your glass for several minutes until the odor is diminished.

Mercaptans and Sulfides

A few wines, especially red wines, have a "skunky" odor caused by the presence of certain sulfur compounds. This occurs because yeast cells use various forms of sulfur in their metabolic processes and some yeasts die and give up hydrogen sulfide (the odor of rotten eggs) to the wine. If this situation isn't detected and corrected early enough the hydrogen sulfide can be further converted to mercaptans and sulfides and these will give a permanent bad odor to the wine.

It is not unknown for certain misguided souls to believe that such bad odors are a sign that a wine has body or character. This probably occurs because even bad smells can, when diluted enough, have an acceptable smell or at least a mildly interesting smell.

For those hardy souls that wish to experience these odors first hand there are several possibilities. The odor of a rotten egg can be obtained by hard boiling an egg and leaving it in a warm place for several weeks before opening it. One way to get a strong mercaptan smell is to find a skunk and molest it. A similar compound is added to natural gas to make the detection of gas leaks easier, so if you turn on a gas burner and take a very quick sniff before lighting the gas you will be able to smell a mercaptan. Sulfides are present in onions and if you cut an onion in small pieces and cover it, then leave it sit for a day or two, you will probably be able to smell a typical sulfide.

Needless to say, none of the above practices is recommended, but they should give you some idea of the quality of the odors that can occasionally be found in red wines. Make up your mind that wines should not smell — even a little bit — like rotten eggs, skunks, gas leaks, or old onions, and you will be on the right track.

Varietal Odors

Having spent some time considering the odors in wines that are generally not desirable, we now come to examine the desirable odors. Foremost among these are the odors that are characteristic of the variety of grapes used to produce the wine.

One of the distinctive types of grape wines found in the U.S. is based on the labrusca varieties. Concord, Catawba, Niagara, and related varieties possess a distinctive odor which is partly due to the ester, methyl anthranilate. Although this pure chemical is not readily obtained, it is found in many foods and products that are supposed to have a grape flavor or odor, including certain candies, chewing gum, and lip ice. Since the Concord grape is the basis of Welch's grape juice, smelling and tasting this juice will give a good idea of what the labrusca character is. Labrusca-derived varieties are found in much of the eastern U.S. and in the northwest and continue to be the basis for much of the eastern U.S. and Canadian wine industries. The main disadvantage of this particular odor and flavor is that it is overpowering and hides other attributes of the wines. Eastern American winemakers have learned in recent years how to minimize this excessive odor and flavor in their wines.

In the southeastern U.S. there are a number of wines produced from the native muscadine grapes. One of the chemicals responsible for the distinctive fragrance of these wines is 2-phenylethanol. Fortunately, one does not have to try to obtain this chemical to learn about this fragrance, since it is the characteristic fragrance of roses.

Most wines produced in the world, including California, are based on vinifera varieties. These wines possess such a wide variety of fragrances that it is impossible to describe them all. Most of them are combinations of very many minor components.

One of the more distinctive vinifera varieties is the muscat grape. One of the chemicals found in the volatile components of this grape is linalool, which has a character that can be approximately described as perfumey. Asti Spumanti from Italy is a wine made from muscat grapes and other muscat wines are produced in the U.S. and in Germany. It is believed that muscat grapes are among the most ancient of the vinifera varieties and the muscat character is present to a small extent in the modern Riesling grape. This character is more noticeable in the Muller-Thurgau hybrid (a cross between Riesling and Silvaner) which is now the predominant German hybrid variety.

Most of the subtle fragrances found in vinifera wines are also found in other plants in varying degrees. It is sometimes useful to characterize these odors as being reminiscent of fruits, vegetables, flowers, leaves, or other growing things. Some French Chardonnay wines have a smell and taste that is akin to that of apples (and both possess sizeable amounts of malic acid). One producer of Cabernet Sauvignon in California managed to get a fragrance and flavor of pears in his wine. The smell of some botrytized Riesling wines from Germany and California has been described as being like apricots.

Recently, one of the chemicals that give rise to the distinctive character of Cabernet Sauvignon wines has been linked to the same chemical in bell peppers. It also appears that certain aldehydes found in leaves can be found in hybrid grapes from the eastern U.S. and Canada.

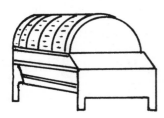

While it is often impossible to exactly characterize the fragrance components of wines, it can be useful to try to analyze them by drawing comparisons with some of the fragrances of flowers, fruits and other materials mentioned above.

Oak

Many premium red wines and dessert wines and a few white wines are aged in oak containers. Oak aging adds complexity to the fragrance and flavor of the wines and also some tannins and coloring matter. Unfortunately, some wines are excessively oaky in character and this detracts from their natural qualities

To experience the taste of wood in a wine shave up some wood (oak if you can find it) and place a teaspoonful in 4 ounces of wine in a small container and allow this to sit for a day, then smell and taste it. The smell and taste of wood should be quite noticeable.

One of the desirable substances that wines, especially red wines, extract from oak is vanillin. Vanillin is, of course, the major fragrance component of vanilla extract. The faint smell of vanilla is a sure sign to the experienced wine taster that a wine has been aged for some time in oak.

To learn what the vanilla smell is like in a wine, dissolve a drop of vanilla extract in a tablespoonful of water and add a few drops of this mixture to 4 ounces of red wine. You may have to vary the amount of vanilla extract depending on how concentrated or old your particular extract is. When you get just enough vanilla smell in the wine so that it is barely noticeable, you will probably find that the result is pleasing.

Oak fragrance and flavor is very noticeable in brandies and whiskeys and smelling and tasting these beverages may increase your understanding of this characteristic.

Overall Wine Quality

Some wine rating forms have an item for overall wine quality. This is rarely defined and one gets the impression that it is merely a way to adjust the total score to make it come out the way the taster thinks that it should.

There is a consensus among wine experts that there is such a thing as wine quality. The problem is that everyone will perceive this factor in a different way, depending on his or her past experiences. Without getting into involved discussions of aesthetics or metaphysics, we can define wine quality as whatever it is that causes us to find pleasure in a wine. Complexity of sensory impressions contributes to wine quality as long as the complexity is not too great. A wine of great quality will be a memorable wine and this is a practical test.

The next time that you have occasion to sample several wines at the same time, pick out those that you find the greatest pleasure in. Set them aside and try to remember what it was about each one that particularly impressed you. It is unlikely that you will be able to exactly name or describe what gave rise to your pleasure, but by doing this exercise you will begin to focus attention on wine quality. The better that you understand wine quality and those things that make you perceive it, the more likely you are to find quality wines in the future.

CHAPTER 19

ORGANIZING & CONDUCTING WINE TASTINGS

Alton L. Long

Introduction

T HIS CHAPTER describes the various types of wine tastings and offers guidelines on how to plan, organize and conduct them. Included are a number of suggestions that will help you conduct a tasting that will permit all participants to become more knowledgeable about wines and at the same time have a pleasant experience.

There are as many ways to conduct wine tastings as there are people willing to host them. While most of the differences may be due to the personal preferences of the host, the basic difference usually lies in the purpose for which the tasting is being conducted. In general, tastings are conducted to accomplish one of the three broad objectives: 1) education, 2) evaluation, or 3) entertainment. A good tasting probably has some elements of each of these three objectives, but it usually has one of them as the primary purpose. Once the objective of the tasting is established, planning enhances the probability of achieving the goal. It therefore behooves the host to decide the purpose of the tasting and then plan and conduct it in a manner that will meet the objectives, remembering that the event should be pleasant and rewarding to all participants regardless of the purposes.

This chapter presents the general considerations for conducting the various kinds of tastings and provides suggestions for tastings that are appropriate for these different purposes. In addition, it provides specific considerations and details regarding tastings in general to help you plan and conduct a successful event.

Tastings For Education

For beginning, but serious, wine tasters, educational tastings hold most interest. In the world of wine, there seems to be no end to the areas that can be explored for the sake of wine education. Basic education usually begins with the comparison of wines produced from different grape varieties (e.g. Cabernet Sauvignon, Baco noir, Chardonnay, and Seyval blanc) or a comparison of the wines from different regions (e.g. Bordeaux and Burgundy or New York and Pennsylvania). As the educational interest of the participants becomes more sophisticated, they may want to explore differences in the same wine or grape variety, such as the effect of age or vintage on quality.

The educational tastings tend to be based on anticipated differences resulting from the different grape varieties, geographical location, the conditions under which the grapes were grown, and the style of the vintner. Table 1 lists some suggested themes for educational tastings.

The educational tasting can be conducted as an open tasting; that is, the identity of the wines are known to the tasters. In addition, it is appropriate for someone in attendance to provide background information relating to the wines being tasted and to explain the characteristics or qualities that should be given special attention.

TABLE 1

Educational Tastings

1. Demonstrating Differences

   A. Grape — Varieties
   B. Regional — California, France, Germany
   C. Attributes — Sweet, Dry, Wood, Vintage
   D. Quality and Style — Regular compared with Reserve or compared with Light

2. Surveys of Broad Topics

   A. Wines of a Nation or Major Region
   B. Wines of a Single Winery or Shipper
   C. Large General Classes — Dessert, Rosé, Sparkling, New Wineries

In educational tastings, general discussion should be encouraged since, to a large degree, articulation enhances memory. Under the guidance of a leader, this will help you develop an understanding of wine related terms. Finally, even though the wines may not be formally evaluated and scored, it is a good idea to record your impressions. Collecting these records in a loose-leaf notebook will provide you with both a history of your wine tastings and a reference of your personal wine preferences.

If you are more serious about wine tasting, you will want to experience a component tasting. This involves tasting specially prepared wine solutions in which one or more of the components that constitute wine are discernible.

A basic component tasting will feature wine solutions having varying percentages of sugar, acid, alcohol, and sulfur dioxide. Tasters can then determine personal thresholds for detecting the presence and differences of these substances. This component tasting experience will help you develop an understanding of the conditions that make a wine sweet, dry, or sour. A component tasting may also be used to demonstrate the interaction of these constituents, such as the balance that can be achieved between acid and sugar.

There are several excellent references for setting up a component tasting, one being Chapter 18 by Philip Jackisch. It is important that the person selected to prepare the solutions and conduct the tasting has a good understanding of the basic chemistry involved, but is not necessary that he or she be a chemist.

Component tastings may be provided in conjunction with a regular tasting. In this case, only one or two components should be investigated. For example, the study of sugar-acid balance could be coupled with a German Wine tasting.

Tastings For Evaluations

How often do we hear the comment, "I don't really understand wines, but I know what I like". "Liking" a wine is the beginning of evaluation, but only the beginning. If you expect to understand wines, you will have to understand what it is that you like about a wine. The understanding will then enable you to identify other wines with similar attributes, wines you might also "like". This is the beginning of wine appreciation.

The evaluation of wines is essentially the identification, description, and rating of the character of these various attributes of the wine being evaluated. You use four of your five basic senses in this process: sight, smell, taste, and touch. The remaining sense, hearing, is of course, used indirectly by listening to comments on the wines being evaluated by other tasters.

Rating or scoring is one process of quantifying how a given wine compares with other wines or how the individual attributes of a wine compare with those of another wine or a predetermined or expected standard. There are literally dozens of rating and scoring systems. In addition, some systems are based on the hedonistic preferences of the taster and provide a simple ranking of the wines tasted or placed into 4 or 5 categories such as Excellent, Good, Fair, or Poor.

Bottles properly prepared for 'blind tasting'.

Conducting a tasting for the purpose of evaluation requires special attention to the arrangements and procedures. These depend upon the purpose and seriousness of the evaluation. In the more serious evaluation tastings, the purpose is to ascertain the "Best" by high score, or "Best Buy" based on score and price of a grouping of similar wines. Under these circumstances it is usually desirable to conduct the tasting "blind"; that is, the labels of the wines being tasted are concealed until after the tasting, rating, and comments have been completed.

The simplest way to do this is to place the bottles in paper bags with only the neck protruding. Tape the top of the bag around the neck and, randomly reorder the sequence of the wines. Then mark the bags with numbers representing the order in which the wines will be tasted. If more than one bottle of each type wine being tasted is required, make certain that the pairs or groups of the same wine stay together. If possible, someone not participating in the tasting should do this. The neck capsule foil should be peeled down below the bag line so tasters can not use this to recognize the wines being presented. Removing the corks in advance reduces the effort required by the host during the actual tasting. It is recommended that corks be replaced if they identify the winery. Use other corks and do not allow the wines to breathe for most evaluation tastings. This accomplishes two things: first, each wine tasted will have had the same exposure to air; and second, the evaluators will be able to ascertain the effect of air-exposure (breathing) for themselves. The surface area-to-volume ratio (which to a large degree determines "breathing" effects) is at least an order of magnitude greater in the glass than in the bottle. Five minutes in the glass provides as much breathing as an hour in an open bottle. For wines that may have a sediment, it is recommended that they be decanted immediately prior to serving.

Some of the most interesting evaluation tastings are conducted to see if the tasting group will agree with recent contest results. For example, find the ranking from some professional competition and select from the same category two gold medal, two silver medal, and two bronze medal winners and see if the palates of your group agree with those of the contest judges.

The best evaluation tastings are those in which the wines are selected with the possibility of producing some really interesting results. Good examples are the demonstration of quality of a relatively unknown winery's product having a low price, in comparison with the same higher priced variety from a better known winery or vice versa. Another is the rating of several moderately priced wines against several more expensive, recognized and accepted wine "standards" in hope of discovering a "Best Buy",

Wine evaluation process showing glasses – fill level and evaluation sheet.

if not for the group then at least for one or more of the participants. The majority of serious wine tasting groups evolve to the point where most of their tastings are evaluation tastings with occasional educational tastings.

By keeping good records and notes, you will observe your progress in wine evaluation and, at the same time, have a record of your opinions and ratings of a large number of wines. This, in turn provides a good reminder of which wines you may desire to purchase in quantity and lay away.

Table 2 offers several suggestions of basic themes for evaluation tastings along with a few specific examples.

TABLE 2

Evaluation Tastings

1. Classic Comparative Evaluations

   A. Horizontal — Same Region, Variety and Vintage; Different Wineries
   B. Vertical — Same Winery and Variety; Different Vintages

2. General Comparative Evaluations

   A. Regional — Same Variety and Vintage; Different Regions
   B. Competitive Events — By Entry Categories

Tastings For Entertainment

While all tastings should have a high degree of pleasure and enjoyment as one of the objectives, entertainment is frequently the primary objective of a tasting. If this is your objective you should plan and conduct the event with the same concern you would have for a more serious evaluation or educational tasting. This occasion can be an opportunity to introduce wine as a possible lifelong interest and pleasure to a neophyte.

For Entertaining Tastings, set up with bread and cheese. Note national flag indicates source of cheese.

Obviously, the key element in having a tasting for entertainment is to make it possible for the participants to enjoy themselves. In some cases, the wine tasting may be only a setting for the gathering; nevertheless, try to assure that the tasting itself will have some meaning to the participants.

For this kind of tasting you should choose a theme, very much like that of an educational tasting, but, in this case, of course, the "education" is subliminal. Since there is an infinite number of settings and circumstances for the "entertainment tasting", it is difficult to establish ground rules. There are, however, a few general guidelines that should prove helpful.

First, there should be some relationship among the wines to provide the theme. One theme might be "Wines of the World" with wines from 6 different countries including red, white, and rose' wines. Some other themes might be "Wines from the Southern Hemisphere" with wines from Australia, Chile, Argentina and South Africa or "Wines from the American Colonies" with wines from Virginia, Maryland, Pennsylvania, New York, New Jersey and Massachusetts.

Provide a list of the wines being tasted to the guests as a reminder of what they are tasting. Serve 6 to 8 wines. There should be enough variety to assure that everyone will find one or more wines they can enjoy. If the gathering involves many persons who lack wine experience you should probably include one less-than-dry wine such as a typical Chenin Blanc or a Mosel. The current popular trend favors white wines, so, unless there is some reason to do otherwise, the selection should include a predominance of white wines.

For the social wine tasting, it is appropriate to offer a variety of accompaniments such as cheese, fruit, bread and crackers.

If your acquaintances know that you have an interest in wines and in conducting wine tastings, you will undoubtedly be asked to "put on a tasting". This is one of the most serious challenges for any friend of wine as this request will entail many constraints, not the least of which will be the cost. This will challenge your ingenuity, your knowledge of wines and your understanding of the tastes of the public.

The arrangements for a large tasting can be quite complicated but proper planning and organization will assure a pleasant and meaningful wine experience. Guidelines for planning are provided in the next section.

Conducting an entertaining tasting for smaller groups and especially for wine friends who have a similar level of experience can be very rewarding for a host. This will give you the opportunity to experience some unusual wines or to play some wine tasting games. A few interesting examples are included in Table 3.

TABLE 3

Entertainment Tastings

1. Assorted Wines

Several Varieties — Foch, DeChaunac, Baco noir, Chardonnay, Riesling, Chenin Blanc, Cabernet Sauvignon, Pinot noir, Zinfandel

Several Countries or States — Wines of the Mediterranean — of the South — Pacific Coast — Balkans

Theme Related — Riesling from Around the World; New Wineries, Golden Oldies (10 or more years old)

2. Wine Tasting Games

Blind Matching — Two bottles each of three similar wines, all tasted blind — match them up

Guessing Games — Six different wines — guess the variety

Pin the Label on the Bottle — Six different wines — tasted blind — label information available, match them up

Blend Your Own — Two or three different red variety wines and one or two whites — try blending

Guidelines For Conducting Tastings

As demonstrated in the previous sections, there is an infinite variety of themes on which wine tastings may be based. In addition, there is a wide range of settings and formats for the various types of tastings. However, there are a few basic guidelines common to most tastings, which, if followed, will help you make your tasting successful. A checklist of these guidelines is provided in Table 4.

TABLE 4

A Checklist For Conducting Wine Tastings

1. Select Purpose, Theme and Wines
2. Set Date, Time, Host and Location
3. Select Overall Tasting Procedure, Serving, Rating, Discussion
4. Procure Rating Sheets, Handouts, Discussion Leader
5. Mail Announcements, Map, Cost, Reservations
6. Procure and Store Wines
7. Procure Glasses, Decanters, Dump Buckets, Palate Refreshers, Cork Screws
8. Arrange Tasting Area, Lighting, Glass Rinsing (Keep Tasting Area Odor-Free)
9. Prepare Wines, Masking (if blind), Opening
10. Conduct Business Meeting, Plans, Reimbursement
11. Provide Coffee and Tea

Announcements and Reservations

For most tastings, some sort of announcement is required. Besides the time and location, it is recommended that the theme, if not the names of the wines, be presented. If the number of attendees is limited, it is appropriate to ask for reservations by phone or mail. Some wine groups require members to respond whether or not they plan to attend. A definite policy should be established regarding how the cost will be covered.

Quantity and Number of Wines

Once you have selected the purpose and theme of your tasting and have established the time and location, you can start the actual preparation. When you know how many will attend (or have set a predetermined limit), you can procure the wines. 6 different wines seems to be an optimum number. The quantity of wine served per person for each type should be no less than one ounce and seldom more than two. In this way a fifth or 750 ml bottle serves from 12 to 20 persons.

If you have 6 different bottles of wine for your group of 12 to 20 persons, each person would be tasting a total equivalent of one half to one third of a bottle of wine.

When you divide a bottle of wine among 15 or more persons it is difficult to pour equal portions. For a standard you may find it helpful to have a wine glass containing colored water representing the portion to be served.

Purchasing the Wines

When you purchase the wines, ask the merchant if he has literature relating to them. Frequently, he can provide you with handouts, maps, and other interesting promotional materials. Record the price of each wine to calculate the cost of the tasting. These costs are also part of the information that should be provided to the participants.

Handling the Wines

After the wines have been purchased, keep them in a location that will avoid heat, extreme cold, and sunlight. If the wines are to be served cold, they should be chilled to 45–50° F. The minimum for chilling is about 6 hours in the refrigerator if you do not intend to use ice buckets. Red wines should be served at 60–65° F.

Final Preparations

The logistics of the tasting are relatively straightforward. Rating sheets, pencils, handouts, special maps, and reference books are useful for most formal tastings. To allow for adequate preparation decide if someone is to lead a discussion or make a presentation related to the tasting.

Be sure that enough clean, clear, wine glasses, at least 6 ounces in capacity, are available. The 8 and 10-ounce, tulip-shaped glasses are ideal even if only 1 to 2 ounces are being served. The additional volume of the larger glasses provides a "chimney" to collect the essential olfactory components of wines. It is best if the size and style of all the glasses are identical. If more than one wine glass per person is available, place a small piece of tape on the base and mark each glass with the taster's initials and a code to distinguish each glass (#1, #2, etc.). This will enable the participants to taste more than one wine at a time and to conduct direct comparisons.

If you can not obtain an adequate supply of wine glasses, then ask the participants to bring their own. As a last resort you can use a high quality clear plastic 6–8 ounce tumbler. For a purely social or entertaining tasting you could use the 4 ounce plastic wine goblet.

There are times when you may want to use decanters: 1) for serving wines that have thrown a sediment, 2) for accelerating breathing for those wines that require it, and 3) for convenience and atmosphere when serving "jug" wines. You should take caution when decanting older wines and decant them just prior to serving. If they are decanted in advance, some may "breathe" away their aroma.

Dump buckets and rinse water should be provided for cleansing glasses and disposing of less than palatable wines. This also encourages tasters to consume no more than necessary to evaluate or become familiar with the wines. This is especially important if the total quantity of wine served exceeds half a bottle per person.

Opinions vary on the advisability of palate refreshers for serious tastings. Some authorities claim that they should be limited to plain bread (French or Italian style), bland crackers or nothing at all. It can be demonstrated easily that food does significantly impact the palate's reaction to wine. Since the majority of amateur tasters still want to enjoy the tastings and since most of us are interested in how a wine goes with food, it is usually appropriate to provide some sort of palate refresher such as cheese, pate', other light meats and fruit, plus a nice array of bread and crackers. In any case, complementary foods should be selected to avoid extremes in acid, sugar, spices, herbs, salt, or aroma. Table 5 lists a few items suitable for most tastings.

The rooms in which the tasting is held should be well lighted, and tables should be covered with white table cloths so that the tasters can evaluate color and clarity. Sheets of white paper will also serve this purpose. It is very important that the area be kept odor-free. If the group includes novices, put a note on the announcement asking the tasters not to use heavy colognes, shaving lotions and hand creams prior to the tasting. If tables are not available you should provide the tasters with a book or magazine on which they can put their rating sheet.

The presentation of the wines for tasting is discussed earlier in the section on Tastings for Evaluation. It is worthwhile here, however, to again stress the need to maintain a positive method for identification of the sequence of wines when conducting a "blind" tasting.

TABLE 5

Suggested Foods For Wine Tastings

Mild Cheddar	Provolone
Swiss Types	Mild Paté
Brie	Sliced Cold Meats
Camenbert	Apples
Gouda	Grapes
Edam	Pears
Munster	Unsalted Crackers
Italian, French and Sourdough Breads	

Stronger flavored and aged cheeses should be avoided with lighter flavored wines.

Procedures

There are several possible procedures available for conducting a tasting. The first and most often used is the simple serial method, tasting one wine at a time. Another way of conducting a tasting is to serve the wines in pairs, taking two wines at a time, thus allowing an A-B comparison. With four or less types of wine, you may pour them all at one time and evaluate each one against all the others. At larger, more informal events, it is appropriate to open all wines and allow the guests to taste them at random.

For educational and evaluative tastings, it is recommended that the participants share their impressions. If there is a discussion leader this can take the form of a question and answer period or the leader can solicit comments from the tasters. For evaluative tastings, the participants should refrain from comments until all have completed rating the wine under evaluation. After the scores have been tabulated and a group average announced, the tasters can share their comments. This can be done by each participant speaking in turn, or at random if under the control of a leader. No one should be coerced to speak.

For a tasting group that meets frequently, take a break in the middle of the program and discuss any business of the group. This can include arranging future events. This is also a good time to announce the cost and method of collection for the current tasting, if this has not been done in advance. Finally, after the tasting is completed, it is a good idea to offer coffee or tea. While coffee or tea does not necessarily counteract the effects of alcohol, the time consumed in drinking the coffee or tea may help the taster dissipate some effects.

Leaders and hosts of wine tastings should discourage anyone who does not appear to have full control, from driving.

Wine tastings can come in many forms. They can range from 2 to 200 persons, from 2 to 20 wines, and cost from $2.00 per bottle to $200.00 per bottle. But there is one thing they must have in common: to be a tasting, the participants must be conscious of the experience and discriminating of the character of the wines being tasted. A successful tasting is the result of proper planning, preparation and implementation. It considers the interest and experience of the participants. It provides you with the opportunity to have an educational, and pleasant experience and at the same time allows you to share this experience with others who have a similar interest in wine. Wine tasting is an activity that can never grow boring, as long as the vintners continue to produce new wines, and each year brings a new vintage.

APPENDIX

Conversion Table for Units (Approximate Equivalents)

1 fluid ounce = 29.573 milliliter

1 quart = 16 fluid ounces = 0.946 liter

1 milliliter = 0.0338 fluid ounce

1 liter = 1000 milliliters = 1.0567 quarts

1 ounce = 2.83 grams

1 pound = 16 ounces = 0.455 kilogram

10 milligrams = 0.000353 ounce

1 gram = 1000 milligrams = 0.353 ounce

1 kilogram = 1000 grams = 2.2 pounds

1 inch = 2.54 centimeters

1 foot = 30.48 centimeters = 0.3048 meter

1 millimeter = 0.1 centimeter = 0.03937 inch

1 centimeter = 10 millimeters = 0.3937 inch

1 cubic centimeter = 0.06102 cubic inch

1 cubic inch = 16.387 cubic centimeters

Sugar Correction

Sugar to add to water to make a gallon:

Add — 1.45 oz. of sugar per point of Brix desired. Most practical use is to add 2 lbs. of sugar to water to make a gallon of mixture. This gives 22% sugar solution (Brix).

Sugar to add to juice to achieve a correction of 22 Brix:

Add 1.5–1.6 oz. of sugar per gallon for each point of Brix short of goal (assumed in this case to be Brix 22).

Note: Although other solids than sugar are involved in the grape juice, these figures are sufficiently accurate. 2 1/2 cups of sugar equals 1 lb.

Potassium Metabisulfite

1 gram = 150 ppm in 1 gallon or 30 ppm in 5 gallons

1 Campden tablet = 30–50 ppm

> Note: A 1/4 teaspoon will approximate 1 gram.

Acid Reduction of Musts

Calcium Carbonate — $CaCO_3$

> 1.5 teaspoons (2.5 grams) per gallon lowers acid 0.1%. Use no more than 2 teaspoons (5 grams) per gallon. More will likely add an undesirable flavor. In red wines there will be a slight color change.

Potassium Bicarbonate — $KHCO_3$

> Same as Calcium Carbonate, but increase the amount to 3.4 grams per point of Brix.

Acid Reduction of Finished Wines

Potassium Carbonate (anhydrous) — K_2CO_3
230 grams in 500 ml water. 5 ml per gallon lowers acid 0.1%.

If we use the formula in Chapter 1 to make a liquid stock solution of metabisulfite of 18.11 grams (4.5 teaspoons) of metabisulfite in 100 ml of water we get the following:

To get	Per liter	Per gallon	Per 5 gallons
20 ppm	.2 ml	.76 ml	3.8 ml
30 ppm	.3 ml	1.14 ml	5.7 ml
40 ppm	.4 ml	1.52 ml	7.6 ml
50 ppm	.5 ml	1.9 ml	9.6 ml
100 ppm	1 ml	3.8 ml	19.0 ml

Example: To get 40 ppm in a liter, use .4 ml of stock solution.

If these quantities are difficult to use, halve the amount of metabisulfite in the stock and double the quantities in the table.

Pearson's square

Proportions are sometimes puzzling when blending wine products. Recently I decided to blend some grape juice (Vidal/Brix of 20) with a so-so finished wine. Because this would be a small scale experiment with no long term storage involved, measurements had to be accurate and consumption relatively soon. Fortunately I remembered an old high school chemistry lesson involving Pearson's square. I applied it this way:

$$
\begin{array}{cc}
A & D \\
& C \\
B & E
\end{array}
$$

A – sugar in juice; B – sugar in wine; C – sugar desired
D – difference between B & C; E – difference between A & C

Therefore:

$$
\begin{array}{cc}
20\% & 2 \\
& 2\% \\
0\% & 18
\end{array}
$$

a 1 to 9 ratio
750 ml = 75 ml juice and 675 ml wine

INDEX

C

D

E

F

Index

JOIN THE AMERICAN WINE SOCIETY

The American Wine Society is a national non-profit consumer organization devoted to educating its members and the general public about all aspects of wine- production, use and appreciation. The society is independent and has no commercial affiliation.

The Society publishes a quarterly Journal containing articles on all aspects of wine appreciation, grape growing and winemaking, Society news, local Chapter news, book reviews and recipes.

Local American Wine Society Chapters have activities such as wine tastings, luncheons, dinners, picnics, lectures, amateur winemaking contests, tours, etc. Each year in November a 2 1/2 day national wine conference offers an opportunity for members to come together and learn more about wine.

Membership is open to any interested person; wine enthusiast, professional in the wine business, amateur winemaker — anyone who wants to learn more about wine. All members receive the quarterly American Wine Society Journal, invitations to attend local, regional and national events, and new technical manuals when they are published. Annual dues are $32.00 per individual or couple. For those who join after July 1, and do not wish to receive the full year's publications, dues are $18.00.

Application for membership in The American Wine Society

Complete and mail with your check to:

AMERICAN WINE SOCIETY
3006 LATTA ROAD
ROCHESTER, NY 14612
(716) 225-7613

_____

Last Name   First Name   Initial

_____

Name of Spouse (if applicable)

_____

Street or Route Number

_____

City   State   Zip Code

_____   _____

Area Code/Phone   Member's Signature

Check type membership which applies to you:

☐ Regular membership (calendar year) (per couple or individual) ($US) $32.00

☐ After July 1 (1/2 year) $18.00

☐ Professional membership (includes wall plaque and special listings) $52.00

☐ Spousal voting privileges $ 2.00

☐ Canada and Mexico add $ 6.00

☐ All other countries add $12.00

TOTAL ENCLOSED _____

Please indicate method of payment:

☐ Check or money order, payable to American Wine Society

☐ Visa   ☐ Master Card   Expires _____

_____   _____

Account No.   Cardholder's signature